GENDER EQUALITY AND SUSTAINABLE DEVELOPMENT

For pathways to be truly sustainable and advance gender equality and the rights and capabilities of women and girls, those whose lives and wellbeing are at stake must be involved in leading the way.

Gender Equality and Sustainable Development calls for policies, investments and initiatives in sustainable development that recognize women's knowledge, agency and decision-making as fundamental. Four key sets of issues – work and industrial production; population and reproduction; food and agriculture; and water, sanitation and energy provide focal lenses through which these challenges are considered. Perspectives from new feminist political ecology and economy are integrated alongside issues of rights, relations and power. The book untangles the complex interactions between different dimensions of gender relations and sustainability, and explores how policy and activism can build synergies between them. Finally, this book demonstrates how plural pathways are possible, underpinned by different narratives about gender and sustainability, and how the choices between them are ultimately political.

This timely book will be of great interest to students, scholars, practitioners and policy makers working on gender, sustainable development, development studies and ecological economics.

Melissa Leach is Director of the Institute of Development Studies, University of Sussex, UK. Between 2006 and 2014 she directed the ESRC STEPS (Social, Technological and Environmental Pathways to Sustainability) Centre.

Pathways to Sustainability Series

Series Editors:
Melissa Leach, Ian Scoones and Andy Stirling
STEPS Centre at the University of Sussex

This book series addresses core challenges around linking science and technology and environmental sustainability with poverty reduction and social justice. It is based on the work of the Social, Technological and Environmental Pathways to Sustainability (STEPS) Centre, a major investment of the UK Economic and Social Research Council (ESRC). The STEPS Centre brings together researchers at the Institute of Development Studies (IDS) and the Science and Technology Policy Research (SPRU) at the University of Sussex with a set of partner institutions in Africa, Asia and Latin America.

Titles in this series include:

Dynamic Sustainabilities
Technology, environment, social justice
Melissa Leach, Ian Scoones and Andy Stirling

Avian Influenza
Science, policy and politics
Edited by Ian Scoones

Rice Biofortification
Lessons for global science and development
Sally Brooks

Epidemics
Science, governance and social justice
Edited by Sarah Dry and Melissa Leach

Regulating Technology
International harmonization and local realities
Patrick van Zwanenberg, Adrian Ely and Adrian Smith

The Politics of Asbestos
Understandings of risk, disease and protest
Linda Waldman

Contested Agronomy
Agricultural research in a changing world
James Sumberg and John Thompson

Transforming Health Markets in Asia and Africa
Improving quality and access for the poor
Edited by Gerald Bloom, Barun Kanjilal, Henry Lucas and David H. Peters

Pastoralism and Development in Africa
Dynamic change at the margins
Edited by Ian Scoones, Andy Catley and Jeremy Lind

The Politics of Green Transformations
Ian Scoones, Melissa Leach and Peter Newell

Carbon Conflicts and Forest Landscapes in Africa
Edited by Melissa Leach and Ian Scoones

Governing Agricultural Sustainability
Global lessons from GM crops
Phil Macnaghten and Susana Carro-Ripalda

Gender Equality and Sustainable Development
Edited by Melissa Leach

Adapting to Climate Uncertainty in African Agriculture
Narratives and knowledge politics
Stephen Whitfield

'Melissa Leach has brought together an outstanding team of practitioners and researchers to produce a crisply written and engaging review of the interlinkages among gender, environment and sustainable development. The forward-looking collection both challenges unsustainable pathways and charts new ones. A must read for all those working in the field of sustainable development.'

Wendy Harcourt, Associate Professor, Erasmus University, The Netherlands

'This is an excellent volume, with both range and depth. It not only brings an essential gender perspective to the issue of sustainable development, but also highlights the insufficiency of recognising women's contributions without providing them resources and voice. The lucid introduction, with its reflections on past and current debates, and on alternative pathways, is a significant contribution in itself.'

Bina Agarwal, Professor of Development Economics and Environment, University of Manchester, UK

'This timely book provides innovative and exciting ideas for both scholars and policy makers, challenging dominant market-led development models. It shows how pathways to achieve sustainable development and gender equality can be built through women's collective action at the grassroots and supportive public investment and services.'

Diane Elson, Emeritus Professor, University of Essex, UK

'This astute group of critical observers and participants dare to question the dominant narratives of capitalism, sustainability and development as well as facile gender and development formulas. They reiterate the critical feminist question "Sustaining what for whom?" and acknowledge the political choices embodied in green technologies, green economies and the feminization of planetary care work.'

Dianne Rocheleau, Professor of Geography, Clark University, USA

GENDER EQUALITY AND SUSTAINABLE DEVELOPMENT

Edited by Melissa Leach

LONDON AND NEW YORK

from Routledge

First published 2016
by Routledge
2 Park Square, Milton Park, Abingdon, Oxon OX14 4RN

and by Routledge
711 Third Avenue, New York, NY 10017

Routledge is an imprint of the Taylor & Francis Group, an informa business

British Library Cataloguing-in-Publication Data
A catalogue record for this book is available from the British Library

Library of Congress Cataloging-in-Publication Data
Gender equality and sustainable development / edited by Melissa Leach.
pages cm
1. Sustainable development. 2. Women in sustainable development. 3. Women's rights. I. Leach, Melissa, editor.
HD75.6.G46 2016
338.90082--dc23
2015009258

ISBN: 978-1-138-92130-6 (hbk)
ISBN: 978-1-138-92131-3 (pbk)
ISBN: 978-1-315-68645-5 (ebk)

Typeset in Bembo
by Saxon Graphics Ltd, Derby

Printed in Great Britain by Ashford Colour Press Ltd

CONTENTS

BOXES

CONTRIBUTORS

Elissa Braunstein is an Associate Professor in the Department of Economics at Colorado State University, USA. In her work she uses a feminist lens to better understand macroeconomic and international economic processes and outcomes, with particular emphasis on issues of economic development, growth and gender equality. She publishes widely in both academic and policy venues, and does regular consulting work for a number of international development institutions, including UN Women, the International Labour Organization and UN Research Institute for Social Development (UNRISD).

Sakiko Fukuda-Parr is Professor of International Affairs at The New School, New York, USA. She is a development economist interested in human development and capabilities, and the broad question of national and international policy strategies. Her current research includes projects on public policies and economic and social rights, and the impact of global goal-setting on international development agendas. From 1995 to 2004 she was lead author and director of the UNDP *Human Development Reports*. She currently serves as Vice Chair of the UN Committee on Development Policy. Her recent publications, in addition to the *Human Development Reports*, include *Fulfilling Social and Economic Rights* (with T. Lawson-Remer and S. Randolph, 2015) and *MDGs, Capabilities and Human Rights: The Power of Numbers to Shape Agendas* (co-edited with A. Yamin, 2015).

Betsy Hartmann is Professor of Development Studies and senior policy analyst for the Population and Development Program (PopDev), a centre for peace, population and the environment located at Hampshire College in Amherst, MA, USA.

Anne Hendrixson is Director of the Population and Development Program (PopDev), a centre for peace, population and the environment located at Hampshire College in Amherst, MA, USA.

Mimi Houston is a PhD student and special instructor at Colorado State University, USA, studying political, environmental and development economics. Her research focuses on the political economic dimensions of global climate agreements, including topics such as inequality and power across negotiating nations, social implications of climate policy, and alternative strategies that integrate community-based resource management.

Melissa Leach is Director of the Institute of Development Studies at the University of Sussex, UK. She founded and directed the STEPS Centre from 2006–14 and is co-Chair of the Science Committee of Future Earth. A social anthropologist and geographer, her research in Africa and beyond has addressed a variety of environmental, agricultural, health and technology issues, often integrating gender and feminist political ecology perspectives. Recent books include *Dynamic Sustainabilities: Technology, Environment, Social Justice* (2010); *Green Grabbing: A New Appropriation of Nature* (2013) and *The Politics of Green Transformations* (2015).

Michael Levien is an Assistant Professor of Sociology at Johns Hopkins University, Baltimore, MD, USA. He is currently working on a book about new forms of land dispossession in post-liberalization India and their implications for development, social inequality and democratic politics. His articles on this subject have appeared in *Politics and Society, Journal of Peasant Studies, Journal of Agrarian Change, Development and Change* and *Economic and Political Weekly*.

Lyla Mehta is a Professorial Research Fellow at the Institute of Development Studies at the University of Sussex, UK, and a Visiting Professor at Noragric, Norwegian University of Life Sciences. She is a sociologist working on gender and displacement, rights and access to natural resources and power/knowledge interfaces in policy debates, water and sanitation, and the politics of scarcity and uncertainty. She has research and field experience in southern Africa and South Asia. Lyla has engaged in advisory work with various UN agencies, and has also been active in advocacy and activist work on gender, environment and development issues with NGOs and social movements in Europe and India. She has authored *The Politics and Poetics of Water: Naturalising Scarcity in Western India*; edited *Displaced by Development: Confronting Marginalisation and Gender Injustice*; and co-edited *Shit Matters: The Potential of Community-led Total Sanitation*.

Preetha Prabhakaran has around ten years' experience in the development sector, principally in the areas of child rights advocacy, feminist social work practice and gender policy research. She is an alumna of the Tata Institute of Social Sciences in Mumbai, India and holds a Master's degree in Gender and Development Studies from the Institute of Development Studies, UK. Her earlier published work includes an analysis of global water discourses (specifically integrated water resources management) from a feminist political ecology perspective. She is currently working on sanitation and hygiene issues focusing specifically on community-led total sanitation in Asia and Africa.

Seemin Qayum is Policy Advisor on Sustainable Development at UN Women. Her areas of interest within the broad domain of gender and sustainable development are the articulation of sustainable livelihoods, access to resources, and community and landscape resilience, and the continuum from unpaid care to decent work. Recent publications include *Cultures of Servitude: Modernity, Domesticity, and Class in India* (with Raka Ray, Stanford University Press, 2009), *Multi-Stakeholder Decision-Making: A Guidebook for Establishing a Multi-Stakeholder Decision-Making Process to Support Green, Low-Emission and Climate-Resilient Development Strategies* (UNDP, 2012), and *The Bolivia Reader: History, Culture, Politics* (co-edited, in progress with Duke University Press).

Isha Ray is Associate Professor at the Energy and Resources Group, UC Berkeley, CA, USA and Co-Director of the Berkeley Water Center. She has a BA from Oxford University, UK and a PhD from Stanford University, CA, USA. Isha's research projects focus on access to water and sanitation for the rural and urban poor, and on the role of technology in advancing sustainable development goals. She has worked on water in India, China, Turkey, Mexico, Tanzania and California's Central Valley. She is co-editor (with Pranab Bardhan) of *The Contested Commons: Conversations between Economists and Anthropologists* (Wiley-Blackwell, 2008), and has extensive experience in the non-profit sector on international development and freshwater issues.

Shahra Razavi is Chief of the Research & Data Section at UN Women. Her work has been on gender dimensions of development, with a particular focus on livelihoods, agrarian issues, social policy and care. Since January 2013, when she joined UN Women, Shahra has been working on two of UN Women's flagship reports, 'Progress of the World's Women 2015' (on women's economic and social rights) and the 'World Survey on the Role of Women in Development' (on gender equality and sustainable development), as well as substantive work on the Commission on the Status of Women (CSW58 and CSW59). Before joining UN Women, Shahra was at the UN Research Institute for Social Development (UNRISD). Her recent publications include *The Global Crisis and Transformative Social Change* (with Peter Utting and Rebecca Varghese Buccholz, eds, 2012) and *Seen, Heard and Counted: Rethinking Care in a Development Context* (special issue of *Development and Change*, 2011).

Jade Sasser is an Assistant Professor in the Department of Gender and Sexuality Studies at the University of California, Riverside, CA, USA.

PREFACE AND ACKNOWLEDGEMENTS

The twin challenges of building pathways to sustainable development and enhancing gender equality have never been more pressing. This book shows why each is so important, but also why they must be addressed together, and how this might be done.

And this is a timely moment. As the world moves towards defining and implementing Sustainable Development Goals (SDGs) for the post-2015 era, there is much talk of integration – of environmental, social and economic dimensions of sustainability; of goals around climate change, water, food and land, health and reproduction, and other issues; and, with these, of gender equality and the empowerment of women and girls. But what does integration mean in practice, and how might it be achieved? In this book we offer an approach to these questions centred on the concept of pathways to sustainability, informed by feminist thinking around rights, relations and power. The book untangles the complex interactions between different dimensions of gender relations and of sustainability, and explores how policy and activism can build synergies between them. But further, it shows how plural pathways are possible, underpinned by different narratives about gender and sustainability, and how the choices between these are ultimately political.

Too often, discussions and action around gender and the environment have followed simplistic stereotypes that focus narrowly on women's roles, and assume them to be either victims or 'sustainability saviours'. These past tendencies have recently been brought to life again in the context of policy concerns with climate change, 'planetary boundaries' and green economies. In chapters focusing on work and industrial production; population and reproduction; food and agriculture; and water, sanitation and energy, the book's authors challenge and move beyond these stereotypes. They analyse the varied interactions between gender relations as intersected by other differences such as class, ethnicity and place, and different views of sustainability, asking 'sustainability of what, for whom'? They explore how gendered livelihoods, work and control of resources – but also identities, bodily integrity, dignity and knowledge – are implicated in pathways to sustainability – or otherwise. Revealed are tensions and trade-offs, and some powerful ways in which dominant market-led development models and policy approaches lead to both gender inequality and unsustainability. But the reverse is also possible: gender equality and sustainability can powerfully reinforce each other in alternative pathways. Women's knowledge, agency and collective action are often central to these, whether in managing local landscapes, adapting to climate change, producing and accessing food, or securing sustainable water, sanitation and energy services.

Drawing from these illustrations, the book calls for policies, investments and initiatives in sustainable development that recognize women's knowledge, agency and decision-making as fundamental. Such gender-equitable approaches can improve resource productivity and efficiency, and enhance ecosystem conservation and sustainable use. They can also build fairer and greener economies, and more sustainable, low-carbon and climate-resilient food, energy, water and sanitation, and health systems. Ultimately, for pathways to be truly sustainable and to advance gender equality and the rights and capabilities of women and girls, the book argues that those whose lives and wellbeing are at stake must be involved in leading the way, through community groups, women's organizations and other forms of collective action; through appropriate forms of investment and public services; and through fostering a linked, progressive politics of both gender and sustainability.

The book emerged from discussions and background papers originally commissioned by UN Women to inform its 2014 World Survey on the Role of Women in Economic Development. In a series of workshops and informal interactions, chapter authors – from different disciplinary, theoretical and sectoral backgrounds, yet sharing a commitment to engaged feminist scholarship – agreed that a common book-length project was both valuable and timely. The process of putting it together has been exciting and rewarding. As Editor I owe deep thanks to UN Women for its initial catalytic role and subsequent support, as well as to the chapter authors for their endeavour and collaborative spirit – it has been a pleasure and a privilege to work together, and a nice example of international feminist networking.

The book's overall conceptualization and individual chapter drafts have benefited greatly from others' comments and insights, both at the World Survey Expert Group meetings in New York and Rome in 2013–14, and in written reviews and informal interactions. Amongst others, particular thanks are owed to Bina Agarwal, Peter Alstone, Wendy Harcourt, Andrew Fischer, Stacy Jackson, Saraswathi Menon, Marjorie Mbilinyi, Mohan Rao, Liane Schalatek, Stephanie Seguino, Gita Sen, Libor Stloukal and Simon Thuo for their inputs to particular chapters or overall. We gratefully acknowledge the helpful comments of anonymous reviewers, while several chapters benefited from excellent research assistance, including from Senti Sojwal and Jessa Orluk (Chapter 3) and Tanya Kar and Larissa Ushizima (Chapter 4).

Finally, I should like to thank Naomi Vernon for her superb and timely copy-editing, and the ESRC STEPS Centre for its support to the process of production and publication.

Melissa Leach
Falmer, Brighton
February 2015

ACRONYMS AND ABBREVIATIONS

AGRA	Alliance for Green Revolution in Africa
AoA	Agreement on Agriculture (WTO)
BC	black carbon
BPO	business process outsourcing
CBD	Convention on Biological Diversity
CEDAW	Convention on the Elimination of All Forms of Discrimination against Women
CESCR	Committee on Economic, Social and Cultural Rights
CLTS	community-led total sanitation
DAWN	Development Alternatives with Women for a New Era
DFID	UK Department for International Development
FAO	Food and Agriculture Organization of the United Nations
FPE	feminist political ecology
GAD	gender and development
GED	gender, environment and development
GMO	genetically modified organism
GVC	global value chain
HAP	household air pollution
HDI	Human Development Index
HGU	land-use concessions (*Hak Guna Usaha*)
HLPE	High Level Panel of Experts
ICN	International Conference on Nutrition
ICPD	International Conference on Population and Development

ICTSD	International Centre for Trade and Sustainable Development
IFAD	International Fund for Agricultural Development
IFI	international financial institution
IFPRI	International Food Policy Research Institute
ILO	International Labour Organization
IT/ITES	information technology and services
IUCN	International Union for Conservation of Nature
LGBT	lesbian, gay, bisexual and transgender
LPG	liquefied petroleum gas
MARA	Malthusian Anticipatory Regime for Africa
MDGs	Millennium Development Goals
MMR	maternal mortality ratio
MWC	Mahindra World City
NAPM	National Alliance of People's Movements (India)
NEP	National Electrification Program (South Africa)
NFPE	new feminist political ecology
NISP	National Improved Stoves Program
NREGA	National Rural Employment Guarantee Scheme
PPP	public–private partnership
SC/STs	scheduled castes and tribes
SDGs	Sustainable Development Goals
SEZ	Special Economic Zone
SIE	semi-industrialized economy
SRHR	sexual and reproductive health and rights
SUN	Scaling Up Nutrition
TFR	total fertility rate
UNCCD	United Nations Convention to Combat Desertification
UNCED	United Nations Conference on Environment and Development
UNDP	United Nations Development Programme
UNEP	United Nations Environment Programme
UNFCCC	UN Framework Convention on Climate Change
UNFPA	United Nations Population Fund
UN-REDD	United Nations collaborative initiative on Reducing Emissions from Deforestation and forest Degradation
USAID	US Agency for International Development
WANTO	Women in Apprenticeship and Nontraditional Occupations
WCD	World Commission on Dams

WED	women, environment and development
WEDO	Women's Environment and Development Organization
WFP	World Food Programme
WFS	World Food Summit
WHO	World Health Organization
WID	women in development
WIEGO	Women in Informal Employment: Globalizing and Organizing
WiRES	Women in Renewable Energy Sector project
WOW	Wider Opportunities for Women
WTO	World Trade Organization

1

SUSTAINABLE DEVELOPMENT

A gendered pathways approach

Melissa Leach, Lyla Mehta and Preetha Prabhakaran

Introduction

Women in Kenya struggle to produce crops to feed their families amidst drying climates and insecure land tenure, on holdings diminished by private sector 'land grabs'.

In many villages and cities, vital work to care for the people who sustain economies and societies is compromised and rendered more difficult, because the basic water, sanitation, health and energy services needed aren't within reach.

Environmental and economic problems are blamed on population growth and the 'excessive fertility' of women – especially in Africa – encouraging a resurgence of coercive policies that undermine their bodily integrity and control.

Forest user groups in India with strong women's involvement render landscapes greener and richer in biodiversity and climate mitigation potential, while also satisfying vital needs for livelihoods, food and fuel.

Waste picker networks with women at their heart combine livelihoods with 'green' circular economies both in their communities and through upscaling into global networks.

Vignettes like these highlight vital interconnections between gender, environment and development. Environmental degradation has different impacts on women and men. Development patterns that neglect everyday environmental and economic needs can worsen women's positions, but so can environment and development discourses that target women inappropriately. Yet in an era when development is becoming sustainable development, women are also leading the way in new practices that combine environmental, economic and social goals. This book highlights the vital synergies between sustainable development and gender equality, but also the need for transformational change if negative interactions are to be averted and positive pathways built.

Accelerating sustainable development, and enhancing gender equality are both current imperatives in research, policy and public debate. Too often, however, they are addressed separately. This book's central argument is that they need to be integrated in both understandings and practices, in ways that appreciate the diversity of women's and men's experiences and contexts. Pursuing either sustainability or gender equality without attention to the other is doomed to failure on practical, moral and political grounds; the challenge, therefore, is to find pathways that build synergies between these concerns, towards sustainable and just futures for all. But how is this to be done, and by whom? How are gender equality, sustainability and their interlinkages to be understood, and how might the challenge of integrating them be addressed? The chapters that follow take up these questions in relation to a variety of issues and settings across the world. In this chapter, we introduce the overall arguments, definitions and conceptual approaches that inform and unite these contributions.

Our starting point is glaring evidence that dominant patterns of production, consumption and distribution are heading in deeply unsustainable directions. In a world in which humanity has become a key driver of Earth system processes, we are seeing over-exploitation of natural resources, the loss of key habitats and biodiversity, and pollution of land, seas and the atmosphere. Scientific understandings are clarifying the huge social, environmental and economic challenges posed by threats such as climate change and loss of essential ecosystem services, as humanity approaches or exceeds so-called 'planetary boundaries' (Rockström et al, 2009a; IPCC, 2013; Steffen et al, 2015). Already, human interactions with the environment are producing unprecedented shocks and stresses, felt in floods, droughts, and devastated urban and rural landscapes and livelihoods, while many people and places have suffered from a 'nexus' of food, energy, environmental and financial crises. These unsustainable patterns add to poverty and inequality today – especially for the third of the world's population directly dependent on natural resources for their wellbeing (Unmüßig et al, 2012) – and create deep threats for future generations. And their effects often intensify gender inequality.

The causes and underlying drivers of unsustainability and of gender inequality are deeply interlocked. Both, we argue, are produced by political–economic relations in late capitalism that support particular types of neoliberal, market-led growth. These involve extreme privatization, financialization and concentration of capital; production geared to short-term profits; unfettered material consumption; and unprecedented levels of militarism – very often at the expense of state regulation and redistribution, reproduction and care. These political–economic relations rely on and reproduce gender inequalities, exploiting women's labour and provision of unpaid care, and often their bodies too. They are leading, in many settings, to crises of social reproduction, while undermining people's rights and dignity. The same political–economic relations also produce environmental problems, as market actors seek and secure profit in ways that rely on the over-exploitation of natural resources and the pollution of climates, land and oceans. Such market-led pathways are leading in directions that are unsustainable in social and ecological terms, and ultimately in economic terms too, undermining the conditions for future progress.

Growing international attention and debate now highlight the need to move economies and societies onto more sustainable paths, whether to avert crisis and catastrophe, or enable prosperity through 'green economies'. Yet often missing in these debates is a sense of the politics involved. The challenge is often seen in technical and managerial terms, as a matter of getting the technologies, prices and regulations right. This overlooks the more profound restructuring of social, economic and political systems that we may require to transform unsustainable patterns. Equally, 'sustainability' is often presented as if it were a clear, uncontested term. Yet many tensions and trade-offs arise: for instance between finance for different kinds of low-carbon energy; between prioritizing food or biofuels in land use, or forests for carbon to mitigate global climate change or to meet local livelihood needs, to name a few. How such tensions are addressed has profound implications for who gains and loses – amongst social groups, and between local, national and global interests. Thus sustainability is a normative and contested term: we must constantly ask 'sustainability of what for whom' (Leach et al, 2010). As this book shows, many instances of policy and intervention today promote sustainability or green economy goals in ways that create tension with, or undermine, women's rights and gender equality.

Yet this is also a time of opportunity. Examples are accumulating around the world of alternative pathways that move towards sustainability and gender equality, uniting these in powerful synergies. Some are rooted in the everyday practices through which women and men access, control, use and manage forests, soils and urban landscapes in ways that sustain livelihoods and wellbeing. Others are evident in movements and collectives, many led by women, to build alternative food and resource sovereignty, agro-ecology, urban transitions or solidarity economies. While some of these offer alternatives or modifications within current capitalist relations, others suggest routes to more profound 'green transformations' (Scoones et al, 2015).

Integrating gender equality and sustainable development is therefore vital for several reasons. First, this is a moral and ethical imperative: building more equitable gender relations that support the human rights, dignity and capabilities of all women and men, intersected by differences of class, race, sexuality, age, ability and circumstances, is a central requirement of an ethical world order. Second, an integrated approach is vital to avoid women becoming victims, redressing the all-too-common pattern whereby women suffer most from environmental, climatic and economic shocks and stresses, undermining their vital roles in sustaining their families and communities. But third, and most significantly, an integrated approach offers opportunities to build on people's agency. Attention to gender offers routes to improve resource productivity and efficiency; to enhance ecosystem conservation and sustainable use, and to build more sustainable, low-carbon food, energy, water and health systems. Not just victims, the chapters in this book show how women have been, and can be, central actors in pathways to sustainability and green transformation. Yet, crucially, this must not mean adding 'environment' to women's caring roles, or instrumentalizing women as the new 'sustainability saviours'. It means recognition and respect for their knowledge, rights, capabilities and bodily integrity, and ensuring that roles are matched with rights and control over resources and decision-making power.

Gender equality and sustainable development can thus reinforce each other in powerful ways (see Agarwal, 2002; Buckingham-Hatfield, 2002; Johnsson-Latham, 2007; UNDP, 2012). Charting what pathways that reinforce gender equality and sustainable development together might look like, and how they might be built, are the central aims of this book. Five key sets of issues provide focal lenses through which the book's chapters consider these challenges. Thus Elissa Braunstein and Mimi Houston explore work and industrial production (Chapter 2); Betsy Hartmann, Anne Hendrixson and Jade Sasser consider population and reproduction (Chapter 3); Sakiko Fukuda-Parr addresses food security and agriculture (Chapter 4); Michael Levien takes up the related question of land rights and 'grabs' (Chapter 5), and Isha Ray examines everyday innovations around water, sanitation and energy (Chapter 6). These issues have been chosen – amongst many possibilities – because each illustrates 'troubling intersections' between dominant development pathways, (un)sustainability and gender (in)equality; each highlights the importance of a range of rights that are key to gender equality, from those involved with bare life and survival to those linked with voice, power and dignity; and each reveals contestation and debate between problematic narratives and pathways, and alternatives that offer pathways to sustainable development and gender equality.

The chapter authors are all eminent scholars and experts in the particular fields and issues they address. They come from diverse disciplinary backgrounds – including anthropology, economics, politics and technology studies – and a variety of positions in gender, development and feminist debates. These differences are reflected in the focus and analytical style of their particular chapters. Yet all share a broad political commitment to greater gender equality and a more sustainable and just world. This sense of the politics involved and their importance, as well as a desire to collaborate to produce a coherent set of analyses of gendered pathways to sustainability, was reinforced during a series of workshops and exchanges during 2013–14. These were hosted by UN Women, the United Nations entity for Gender Equality and the Empowerment of Women, to inform the preparation of the 2014 World Survey on the Role of Women in Economic Development (UN Women, 2014). While several of the book's chapters originated as background papers from which the report drew material, the analysis and arguments developed during these dialogues went far beyond what a UN report could hope to include. Shahrashoub Razavi and Seemin Qayum (Chapter 7) reflect on these issues of inclusion and translation, as an exemplar of the wider challenges of bringing a feminist political perspective to bear on sustainable development debates. Meanwhile, this book emerged as a collective effort to present a deeper set of contributions that, together, could demonstrate the importance of building pathways to sustainability and gender equality.

The dialogues that led to this book shared and developed a common set of definitions and approaches to gender equality, sustainability and their interlinkages. Central to these is a 'gendered pathways approach'. Building on the pathways approach developed by the STEPS Centre as a guide to thinking and action around sustainability challenges in a complex, dynamic world (Leach et al, 2010), this offers a conceptual framework for addressing the intersections, tensions and trade-offs between different dimensions of gender and of sustainability. The gendered pathways approach offers guidelines for analysing current pathways of change, and imagining and appraising alternatives.

The next two sections of this chapter introduce these core concepts in general terms, indicating their broad relevance for understanding the interlocking of gender (in)equality and (un)sustainability in pathways related to work, population, food, land, water and energy – thus introducing core themes dealt with in detail in subsequent chapters. The chapters themselves all apply this conceptual approach and illustrate it in action, although to different extents and in different ways, as befits their authors' focal issues and perspectives.

Tracing interlinkages between gender and sustainability is nothing new, however. The subsequent section reviews how diverse concepts – or narratives – about women, gender and sustainability have emerged and come to co-exist. Tracing shifting sustainability debates from colonial times to the present, we consider how and to what extent gender has been conceptualized, and the gendered outcomes of sustainability-focused policies and programmes. This includes a review of gender thinking – and silences – in current approaches to climate change, green economies and planetary boundaries. As it shows, powerful narratives have sometimes worked to hide or misrepresent gender–sustainability linkages. In the name of environmental protection, women have sometimes been dispossessed from their lands, forests and water resources. Women's roles as so-called 'carers' of nature have sometimes been essentialized, making women responsible for environmental chores that draw on their voluntary labour – in narratives that cast them as 'sustainability saviours'. Revisiting a longer history of sustainability thinking and feminist scholarship highlights problems to avoid and potentials to build on in developing a fully gendered pathways approach.

Building on this review, we go on to elaborate the gendered pathways approach more fully, drawing particularly on insights from feminist political economy, feminist political ecology, and studies of gendered subjectivities and embodiment. We also emphasize the significance of tensions and trade-offs in different pathways. Some will promote sustainability at the cost of gender equality; some may promote gender equality and neglect key dimensions of sustainability. Since pathways are dynamic, they can also have unintended social, technological and environmental consequences which effect gendered outcomes. Negotiating such dynamics requires inclusive learning and deliberation processes and ways to monitor exclusions, trade-offs and emerging opportunities, as well as ongoing awareness of the complex politics of both gender and sustainability.

The final section addresses the policy and political challenges of transforming pathways towards greater gender equality and sustainability. Strengthening and refining public policies and investments is key; but beyond and complementing these lies scope to build gender-progressive alliances between public and private actors, state and civil society institutions, and formal and informal practices. Ultimately, feminist movements and collective organizing, emerging in diverse ways and places across the world, may offer the greatest hope both for challenging unsustainable pathways and charting new ones that lead us in more sustainable, gender-equal directions.

Conceptualizing sustainable development, gender equality and pathways

Sustainability, and sustainable development, are historically changing and much debated concepts. Since the 1990s, mainstream views have generally defined sustainability in normative terms, to refer to a broadly identifiable set of social, environmental and economic values. Our definition is broadly in line with the view, since Brundtland (1987, p43), that sustainable development should 'meet the needs of the present without compromising the ability of future generations to meet their own needs'. This involves integrating three 'pillars' of sustainability: environmental, economic and social. Yet we go beyond these broad emphases in several important ways. First, we emphasize the need to be more specific about the values and goals at stake around different issues and contexts, across temporal and spatial scales, and according to the perspectives and priorities of different groups. Thus there may be multiple possible sustainabilities at stake, and negotiating these is a political, not just a technical and managerial, challenge. Second, in such negotiations, the social dimensions of sustainability – too often played down or ignored – must be fully integrated. And third, we must attend to equity not just across generations, but within them. Here gender equity and equality are central.

In this book, then, sustainable development is development that ensures human wellbeing, ecological integrity, gender equality and social justice, now and in the future.

Pursuing sustainable development for all requires upholding human rights principles, widening freedoms and promoting peace – in combination with respect for the environment. It requires redressing discrimination and disadvantage at household, local, national, regional and global levels.

This in turn requires redirecting interconnected environmental, economic, social and political processes, challenging current unsustainable pathways of production, consumption and distribution and finding new ones. It requires action and accountability by the state, civil society, the private sector, communities and individuals, building alliances to transform institutions and power relations, and to democratize knowledge.

In this conceptualization, gender equality is therefore integral to how sustainable development is defined and pursued. We consider gender equality in relation not just to women and men, but also to the ways that gender intersects with class, race and ethnicity, sexuality, place and other significant axes of difference. The concept of substantive gender equality emphasizes the importance of human rights, capabilities and the ways these intertwine and overlap (Goldblatt and McLean, 2011; Vizard et al, 2011). Building on this, we recognize multiple dimensions to pursuing gender equality. They include first, redressing socio-economic disadvantage in the domains of work, wellbeing and access to resources. This encompasses ensuring equal access to decent work and secure livelihoods; the recognition, reduction and redistribution of unpaid care work; equal access to quality education, health and other social services and public goods; and equal access to and control over resources and their benefits – including ecosystem-based resources. A second dimension is enhancing recognition and dignity. This includes challenging stereotypes around masculinity and femininity; assuring freedom from violence and violations of dignity and security; assuring bodily integrity and sexual and reproductive health and rights; and recognition and respect for diverse forms of knowledge production and application. Third, greater gender equality means enhancing equal participation in decision-making at multiple levels. This includes supporting agency, power and voice in institutions and decision-making; building deliberative forms of democracy that can debate sustainability goals and values in inclusive ways; and assuring space for feminist collective action.

Gender equality ultimately requires the realization of all human rights. In relation to work, we see the importance of women's rights to decent employment and livelihoods, and the significance of multiple rights while at work (see Chapter 2). In relation to population, we see the importance of assuring sexual and reproductive rights, as well as rights to freedom from violence and coercion (Chapter 3). Chapters 4 and 5 on food and agriculture highlight the right to food, as well as the importance of rights to land and natural resources in order to produce it. In relation to water, sanitation and energy, we see the importance of the right to water and sanitation as well as rights to basic infrastructure and services, and their vital links to rights to bodily integrity, dignity and security (Chapter 6). Yet in each of these areas, different kinds of rights and capabilities overlap and reinforce each other. Rights on their own are often not enough; making them real also requires recognition and respect (Fraser, 2013), power and voice, and challenges to dominant institutions and forms of knowledge. It is here that we see the critical role of collective action and women's mobilization in challenging stereotypes, making states accountable for the realization of rights, and in providing alternatives.

Our pathways approach helps in conceptualizing how institutions, power and knowledge can interact to create and sustain pathways that are either unsustainable, or – alternatively – that offer routes to sustainable development. Pathways are alternative directions of intervention and change. They refer to the ways that 'systems' or assemblages of social, political, economic, institutional, ecological and technological processes, interacting in dynamic ways in particular environments, might develop over time (Leach et al, 2010). Such systems operate at different scales. Thus a local example might be the interactions of land and tree ecologies, gender divisions of labour and responsibility, and cooking technologies involved in fuelwood use. Nationally, we might be concerned with the interactions of state policies and markets involved in food systems. And a global example might be the interactions of dynamic climate processes with international regulation, carbon market schemes, and finance aimed at curbing greenhouse gas emissions and impacts. Yet most sustainability challenges involve interactions across scales. Thus we might be concerned with the impacts of global climate processes on local land ecologies and uses, or with the ways that household, state and market institutions interact to shape the dynamics of food access. Pathways might involve systems moving in unsustainable directions or, alternatively, towards sustainable development.

Central to the pathways approach is to recognize that there are multiple ways of understanding and representing – or 'framing' – systems and change. Issues such as which scale is important, which processes are highlighted, the nature of problems and possible solutions, and which goals or dimensions of sustainability to highlight, can all be framed in different ways. Different actors – whether different local people, scientific, policy or business actors – will often hold different views depending on their particular backgrounds, perspectives, interests and values, and such framings often become part of narratives, or storylines, about a problem or issue, why it matters and what is to be done (Roe, 1995). 'Labelling' of particular people and groups – as responsible for the problem, or key to the solution – is often part and parcel of this.

Most sustainability issues involve multiple, contested framings and narratives. Thus, for example, environmental problems may be attributed to rising populations in Malthusian narratives that blame women's excessive fertility; or alternatively as the result of political–economic processes that lead to poverty-related resource degradation (see Chapter 3). Food sustainability challenges may be framed as problems of production, to be solved by new agricultural technologies and enhanced markets; or alternatively in terms of distribution, access and entitlements (Chapter 4). Different narratives, as we shall see, implicate and label gender and women in highly contrasting ways. The point is that not all narratives are equal; some dominate, supported by powerful institutions and relations, while others remain marginalized or hidden. And narratives have material consequences: they underpin and legitimate particular policies, institutions, interventions and patterns of investment, while excluding others.

The pathways approach thus highlights the narratives, institutions and political–economic processes that shape pathways towards, or away from, sustainable development and gender equality. It highlights the multiplicity of possible narratives and pathways in any setting, the tensions between these, and the importance of looking beneath the dominant 'motorways' to recognize and validate alternatives – the bush paths or faint footprints of the global development scene.

Pathways of (un)sustainable development and gender (in)equality

It is increasingly clear that dominant pathways of development are unsustainable in economic, social and environmental terms. The decades since the 1950s have seen huge growth across many indicators of production and consumption (Steffen et al, 2004). Since 1950 the global economy has increased by more than a factor of 15, and real world gross domestic product (GDP) grew from US$2 trillion in 1965 to US$28 trillion in 1995 (UNDP, 2000; UNEP, 2000; Steffen et al, 2004). This has depended, for the most part, on a development model focused on market-led economic growth under late capitalism. This is supported by powerful narratives, deeply entrenched amongst many international agencies and market actors, in which economic growth is the core goal, and market-led approaches the best way to achieve it. Such narratives have co-developed with patterns of production and consumption generally geared to increasing monetary accumulation. Hyper-consumption and materialistic lifestyles are encouraged. Neoliberal policies and logics emphasize the pursuit of private profits by firms and individuals, in markets left as free as possible from state involvement. Business competition and free trade are encouraged nationally, regionally and globally, but monopolistic practices are left largely uncurbed. There is increased financialization of many resources and sectors of the economy – and trade and speculation in those financialized resources. While there is obviously variation between countries, regions and sectors, much has been variation within the broad parameters of this kind of market-oriented, neoliberal growth model.

Increasingly, though, the economic sustainability of such pathways is in question. Financial crises and recession, taking hold in many countries and sending shock-waves around a globalized world, have laid bare the risks and vulnerabilities, bubble-like and boom–bust tendencies inherent to financialized market models, which undermine their viability even on their own terms. The fruits of this growth have also been deeply unequal. As GDP has grown, the economic disparities between countries and regions and within individual societies have increased. The poorest 20 per cent of the world's population control only 2 per cent of global income (Unmüßig et al, 2012), while the world's most rapidly growing economies – including the rising powers of Asia, South Africa and Latin America – have also seen rapid rises in inequality (Piketty, 2014). Inequality itself threatens economic sustainability, fuelling unrest and conflict, and undermining the stability, level playing field and consumer demand on which growth relies (Stiglitz, 2012).

Many dominant market-led pathways are also socially and environmentally unsustainable. Indeed mainstream growth-focused models frequently rely on, and thus perpetuate, both gender inequality, and pollution and over-exploitation of the environment. In terms of gender, a central dynamic includes reliance on a separation between productive and reproductive labour – the latter including unpaid and volunteer labour for care, subsistence and reproduction, much of it carried out by women. While productive labour is valued, capitalist pressures often force wages down. Growth in many areas of industry and commercial agriculture has unfolded along with a feminization of labour. While economic globalization has created employment opportunities for women across various classes, many of these have been provided within and reproduce patterns of discrimination and segregation that are embedded within labour markets. Thus poorer women undertake work that is seen to be an extension of their traditional gender roles, in low-end retail jobs, domestic service, assembly lines and labour-intensive agricultural work. Such jobs tend to be characterized by low wages, instability of employment, and poor working conditions. Many are informal. They reinforce the status of women as secondary earners within their households, and may remain invisible within the economic system.

Even more significantly, capitalist markets and production can continue to function as they do only because they constantly make use of unpaid labour, mostly by women, in caring for children, the sick and the elderly. Nancy Folbre argues that market economies are sustained not by the 'invisible hand of the market' alone, but also by the 'invisible heart of care' (Folbre, 2001). The nature of work that underlies care and the fact that it is unpaid often essentializes women as care-givers. Women's obligation to fulfil these socially prescribed roles not only places burden and stress on them, but also limits their opportunities, capabilities and choices to participate in paid employment outside the home, with negative consequences for their rights, dignity and status. This care work, which is essential to reproduce both the labour force and the wider communities and societies in which they are embedded, is consistently ignored, undervalued or 'externalized' in capitalist economic models. Gender inequality is therefore a constitutive element of this dominant development model, and reinforced through it. However, by eroding values of care and social security, and by over-exploiting human 'capital', this model risks becoming socially unsustainable; indeed there is growing evidence of an emerging crisis of social reproduction.

In ecological terms, people and their activities have become the dominant drivers of change in the 'anthropocene' (Steffen et al, 2004). Mainstream models of capitalist growth rely on the exploitation of natural resources as if they were unlimited, and on 'externalizing' the environmental costs of production – such as pollution and the release of greenhouse gases. Competitive pressures have led firms and market actors to a relentless search for economic efficiencies at the expense of nature. Economic incentives, technologies, infrastructures and political institutions have often combined to create and 'lock in' pathways that create profit at environmental expense – whether the entrenched fossil fuel systems that dominate energy supplies while creating carbon emissions and climate change, or commercial agricultural schemes that create short-term gain by over-exploiting soils and water supplies. Such pathways are unsustainable in their own terms, threatening to run up against resource limits that will undermine future production and consumption. They threaten the integrity of ecosystems, damaging water, soil, biodiversity, vegetation and air, reducing their life-supporting capacities, resilience and robustness. Declines in ecosystem services and productive capacity undermine people's livelihoods and health in the present, and threaten future generations. Local ecosystem degradation often interacts with global threats and processes, for instance in climate and ocean systems, resulting in shocks and stresses such as floods and droughts that damage further both ecosystems and the people and activities that depend on them.

By ignoring social and ecological limits to growth, the political economy of market-led growth and the narratives that underpin it thereby destroys its own living foundations – humans and nature – through over-exploitation (Wichterich, 2012). The capitalist market economy drives a constantly intensifying use of human, social and natural resources, in a vicious cycle in which hyper-resource extraction, production and consumption reinforce each other. In order to increase profits, capitalist production shifts social and ecological costs onto private households and local communities, or onto nature, along pathways that rely on and perpetuate gender inequality. In this process, local ways of living with environments in socially and ecologically sustainable ways – whether in rural or urban settings, amongst pastoralist, agricultural or forest communities – are often ignored or undermined, along with gendered local knowledge of ecologies and ways to manage them.

The costs and consequences of environmental change are also felt in gendered ways that can further fuel inequality. Disasters, including those related to climate change, often disproportionately affect poor women (Neumayer and Plumper, 2007). Women often bear the brunt of coping with climate-related shocks and stresses, or the health effects of urban pollution, adding to their care burdens. As land and forest resources once held in common are increasingly enclosed, privatized or 'grabbed' for commercial investment, so poorer women and indigenous people, who often depend on these places to produce and gather food and fuel for subsistence and incomes, find themselves marginalized and their livelihoods, rights and status further undermined. As scarcities of land, food, energy and water – created by their privatization and over-exploitation in competitive markets – interact and intensify, the resulting 'nexus' of pressures is also felt in gender-differentiated ways. Women often struggle to sustain livelihoods under more constrained conditions, adding to their care burdens and threatening their health and status.

As policy-makers and businesses seek to respond to environmental change within a market model, nature and ecosystems are increasingly commoditized and financialized, so that their carbon, biodiversity and other ecosystem services can be traded in markets, payment and offset schemes. While such schemes aim to 'put a proper price' on natural capital, so that it can be included within rather than externalized from economic calculations, the resulting markets have often proved to work against the interests of the poor and women, and have further intensified resource pressures, land, water and green 'grabs' (Fairhead et al, 2012; Mehta et al, 2012).

The rise and character of militarism adds a further dimension to pathways of unsustainability and gender inequality. The financial, political and policy relationships that link government agencies, armies and the industrial base that supports them – the so-called military–industrial complex – is a pervasive feature of late capitalism. Spending on defence dwarfs that on social or environmental investments in most countries. Concerns with national military security and defence encourage environmental change to be addressed in terms of its threats to national security – as when climate change is seen to create problematic environmental refugee flows across borders, or armed conflict is attributed to resource scarcity. This military 'securitization' takes attention, policy and investment away from the social, and gender-related, causes and impacts of environmental change. Meanwhile, military interventions are often associated with the perpetuation of violence in ways that rely on and entrench patriarchal values, and often damage women's rights, dignity and bodily integrity.

Such troubling intersections, or mutually reinforcing pathways, between unsustainability and gender inequality are evident in each of the chapters in this book. Yet the chapters also reveal how powerful narratives have often obscured such troubling intersections, hiding them under a gloss that market-oriented growth models can continue unproblematically, and need only to be implemented with greater force. Thus Chapter 2, on work, elaborates on the fundamental political–economic interactions between global growth and economic competitiveness, and the exploitation of women's labour through low wages and reliance on unpaid care. With a focus on industrial production, the chapter shows how this dynamic has played out in varied ways across sectors and in different countries, but has tended to produce both financial unsustainability and gender inequality.

Chapter 3, on population, shows the continued – and indeed renewed – dominance of Malthusian narratives that attribute environmental degradation and ecological threats to growing populations. This conveniently detracts attention from – and thus supports the continuation of – political–economic processes and relations that are actually far more significant in producing environmental problems than are sheer numbers of people. The chapter also shows the interconnections between neoliberalism and the rolling back of the state, and the rise of political economies and policies that treat women as self-disciplining reproductive subjects, blaming them for problems such as rising population growth, without support for – and often undermining – their rights, dignity and control over their bodies. It reveals interconnections between rising militarism and violence to both women and environments.

Chapter 4, on food, illustrates how systemic dynamics in the global economy and markets are intersecting with gender relations to have deleterious consequences for both household food security and gender equality. Yet dominant narratives – in this case the productionist focus that has dominated much international thinking and policy since the 1980s – marginalize questions of food rights and access. Focusing on these questions, the chapter shows how the volatility of world cereal markets and the operation of global value chains are interacting with gender-specific constraints around resource rights, access and control. Women farmers are central in producing food for their families and in sustaining the ecologies that enable this, but must often do so under increasingly constrained conditions. Meanwhile, in some settings food distribution within households works against women and girls. Gender relations, the chapter shows, are key to the distributional patterns and pathways that shape who gets access to food and adequate nutrition, and who goes hungry. They also shape the environmental sustainability, or otherwise, of the pathways involved in food production and access. Levien (Chapter 5) adds to the debate by exploring the gendered nature of dispossession from land, water and forest resources due to the different dimensions of land grabs, where the actions of powerful domestic and international players (often in cooperation with the state) lead to the marginalization of already powerless women and men. Thus the chapters bring to light the crucial, yet too often underplayed, intersections between prevailing political economies and the production of unsustainability and gender inequality.

Yet alternative pathways that move in sustainable directions – economically, socially and environmentally – are possible. They are underpinned by alternative narratives that emphasize not just profit and growth, but the importance of sustainability, inclusivity and social justice. Typically, these pathways do not rely solely on markets; instead they involve different combinations of public, private and civil society action and institutions. Social movements are key in initiating and demanding these pathways, and shaping forms of collective action that maintain them. And states play central roles – in providing appropriate policy contexts, regulating standards and resource use, holding private actors to account, and providing public services and investments crucial to social and ecological sustainability.

Thus, in relation to work, we see new public and private alliances pushing for and building green economies and green transformations (Chapter 2). Here pathways are emerging that link financing, technologies, and investments in areas such as renewable energy and waste recycling to styles of growth that respect ecological limits. Others, questioning whether continued high growth rates and market systems can ever be sustainable, are pioneering alternative pathways around ideas of sufficiency, solidarity and wellbeing.

In relation to food (Chapter 4), we see pathways emerging that focus on securing the right to food. These include policy and public support for needs-oriented smallholder farming, enabling people to secure ecologically sound cultivation, maintain soil fertility and ensure their livelihoods. Successful pathways often incorporate local knowledge of ecological conditions, soils and seeds, cooperatives for production and marketing, and support such as credit to enable poorer farmers to access appropriate inputs. Pathways to support food access and rights also benefit from state interventions, for instance in setting minimum wages, labour market policies and price regulation, and negotiating internationally around issues such as export subsidies and the maintenance of reserve stocks to offset price volatility. Social movements are campaigning actively for such structural changes to the political economy of food, while demonstrating alternative pathways centred on local food system autonomy and sustainable agro-ecological practices.

Chapter 6, on investments, highlights pathways through which the poorest people can secure rights to products and services that meet essential everyday needs – for water, sanitation and clean cooking. These bring vital benefits both in environmental sustainability and in enhancing people's capabilities, dignity and health. Public investment is key to such pathways. But so too is innovation to find appropriate water, sanitation and stove technologies and attune them to local social and ecological conditions. The role of local knowledge and grassroots innovation and action therefore proves fundamental for these pathways too. The challenge is then to scale-up equitably, maintaining a focus on gender justice and sustainability, and here state and public policy interventions are key.

Women's agency is central to many of these alternative, sustainable pathways. Women are often at the forefront of social movements resisting unsustainable pathways and demanding alternatives. Their knowledge, action and agency are central to finding, demonstrating and building more ecologically, economically and socially sustainable ways to manage local ecologies, adapt to climate change, produce and access food, and secure sustainable, appropriate water, sanitation and energy services. Increasingly, women's centrality is recognized in policy and politics. Thus governments and donor agencies target women as key in community adaptation to climate change; in addressing assumed population–environment problems (through their reproductive capacities); and in sustainable food production (as smallholders). Indeed, narratives that see women as 'sustainability saviours' are evident in many areas of debate, from those focused on green care economies or population–environment linkages, to those addressing conservation of climate, biodiversity, water and soils, to those building socially and environmentally sustainable services.

Yet such narratives carry dangers. They often assume, again, on women's unpaid care and reproductive work – sustaining people and ecologies – without granting this due recognition, support and consideration of redistribution with men and others. They frequently treat 'women' as homogeneous, ignoring the vital intersections with class, ethnicity, age and identity that shape their interests, knowledge, values, opportunities, capabilities and rights. They ignore the gender relations – in rights, resource access and control, voice and power – that shape whether women's action and work towards economic or environmental sustainability translates into benefits – in enhanced rights, capabilities, dignity, bodily integrity. Thus women's involvement in pathways to sustainability does not necessarily mean greater gender equality; on the contrary, as the examples of population and agriculture show, 'instrumentalizing' women to save the planet can entrench and worsen gender inequalities.

This is why it is important, always, to attend to the politics of sustainability – asking 'sustainability of what, for whom', and to avoid trade-offs in which economic or environmental sustainability is secured at the expense of gender equality and women's rights and capabilities. Sustainable development, as we define it, must include gender equality as integral; the challenge is to identify and support alternative sustainable development pathways that promote gender equality and women's rights, voice and bodily integrity. This requires analysis and action based on a truly gendered pathways approach.

What areas of theory, policy and debate are most helpful in developing and enriching such an approach? The next section examines the intellectual underpinnings of a range of key concepts and policy debates around sustainability and sustainable development, considering how gender has been conceptualized within these.

Gender and sustainable development: Reviewing concepts and debates

Although 'sustainability' has become a key concept guiding global, national and local institutional frameworks, policies and interventions, the concept is ever-changing, deeply debated and contested. Gender has been variously ignored by, or incorporated into, conceptualizations and policy debates in a diversity of ways. A brief review highlights the historical roots of some key concepts and approaches that continue to co-exist and compete today, albeit in contemporary forms. Specifically, we draw on a long and rich history of work on gender, environment and sustainable development over the past 30 years, with feminist theory co-evolving with feminist movements. We highlight the origins of both continuing problematic narratives about women, gender and sustainability; and also strands of feminist analysis that offer valuable insights to enrich a gendered pathways approach and inspire a transformative politics of sustainable development.

Colonial and neocolonial economic and environmental policies

The term 'sustainability' was first coined in an environmental context by a German forester (von Carlowitz, 1712) to prescribe how forests should be managed on a long-term basis. The emphasis on conserving economically valuable natural resources to sustain European powers was a key thread in imperial and colonial environmental policies, along with aesthetic and moral desires to preserve an imagined, remaining pristine nature and wilderness in the tropics. Colonial conservation policies and practices ranged from forest reserves and 'scientifically managed' plantations to protect supplies of commodities such as timber and rubber (Sivaramakrishnan, 1999) to watershed protection policies and the creation of wildlife reserves (Anderson and Grove, 1987). They were frequently justified by narratives that local populations were incapable stewards of natural resources, whose 'primitive' agricultural hunting, gathering and fire-setting practices caused environmental degradation. The practices of colonial science and administration often went hand-in-hand to label local people as environmental destroyers, justifying their removal, restriction or re-education (Fairhead and Leach, 1996; Leach and Mearns, 1996; Beinart and McGregor, 2003; Adams, 2004). They often had devastating social consequences, dispossessing local women and men of land and livelihoods, and supporting exploitative and degrading labour practices.

Ecofeminists have argued that the colonial period – building on Enlightenment ideas – led to the simultaneous domination of women and nature (Merchant, 1980; Mies, 1986; Mies et al, 1988; Shiva, 1988). Thus Shiva argues that colonial development in India led to the subjugation of a pre-colonial 'feminine principle' that had underpinned harmony with nature and equitable social and gender relations. Mies and Shiva (1993) characterize imperialism and colonialism as bearers of a particular western, mechanistic, 'masculinist' science and rationality, 'doing violence' to women and nature. Other anthropological and historical analyses, while critical of such generalizations about femininity and nature, nevertheless highlight diverse ways of living sustainably with dynamic local ecologies to which women were often central (e.g. Boserup, 1970; Appfell-Marglin and Simon, 1994). They have documented the complex and variegated gender relations in these systems, the gender-differentiated effects of colonial policies (e.g. Mackenzie, 1998) and women's tactical negotiations in response (Allman et al, 2002).

Such analyses are deeply relevant today. Forms of economic development that dispossess people of rights and livelihoods still abound, such as large dams – now often justified as bringing environmentally 'clean' hydropower, yet with negative local ecological as well as social and gendered impacts (see Mehta, 2009a). Neocolonial 'fortress'-like conservation policies and enclosures continue to be implemented in areas such as forest and wildlife conservation (West et al, 2006; Brockington et al, 2008), while the past decade has seen a new wave of large-scale foreign investments in parts of Asia, Africa and Latin America in commercial crops and biofuels for export. Although the actors and dynamics are different, these global land, water and 'green' grabs – and the narratives of local resource mismanagement that underpin them – offer striking similarity (Fairhead et al, 2012; Mehta et al, 2012). Unpicking gendered effects of dispossession, and bringing to light alternative pathways, is more critical than ever.

Social and environmental movements

The colonial period also illustrates the start of emerging tensions, between short-term economic profit and long-term environmental implications, that have continued to the present. Social and environmental movements have been key in identifying and responding to such tensions.

In the global North, movements from the 1960s and 1970s focused on pollution, resource depletion and habitat loss. Together with cornerstone publications such as *Silent Spring* (Carson, 1962) and *The Limits to Growth* (Meadows et al, 1972), they fuelled a growing public and political consciousness of the environmental downsides of economic growth. Social and environmental movements in Asian, Latin American and African settings, in contrast, focused mainly on the negative impacts of economic and environmental policies on local livelihoods, and the protection of local social and indigenous people's rights and wellbeing. Examples from the 1970s include movements resisting large dams and displacement, mining and forest destruction (Doyle, 2005). The 1974 Chipko movement resisting industrial logging in the Himalayas was primarily a livelihood-protection movement, but went on to become a celebrated exemplar and symbol for non-violent environmental protest and women's roles in it. Similar symbolism attached to Kenya's Green Belt Movement, founded by Professor Wangari Maathai in 1977, which encouraged rural women to work together to plant trees for livelihoods and conservation. Women's central involvement in many movements encouraged analysts later to make stereotyped linkages between women and 'nature'. Nevertheless, most shared a general and important narrative critiquing dominant economic development pathways and their social and gendered consequences, and forwarding alternatives. This set the stage for many further forms of feminist mobilization for sustainable development to the present.

Sustainable development; women, environment and development; and ecofeminism

Against this backdrop, in the 1980s the term 'sustainability' came into wider currency in efforts to show how environmental issues might be linked to mainstream questions of economic and social development. The landmark UN Commission report *Our Common Future* (Brundtland, 1987) established what is still the most widely accepted concept of sustainable development (discussed above). This linked sustainability firmly to questions of human economic and social needs, 'in particular the essential needs of the world's poor, to which overriding priority should be given' (Brundtland, 1987, p43). Yet, in its static notion of 'needs', the concept stops short of concern with capabilities, rights and justice as goals of sustainable development. The Brundtland report also paid little attention to intra-generational equity, including gender equality.

The United Nations Conference on Environment and Development in Rio, 1992 provided a landmark forum where diverse approaches to sustainable development were debated by governments, civil society and social movements. It launched high-level convention processes around global environmental issues – including the UN Framework Convention on Climate Change (UNFCCC), the Convention on Biological Diversity (CBD), and the UN Convention to Combat Desertification (UNCCD), setting in train intergovernmental negotiations and related national action plans that have continued to the present. Yet global negotiations have failed to meet targets, while many national sustainability plans became forms of managerialism that failed to challenge the political–economic processes supporting unsustainable pathways (Berkhout et al, 2003).

Agenda 21 at Rio envisaged sustainability being built from the bottom up through initiatives by local governments, community groups and citizens (Lafferty and Eckerberg, 1998; Selman, 1998). It stimulated a plethora of 'community-based' and joint state–local sustainable development projects and programmes across the world, around water, fisheries, forests, wildlife, urban environments and other issues. These initiatives embodied important recognition of local resource rights and collective action. Yet many suffered from an overly homogeneous and romanticized view of 'the community' that failed to account for socially and gender-differentiated perspectives and priorities (Leach et al, 1999; Dressler et al, 2010), or involved women only tokenistically in project management committees. This tendency has continued in much community-based sustainable development to the present.

Around Rio 1992, a wide coalition of NGOs and social movements, including the Women's Environment and Development Organization (WEDO), Development Alternatives with Women for a New Era (DAWN) and others lobbied hard to integrate gender concerns into emerging sustainable development debates. Women's Action Agenda 21 was produced and fed into the 1991 Miami World Women's Congress for a Healthy Planet. This critiqued existing development pathways and free-market thinking, instead embracing the concept of 'sustained livelihoods' and flagging the need to link everyday practices of care, social reproduction and resource justice (see Wichterich, 2012). Yet many of the alternatives put forward by women's groups and networks in the 'Global Women's Lobby' in Rio were overshadowed by the optimism towards economic efficiency, technology and markets (Wichterich, 2012). DAWN and other groups called 'sustainable development' a huge contradiction, calling for transformation of growth-based development models towards gender-equitable development (Wiltshire, 1992).

Agenda 21 and post-Rio debates did recognize women as important actors in environmental protection and poverty alleviation, but treated gender in an instrumentalist rather than a transformative way – following dominant 'women, environment and development' (WED) approaches. In the 1980s, a plethora of publications by scholars, NGOs and donor agencies had forwarded a strong narrative that women were the primary users and managers of the environment at the local level (e.g. Dankelman and Davidson, 1988; Rodda, 1991). What came to be termed the WED approach translated 'women in development' (WID) perspectives into the environmental domain. WED discourse valuably highlighted the significance of local environments to women's lives and livelihoods, and underlined the importance of alternative pathways in which women were central. However, like WID, WED gave a rather homogeneous, static view of women and their roles, ignoring their shaping by gender and social relations. Women–environment connections – especially in reproductive and subsistence-focused activities such as collecting fuelwood, hauling water and cultivating food – were often presented as if natural and universal.

In early WED debates, women often appeared as victims of environmental degradation – imagery revived in recent narratives about climate change impacts. Later, the positive image of women as agents – effective environmental managers and conservers of resources – gained ground. This underpinned narratives that women should be harnessed as 'sustainability saviours'. Thus the World Bank developed a 'synergistic' or 'win–win' approach, arguing for a general identity of interest between women and environmental resources (see Jackson, 1998 for a fuller discussion). Women were also conceptualized as the central agents of community-based conservation and 'primary environmental care'. Yet the ensuing projects and policies often mobilized women's labour, skills and knowledge, 'instrumentalizing' women and adding to their unpaid care roles without addressing whether they had the rights, voice and power to control project benefits. This tendency persists to the present in recent approaches to population and environment, and to green economies.

WED also had strong synergies with ecofeminism, which emerged as a powerful discourse in the late 1980s and early 1990s, based on the notion that women are especially 'close to nature' (e.g. Plumwood, 1986; Shiva, 1988; Mies and Shiva, 1993). Ecofeminism has many strands, some naturalizing and essentializing a femininity–nature connection, others seeing this as a social, cultural or ideological construct. Most assume that violence against nature goes hand-in-hand with violence against women; hope for sustainable and equitable development therefore lies in recovering people–nature interdependence grounded in a 'feminine principle'.

Ecofeminist views of natural linkages between women and nature sometimes served to justify WED-type projects that instrumentalized women's roles – yet these linkages rarely stand up to historical or anthropological scrutiny (Joekes et al, 1996). Equally problematic is the assumption that sacralized views of 'nature' go hand-in-hand with harmonious environmental practices and egalitarian gender relations (Croll and Parkin, 1992). Such critiques and debates around WED and ecofeminism circulated intensely in the 1990s, a vibrant period for feminist analysis of sustainable development (Braidotti et al, 1994; Harcourt, 1994a,b; Leach, 1994). Nevertheless ecofeminism inspired – and continues to inspire – valuable critiques of modern science, endorsement of local and indigenous knowledges, and social movements and political action, for instance around energy systems and peace (see also Wichterich, 2012), highlighting alternative narratives and pathways.

Feminist political economies and ecologies

From the early 1990s, feminist scholars advanced social relational perspectives on environment and sustainable development. Many of these drew their grounding from feminist political economy analyses, especially of households and agrarian change, and of states, markets, production and reproduction (e.g. Benería and Sen, 1981; Young et al, 1984; Folbre, 1994), as well as from gender and development (GAD) scholarship. Up to the present, feminist political economy offers invaluable critiques of dominant development pathways and the ways they produce social unsustainability and gender inequality, advocating transformational alternatives based on rights, capabilities, and social and gender justice (Rai and Waylen, 2013). Integrating ecological dimensions, several important approaches emerged including feminist environmentalism (Agarwal, 1992); gender, environment and development (Braidotti et al, 1994; Leach, 1994; Joekes et al, 1996); and feminist political ecology (Rocheleau et al, 1996).

Despite their differences, these perspectives share a number of core ideas. First, women's (and men's) relationships with the environment are seen to emerge from the social context of dynamic gender relations – not an a priori special relationship with nature. Thus women's close involvement in gathering wild foods, for instance, might reflect labour and tenure relations, and lack of access to income from trees on private holdings (cf. Rocheleau, 1988; Agarwal, 1992). Second, different women – and men too – have very different interactions with land, trees, water and so on, associated with class, age, ethnicity and kinship positions. Third, unlike WED, which focused on roles, importance is given to relations of tenure and property, and control over labour, resources, products and decisions. Environmentally related rights and responsibilities are almost always contingent on class, kin, household and state arrangements and the negotiations these entail; arrangements that need to be understood and addressed if the aim is to enhance women's rights and agency. Finally, gender analyses of environmental relations point out the fallacy of assuming that women's participation in environmental projects is coterminous with benefit. Allocating women responsibility for 'saving the environment' could increase their workloads or reinforce regressive gender roles, rather than representing progressive change or enhanced gender equity (Leach, 1992; Jackson, 1998).

Feminist political ecology (FPE) fused feminist political economy and broader political ecology approaches to address the intersections between ecology and gendered power relations on scales from household up to global. Building on feminist critiques of science (e.g. Haraway, 1988), FPE emphasized the significance of alternative and gendered forms of knowledge, challenging epistemology, objectivity and rationality whilst embracing the gendering of knowledge, human embodiment, subjectivity and political agency (Wright, 2010, p819). And it drew attention to the power of emancipatory social movements, often grounded in alternative knowledges and collective action, in struggles for rights and environmental protection (Rocheleau et al, 1996; Nightingale, 2006, 2011). While most feminist political ecologists are critical of romanticized visions of 'community' that side-step questions of class, gender or other social divisions (e.g. Rocheleau et al, 1996; Agarwal, 2001; Asher, 2004; Resurreccion, 2006), at least in some conceptions of FPE there are dangers of romanticism (and sometimes essentialism) in ideas of 'the indigenous' and indigenous movements.

In recent years, new feminist political ecology (NFPE) has added to these debates, emphasizing how gender is 'performed' in different contexts, thereby encompassing multiple and complex subjectivities (Butler, 1994; Resurreccion and Elmhirst, 2008). It turns attention to 'the entangled processes of the production of nature and subjectification/subjection as this relates to gendered roles, landscapes, bodies, livelihood strategies…' (Hawkins and Ojeda, 2011, p250). NFPE has also drawn on gender with a lesbian, gay, bisexual and transgender (LGBT) perspective, going beyond dualisms in discourses, bodies and subjectivities to highlight problems with the dominant heteronormative lens in environment and development debates. A performative approach to gender draws attention to the multiple processes by which the 'gendered subject' is continually constructed and reconstructed through social, political–economic and ecological engagements, extending from the most intimate and emotional to the global (Elmhirst, 2011; Sultana, 2011, Truelove, 2011). It connects with feminist work on embodiment (e.g. Braidotti, 1994) and on the changing character of masculinities, femininities and 'intersectional' identities, including in the hyper-materialist contexts of late capitalism (e.g. Edström et al, 2014).

Sustainability politics: Whose futures count?

As the world approached the run-up to Rio+20, the 2012 United Nations Conference on Sustainable Development, narratives around the meanings of, and potential pathways to, sustainable development were even more divided and contested than 20 years earlier. The 1990s and 2000s had seen the consolidation of neoliberal policies and practices, the rise of corporate power, and growing political and economic strength amongst 'rising powers', creating an even more challenging landscape for international cooperation. At the same time, the real impacts of shocks and stresses in climate, food and finance were increasingly felt throughout the world. In this context, many policy and business actors, cynical about the prospects of sustainable development, instead embraced apparently positive alignments between economic growth and environment through notions such as the green economy. Yet, in parallel, social movements and activism around environment and development have flourished, contesting dominant perspectives on issues such as climate change, water privatization, genetically modified organisms, biodiversity and land grabbing, and advocating alternative pathways that link sustainable development firmly with questions of social justice.

Compared with 1992, feminist visions and contributions were notably less vocal in Rio 2012's debates about *The Future we Want* (Wichterich, 2012). Indeed, many current mainstream sustainability literatures and policy debates are remarkably gender blind, or continue to mobilize problematic narratives that see women narrowly as environmental victims or sustainability saviours. This is the case for three key sets of contemporary discourse and practice – around climate change, planetary boundaries and the green economy. Yet in these, too, important feminist and gendered critiques and alternatives are emerging from the margins and from social movements.

Since the 2000s, climate change has been taken seriously as a major issue involving politics, economics and injustice. The relative successes and setbacks of global climate change frameworks and negotiations, difficulties in implementing principles of 'common but differentiated responsibility' in mitigating far-reaching threats, and the plight and coping strategies of people already faced with the need to adapt to climate-related shocks and stresses have galvanized public reaction, and a renewed and globalized environmental politics involving movements and campaign groups stretching across local and global scales. Yet the 1992 UNFCCC was a remarkably gender-blind document, and subsequent efforts to mainstream gender issues into climate change debates have been very piecemeal (Denton, 2002; Skutsch, 2002). The focus on universal issues and consensus has compromised a focus on gender, while even discussions of equity and climate change have downplayed its gender dimensions (Lambrou and Paina, 2006). Only in 2008 did the UNFCCC Secretariat call for gender-sensitive measures. 'No climate justice without gender justice' was a rallying cry for feminist lobbyists at the 2008 Bali conference, which launched groups such as the Women for Climate Justice Network and Global Gender and Climate Alliance (see Terry, 2009).

To the extent that they address gender, climate policy documents often repeat WED-type problematic narratives, either stereotyping women as victims, or assuming them saviours in keeping their communities resilient or adopting low-carbon technologies (for critiques see MacGregor, 2010; Arora-Jonsson, 2011). Yet feminist political economy/ecology analysis underscores how gender and class relations, rights and inequalities shape differences in women's and men's vulnerability to climate change, and opportunities to be agents in mitigation and adaptation (Agarwal, 2002). For instance, in contexts of entrenched discrimination, women's inclusion in technical committees for low-carbon technologies can increase women's workloads and reinforce gender stereotypes, as Wong (2009) shows for solar home systems in Bangladesh. Women can be key agents in low-carbon development, but only with attention and support to their specific knowledge and capacities (Otzelberger, 2011).

Much of the debate on gender and climate change has focused on adaptation and local-level vulnerabilities, with much more limited, and only recent, attention to gender in debates around large-scale technologies, market initiatives and climate finance (see World Bank, 2011; Schalatek, 2013). International agreements on gender equality, such as the Convention on the Elimination of All Forms of Discrimination against Women (CEDAW), are insufficiently reflected in national adaptation or low-carbon development plans (Otzelberger, 2011). This poor integration is a reflection of, and in turn reinforces, the tendency for policy to focus on simplistic imagery and apparent quick wins, rather than the more structural political–economic changes needed to re-steer pathways of climate unsustainability and gender inequality.

A second contemporary debate centres on notions of planetary boundaries. Influential scientific analyses suggest that we have entered the anthropocene, a new epoch in which human activities have become the dominant driver of many Earth system processes, including climate, biogeochemical cycles, ecosystems and biodiversity. A series of nine planetary boundaries has been identified, referring to the biophysical processes in Earth's system on which human life depends (Rockström et al, 2009a), which together serve to keep the planet within Holocene-like conditions and thus define a so-called 'safe operating space' for humanity. Potentially catastrophic thresholds are in prospect, it is argued, providing a new urgency and authority to arguments that development pathways must reconnect with the biosphere's capacity to sustain them (Folke et al, 2011). A recent update (Steffen et al, 2015) identifies two core boundaries – climate change and biosphere integrity – each of which, it is claimed, could on its own drive the Earth system into a new state, should they be substantially and persistently transgressed.

While the science is still developing, the concept of planetary boundaries has become influential within policy debates – but is also critiqued. Some actors, including some developing country governments, interpret it as anti-growth and development. Others suggest that planetary boundaries thinking privileges universal global environmental concerns over diverse local ones, justifying top-down interventions that protect the environment at the expense of people and their livelihoods. The renewed narratives of impending scarcity and catastrophe implied by some interpretations of planetary boundaries arguments risk a return to draconian policies and unjust responses that limit people's rights and freedoms, as Hartmann et al show in relation to population (see Chapter 3). That steering development within planetary boundaries should not compromise inclusive development that respects human rights has been proposed by Raworth (2012), whose 'doughnut' concept takes the circle of planetary boundaries and adds an inner 'social foundation'. In between these is a 'safe and just operating space' for humanity, within which sustainable development pathways should steer (Leach et al, 2013). Raworth (2012) notably introduces gender equality as one dimension of this social foundation, but otherwise discussion and advocacy arising from the planetary boundaries concept has been largely gender-blind.

Finally, a focus on green economies is now capturing the attention of governments, businesses and NGOs alike. According to the United Nations Environment Programme (UNEP), which launched its Green Economy Initiative in 2008, a green economy is one that results in improved human wellbeing and social equity, while significantly reducing environmental risks and ecological scarcities; it is low-carbon, resource-efficient and socially inclusive (UNEP, 2013a). This general definition integrates social, ecological and economic concerns in ways akin to sustainable development. Yet, in practice, there are many versions of green economy thinking. Dominant ones assume continued, even enhanced market-led economic growth, through green business investments and innovations that enhance energy and resource efficiency, and prevent the loss of ecosystem services. It has been argued that the emerging green technology economy will be worth US$4.2 trillion annually by 2020 (Clancy, 2009). Other strands emphasize market-based approached to environmental protection through financial valuation of 'natural capital' (e.g. Natural Capital Committee, 2013), payments for ecosystem services, and schemes for trading carbon and biodiversity credits and offsets.

However, others argue that environmental constraints require a rethink of growth and market strategies. UNEP's 'decoupling' (Fischer-Kowalski et al, 2011) suggests that economic growth should be de-linked from the increasing consumption of material resources such as construction minerals, fossil fuels and biomass. Jackson (2009) argues for a shift in focus towards prosperity and wellbeing with reduced or no growth, in which investments in services and care, as well as in 'green' action in the areas of sustainable food production and marketing and clean energy, are key.

Mainstream approaches to defining and developing green economies have paid little attention to their differentiated implications for women and men (see Naret Guerrero and Stock, 2012). Feminist analysis and activists are critical, arguing that Rio+20 missed a chance to break with the business-as-usual global economic model, which produces environmental destruction, social exploitation and inequality (Unmüßig et al, 2012; Wichterich, 2012; Schalatek, 2013). They see the green economy as a market-based approach that justifies the commodification and enclosure of resources and commons, undermining livelihoods, justifying land and green grabs (Borras et al, 2011; Fairhead et al, 2012; Mehta et al, 2012) and dispossessing local people – especially women food producers. Feminists variously call instead for 'green development' that respects commons and livelihoods (Agarwal, 2010); for recognition and value of care and social reproduction in green economy debates (e.g. Vaughan, 2007; Mellor, 2009); for replacing efficiency with sufficiency (Salleh, 2009; Mehta, 2010); and for a focus on commons and communing and 'enough' and more fundamental 'green transformations' that restructure production, consumption and political–economic relations along truly sustainable pathways (Wichterich, 2012, 2015). The Women's Major Group at Rio argued for social equity, gender equality and environmental justice to be placed at the heart of a 'sustainable and equitable' (as opposed to green) economy, grounded in ethical values such as respect for nature, solidarity, caring and sharing (see also UNDP, 2013a). These arguments link with growing narratives and action around alternative economies and solidarity economies (Unmüßig et al, 2012), and powerful examples of feminist collective organizing and social movement activism around the world.

The contradictory processes after the 2008 global financial crash and the accompanying food, climate and resource crises highlight the need to interweave both feminist political economy critiques of macroeconomics, trade and labour relations, and feminist political ecology approaches that highlight gendered access to and control over resources and links with subjectivity, identities and the politics of knowledge. As Wichterich (2015) eloquently argues, both approaches deconstruct 'othering' (be it of women as carers of unpaid work, or of nature) and provide an intersectional and context-specific analysis of gender in global and local power structures. Both also understand gender as a key social category of inequality, and are concerned with processes of inclusion, exclusion and othering in this new landscape of neoliberalism and resource commodification (Wichterich, 2015). Using both approaches to revitalize debates concerning care, commons, commoning and cultures of sufficiency, solidarity or enough can thus provide powerful critiques of current growth-oriented paradigms and their destructive impacts on ecosystems and local people.

This account of the past few decades of thinking, policy and practice has also clearly highlighted that sustainability and sustainable development are political. An array of concepts, approaches and associated policies and actions have emerged, and continue to co-exist to the present, with much contestation. Feminist and gender-based analysis and action has been and remains key, although capacity to shape the mainstream has varied. Yet feminist thinking is also varied, producing a variety of different narratives about women, gender and sustainability. Which concepts and approaches offer the most helpful insights and contributions to a fully gendered pathways approach?

Elaborating a gendered pathways approach

Returning to our definition, the challenge is to identify and build pathways of sustainable development – that is, development that ensures human wellbeing, ecological integrity, gender equality and social justice, now and in the future. Pathways, as defined and illustrated earlier, are alternative directions of intervention and change, underpinned by particular framings and narratives, which embody selective values, knowledge and power relations. As previous sections have shown, there are urgent needs to challenge current unsustainable pathways of production, consumption and distribution, and to recognize and support alternatives.

Insights from feminist scholarship offer valuable ways to enrich and elaborate a pathways approach, integrating a concern for gender equality into both the processes through which pathways develop and unfold, and their outcomes. Recent gender analyses underscore the importance of addressing not just women and men, but the ways that gender intersects with class, race and ethnicity, sexuality, place and other significant axes of difference. Feminist political economy and gender, environment and development (GED) approaches highlight the significance of gender relations and institutions – from households and kinship to states and markets – as part of pathways. Together with rights-based and capability approaches, they emphasize the importance and ingredients of substantive gender equality as key pathway goals or outcomes. These need to include equal access to decent work and secure livelihoods; the proper recognition and redistribution of unpaid care work; and equal access to key social and environmental services and benefits. Linking with ideas around green transformations, feminist political economy also underscores that sustainable development may not be possible without quite fundamental restructuring of political–economic–environmental relations.

Feminist and new feminist political ecology approaches highlight the importance of selective knowledge and power, underscoring the importance of challenging problematic narratives about gender and sustainability, and making space for alternative narratives and pathway processes built on alternative, gendered forms of knowing and being. They highlight the diversity and performative, embodied character of femininities, masculinities and related identities. This offers insights into the enhancement of recognition and dignity as key pathway goals. As we have seen, this requires challenging stereotypes around masculinity, femininity and their interconnections with ecology and economy, as well as assuring freedom from violence and violations of dignity and security, and assurance of bodily integrity, and sexual and reproductive health and rights. Finally, feminist political ecology – along with feminist analyses of politics and governance – emphasizes the importance of equal participation in decision-making, and that this must happen at multiple, interconnected scales. They highlight the positive outcomes – in terms of alternative narratives and visions of the future linked to pathways that generate sustainable and gender-equal outcomes – that come from support to women's agency, power and voice, and assuring space for feminist collective action.

For gender equality to flourish, pathways therefore need to generate multiple capabilities and freedoms that go beyond basic material needs and rights. They also need to include opportunity and process freedoms that allow people to convert resources to multiple capabilities. The hope is that these then feed back to sustain ongoing processes of pathway generation and maintenance, that further reinforce sustainable development and gender justice. But this will often not be a linear process; there will be unexpected events, opportunities and setbacks, to which people, institutions and ecologies will need to adapt and respond.

Moreover, just as many pathways have converged in current, unsustainable directions, so too there are multiple possible sustainable development pathways. These may be associated with the values and goals of different groups or places, or across spatial and temporal scales; they may refer to particular dimensions of ecological integrity, or they may prioritize particular dimensions of gender equality. We need to respect diversity – to suit the hugely varying circumstances, lives, identities, perspectives and priorities of different women and men in different places across the world. We also need to recognize tensions and trade-offs between pathways; not all pathways that move towards ecological integrity or economic sustainability promote gender equality, and vice versa.

The interactions, feedbacks, non-linearities, trade-offs and tensions involved as pathways unfold are illustrated well by the examples of forest governance and sanitation (Boxes 1.1 and 1.2). They highlight that the process of adjudicating between pathways is a deeply political one, that needs to involve inclusive deliberation around choices and outcomes. Reflective learning processes – about what is working to sustain what for whom, with what implications for gender equality – should also be part of pathway creation processes, and these too need to be fully inclusive of women's and men's diverse forms, knowledges and perspectives.

BOX 1.1 FOREST PATHWAYS AND GENDER EQUALITY

Forest landscapes illustrate well the interaction of ecological, social, technological and political–economic processes in shaping change. Whether in humid forests in Africa or the lowland and montane forests of South Asia, vegetation cover and quality reflect the dynamic interaction of ecology, soil and climate with people's uses and practices, the latter shaped by livelihoods, social relations, knowledge and understanding, and forms of property and tenure. The same forests and trees may be variously valued by different people for their timber and gathered products, for their services in shade and ecosystem protection, or for their cultural values as places of ancestors, spirits, aesthetic meaning or social memory. Forest conditions have co-evolved, often over long periods, with gendered capabilities and relations in resource access, use and control (Leach, 1994), resulting in a wide diversity of historically embedded forest pathways in different settings, associated with a variety of gendered values and outcomes.

Forests have been subject to many forms of policy and intervention, and as these have interacted with ongoing processes of change, so new pathways have emerged, with varying outcomes for gender equality. From colonial times onwards, successive state, donor-led and non-governmental programmes have focused on goals from sustaining supplies of timber and non-forest products to protecting watersheds and biodiversity, geared variously to local, national or global economic or environmental interests. The latest round of interventions focuses on carbon and climate change, gearing forest management to protecting and enhancing carbon stocks and sequestration to mitigate a perceived global climate crisis by offsetting emissions produced in industrialized settings. The many schemes that have emerged – associated variously with the UN-REDD (United Nations collaborative initiative on Reducing Emissions from Deforestation and forest Degradation) process, Clean Development Mechanism, Voluntary Carbon Standard or unaccredited private deals – all revalue forests as a source of a carbon commodity to be exchanged in emerging markets. They involve knowledge, values, institutions and practices aligned with broader neoliberal environmentalism, geared to solving global sustainability challenges through financializing ecosystems and nature (Büscher et al, 2012). Projects are often justified through Malthusian narratives and associated methodologies that see forests as undergoing one-way degradation, with local users to blame (Leach and Scoones, 2013). As these forest carbon projects play out on the ground, they have often created pathways that aim to meet global sustainability needs but exclude local forest users and their livelihoods, contributing to dispossession (Corbera and Brown, 2008; Corbera and Schroeder, 2010) and becoming 'green grabs' (Fairhead et al, 2012). The result is often greater inequality and injustice for local users vis-à-vis external agencies and global actors, and sometimes along gendered lines as well. Fostering greater justice in forest carbon pathways requires shifts in the institutional, knowledge and power relations through which they are designed and conceived, and far greater inclusion of local women and men.

An alternative set of forest intervention pathways has focused on community-based and joint forest management. From the 1980s to the present, these generally conceive of sustainability in relation to local livelihood goals and cultural values, where necessary reconciling these with national and global priorities through collaborative institutions and decision-making. Such approaches thus have the potential to foster pathways that support local rights and capabilities. Yet the outcomes of community forest management for gender equality have varied considerably. In many cases, gendered interests and values in forest management have been subordinated to a generalized notion of 'the community', through institutions dominated by men and community leaders. Gender relations and gendered forms of forest knowledge have not always been appreciated. However, Agarwal's (2010) work in Nepal and Gujarat, India provides evidence to show that gender equality in joint forest management processes is associated with positive outcomes for both forest ecology and gender equality. Gender-related inequality (unless mitigated by specific measures) is often associated with low or failed cooperation within forest management committees. Yet where women are full participants with voice and power in more gender-democratic committee structures (women's attendance rates and effective presence in the executive committees of community forestry institutions is found to improve significantly once more than a quarter of the committee consists of women), and gendered resource access is enabled with less strict forest closure regimes, voluntary cooperation by women and greater gender equity in benefit-sharing can be promoted along with better forest quality. This supports pathways that simultaneously promote sustainability according to local values, and gender equality.

BOX 1.2 DIFFERENT PATHWAYS IN SANITATION

Access to improved sanitation has multiple benefits for women and girls. The privacy and dignity afforded through proper, separate sanitation and menstrual hygiene facilities can improve girls' school attendance. Access to sanitation also prevents both men and women from losing critical days from work and livelihood activities due to ill health. Sanitation processes and outcomes are determined by a range of social, technological and ecological dynamics. Cultural practices and perceptions of digestion, purity and pollution differ tremendously around the world and profoundly influence whether externally driven sanitation initiatives get local uptake or not. Technological aspects (space, materials, design) often interact profoundly with ecological considerations (e.g. proximity to groundwater sources, presence of pathogens, contamination possibilities) to shape sanitation outcomes (see Movik, 2011).

Until recently, dominant pathways around sanitation have tended to neglect these multi-dimensional and gendered aspects. Dominant pathways have also tended to be top-down and prescriptive, focused on providing people with ready sanitary technology/infrastructure involving subsidies for hardware, usually accompanied by public health behaviour-change campaigns to encourage women and men to use the toilets. However, many top-down initiatives have failed miserably, especially in countries such as India, with local people preferring open defecation and using toilets for purposes such as storage.

Community-led total sanitation (CLTS), initiated by Dr Kamal Kar in 2000 in Bangladesh, has offered some powerful alternatives to mainstream sanitation pathways (see Kar and Pasteur, 2005; Mehta and Movik, 2011). CLTS aims at encouraging local people to build their own toilets according to the resources available, and to stop open defecation. This takes place through processes of self-analysis concerning the harmful impacts of open defecation, and changes initiated and sustained through local knowledge and people's collective action. The processes of change in CLTS aim to encourage ownership, leadership, and capacity among community members to bring about their own development. Gains made are both individual – in terms of improved health, more income arising from better productivity and reduced medical expenses, privacy and security for women; and collective – in terms of clean environments requiring the cooperation of every woman, man and child – leading to solidarity and social inclusion. When facilitated well, CLTS processes have the potential to trigger emotions within people that can bring about immediate and sustained change for people and communities (Kar and Pasteur, 2005; Mehta and Movik, 2011).

Gender equality is a prerequisite for sustainability in CLTS. For example, expecting women to shoulder responsibilities for fetching water and cleaning toilets can have an impact on sustainability. Women who are already burdened with work and have less time on their hands might not want to take on extra responsibilities which affect the continued behaviour change of using toilets and handwashing. In terms of gendered outcomes, CLTS can be empowering in terms of improved reproductive and sexual health, work productivity, more income and bargaining power. Women have also been encouraged to play an important leadership role in many communities, and emerge as 'natural leaders' with the potential to develop into women's collectives, district-wide sanitation and school hygiene leaders. Once CLTS has been introduced in an area, there have been many cases where it can increase women's negotiating power in marriage, as many women refuse to marry into a household that defecates in the open. This is important for the sustainability, spread and scaling-up of CLTS.

However, there is a risk that certain groups could be excluded on the basis of the generation of powerful emotions, such as shaming when non-compliance takes place. Gender inequality could also increase, or not be addressed at all, because most often CLTS is implemented within pre-existing relations in a society. CLTS has the potential as an outcome to achieve solidarity and collective action, but it is not deliberatively designed to address social inequalities. Furthermore, while CLTS has mobilized women en masse as so-called 'natural leaders' and enabled women in deeply hierarchical societies such as Haryana in India to assume leadership roles, it also builds on traditional notions of women as the keepers of cleanliness and order in the family. Maintaining toilets can also add to women's existing labour. Finally, CLTS contains some unknown risks around groundwater and soil contamination, issues that were not considered when the approach was conceived.

Towards gender-equal sustainable development: Policy frameworks and political strategies

To challenge unsustainable pathways and move towards sustainable development and gender equality will require action at many levels, by a diversity of actors. As the discussions of work, population, food, land, water and energy illustrate, states and intergovernmental processes must be central. However, key opportunities for transformation also lie in the ideas and actions of civil society and social movements, businesses and the private sector, communities and individuals – and in building gender-progressive sustainable development alliances between them.

States are the key arbiters and upholders of rights and freedoms for their citizens. Rather than leave everything to the market, states need strengthened capacity and ability to deliver on these in ways that respect sustainability and gender equality. This requires accountable frameworks that secure human rights, including gender-based rights in areas such as work and employment, reproduction and health, food and land, natural resource tenure, and rights to uphold and practise particular identities and sexualities. Governments also have central roles to play in providing public services, supporting the health, education and care for children, the elderly and the sick so essential to people's capabilities, and for assuring social dimensions of sustainability and continued social reproduction. As Ray shows in Chapter 6, public investment is also key in nurturing and scaling-out key innovations that offer vital prospects for improving sustainable development and gender equality, in areas such as the provision of modern energy services, water supplies and appropriate sanitation facilities.

There are, to be sure, growing opportunities for businesses and the private sector to contribute to sustainable development solutions – as emerging 'green economy' discourses emphasize. Nevertheless these often require state support to be viable, at least in the early stages. Meanwhile, growing evidence shows that partnership and 'co-production' arrangements – in which private, public and civil society actors work jointly to deliver health, housing or energy services, or manage forests, biodiversity or water – are often most effective. For such state or co-produced arrangements to work effectively for gender equality and sustainability, it is vital that women are involved centrally in planning and implementation – as Box 1.1, highlighting the advantages of women's involvement in forest management committees, exemplifies. Adequate financial resources are also required to achieve the goals of sustainable development (Schalatek, 2013).

National policies are increasingly shaped by international regimes and frameworks, globalization processes, and transnational policy transfer and learning. International human rights frameworks, those dealing with particular sectors (e.g. the right to water and sanitation, the right to food), and the CEDAW offer important frameworks within which states should be held to account. However, to achieve sustainable development, gender equality and human rights need to be brought far more fully into policy frameworks dealing with environment, development and sustainability questions. As we have shown, global efforts to integrate gender and sustainable development thus far have been mixed, ranging from 'total exclusion to minimal inclusion' (UNDP, 2012, p30). The Millennium Development Goals (MDGs) made strong commitments to both environmental sustainability (MDG 7) and gender equality (MDG 3), but goals, targets and implementation remained separate. Joined-up, integrated thinking and action is a key challenge and opportunity for the post-2015 Sustainable Development Goals framework. Meanwhile, there needs to be far more inclusion of gender equality concerns and women's participation in ongoing international policy processes around climate change, biodiversity, land, energy and green economies, whether in Conferences of Parties and other intergovernmental processes, or policy-influencing global fora and assessments. Ongoing efforts to mainstream gender, for instance by UNEP, UNDP (2013b) and the International Union for Conservation of Nature (IUCN, 2013), need to be strengthened and intensified, and connected more strongly with an equality and rights-based approach.

Growing evidence and analysis shows that sustainable development requires governance and action that extends from global across national to local scales. If well co-ordinated, such 'nested' or 'polycentric' approaches are best placed to address environmental and economic challenges (Agarwal, 2010; Ostrom, 2010). This suggests a need for questions of gender equality and for representation of women's interests to be included, from local to global institutions.

Formal policies and rights frameworks are clearly insufficient unless policies are implemented and rights are made real, however. Equally, women's participation has too often translated into tokenism or co-optation. Feminist analysis and experience therefore points to the importance of informal political strategies and tactics in engaging with policy processes: resisting, reshaping, subverting, reclaiming (Calas and Smircich, 1999; True, 2003). Feminist action is also central in challenging and reworking the discourses, cultures, practices, biases and stereotypes that beset policy institutions and organizations, as Razavi and Qayum emphasize in Chapter 7. This can happen through feminist action within bureaucracies (Goetz, 1997; Rao, 2006; Sandler and Rao, 2012; Smyth and Turquet, 2012), where 'insider–outsider' strategies, informal alliances and relationship networks prove key in the complex process of translating policy into practice for desired outcomes. It can also be assisted by 'external' pressure from social movements and activism.

Indeed, the growth of movements around gender equality and 'green' issues – and their coming together in forms of collective organizing around sustainable development and social justice – is one of the most exciting developments of recent years. Building on long histories of movement activism, in many countries and regions citizens, informal economy workers, producers and consumers are organizing collectively, both to contest dominant pathways and to advocate for – and demonstrate – alternative pathways. Examples are multiplying rapidly. They include, for instance, La Via Campesina, which from the 1990s has built into a globally networked movement to defend the rights of small farmers in the face of pressures from large-scale corporate agriculture.[1] Promoting a vision of small-scale peasant farming rooted in agro-ecological techniques, local markets and 'food sovereignty' (Borras, 2004; McMichael, 2009), some, though by no means all, strands emphasize central recognition of, and support to, the rights of women as small-scale food producers. They include movements initiated by groups of poor urban dwellers in many cities in Asia, Africa and Latin America, linking wellbeing and rights to homes and livelihoods with the design of decent, sustainable urban spaces (Satterthwaite et al, 2011). In the case of Slum and Shack Dwellers' International,[2] groups initiated around women's savings, credit associations and waste-pickers' cooperatives have networked into a federated global structure that now covers 30 countries, linking local action with campaigning around global agendas. Many other examples are emerging around alternative and 'solidarity' economies, food and land, water and energy.

In such examples, collective action, organization and cooperation provide the basis for alternative pathways that provide routes to social, economic and political empowerment, and environmental sustainability. Networking and alliance-building provide routes through which the everyday actions and knowledge of women and men around work, industry, land, food, water, energy and climate, in diverse places around the world, can begin to add up and scale-out into broader pathways. With appropriate state support, they offer powerful complements or correctives to current mainstream approaches that rely just on individuals and businesses linked through markets as the focus of sustainability and green economies, and offer powerful hopes for transformed, more sustainable and gender-equitable futures.

Conclusion

In this chapter, we have argued that gender equality must be integral to sustainable development. We have demonstrated many reasons why: apart from the moral and ethical imperatives involved, attention to gender differences and relations is vital to avoid the costs of economic and environmental change undermining gendered rights and capabilities, undermining further the sustainability of households, communities and societies. And it is crucial in order to recognize and build on the agency and knowledge of diverse women and men towards sustainable pathways.

Around many issues – whether work and industrial production, population and reproduction, food and agriculture, or water, sanitation and energy, dominant development pathways have proved both unsustainable and gender unequal. Economic, social and environmental unsustainability, and gender inequality, are both produced by, and yet threaten to undermine, market-focused, neoliberal patterns of growth. As troubling intersections of unsustainability and gender inequality threaten or exceed planetary boundaries around climate change, biodiversity and pollution, so shocks, stresses and feedbacks may undermine gendered rights and capabilities even further. Yet, as we have shown, the reverse is possible – gender equality and sustainability can powerfully reinforce each other in alternative pathways.

Integrating gender equality with sustainable development requires sharp conceptual understanding of both concepts and their interlinkages. This chapter has developed a 'gendered pathways approach', offering this as a conceptual framework for addressing the interactions, tensions and trade-offs between different dimensions of gender equality and sustainability. Enriched through insights from several decades of feminist thinking and practice, especially in feminist political economy and political ecology, the gendered pathways approach offers guidelines to analysing current pathways of change, and imagining and appraising alternatives. Applying elements of the pathways approach to issues of work, population, food, land, water and energy, subsequent chapters in this book demonstrate that there are multiple ways to challenge current unsustainable pathways, and multiple alternative pathways to sustainability that embrace gender equality. They also reveal that powerful narratives have sometimes worked to hide or misrepresent gender–sustainability linkages, justifying dispossession and essentializing women as 'sustainability saviours'.

As we have demonstrated, and as the chapters illustrate, there will always be tensions. Some pathways will promote sustainability at the cost of gender equality; some may promote gender equality and neglect key dimensions of sustainability. Since pathways are dynamic, they can also have unintended social, technological and environmental consequences, which also affect outcomes in terms of gender (in)equality. Negotiating such dynamics requires inclusive learning and deliberation processes, and ways to monitor exclusions, trade-offs and emerging opportunities, as well as ongoing awareness of the complex politics of both gender and sustainability.

We want to end with hope, however. There are many alternative pathways to sustainability and gender equality, albeit currently under-appreciated. They exist in urban and rural spaces where women and men make and sustain their livelihoods, in women's cooperatives and movements, in the writings of feminist scholars, and in the margins of bureaucracies and global institutions. We need to seek out these champions and create conceptual and policy space for their ideas and practices. These offer powerful challenges to the logic of 'homo economicus' and to dominant patterns of consumption and production that are promoting structural inequalities and unsustainability. They offer alternatives with the potential to create green transformations that are gender and socially equitable. And an emerging politics of alliance-building for gender equality and sustainable development, combining movements, states and enlightened businesses, and formal and informal practices, offers the potential to make them real. Feminists have often been the ones to provide the most trenchant critiques of dominant thinking and ways of life, usually from the margins. It is now time to reclaim those margins and promote new ways of being.

Notes

1   http://viacampesina.org/en/
2   www.sdinet.org/about-what-we-do/

2

PATHWAYS TOWARDS SUSTAINABILITY IN THE CONTEXT OF GLOBALIZATION

A gendered perspective on growth, macro policy and employment

Elissa Braunstein and Mimi Houston

Introduction

This chapter considers sustainability from an economic and social perspective, explaining how the dominant global economic paradigm fails to deliver growth and development in ways that generate sustainable livelihoods, decent employment and gender equality. The issue of environmental sustainability is taken on in this context, assessing how prevailing models of green growth measure up to the visions of sustainable development and gender equality detailed in this book. Ultimately, the chapter's goal is to identify sustainable pathways for development in terms that directly reflect the roles of economic growth and macroeconomic policy in achieving gender equality and environmental sustainability through decent work.

Providing opportunities for decent work and secure livelihoods is an essential feature of sustainable development. Decent employment helps ensure and improve wellbeing, safeguards human rights, widens the scope of capabilities, and provides a key pathway for alleviating poverty, protecting the environment and realizing social justice. Gender fundamentally structures whether and how development processes create opportunities for decent work and sustainable livelihoods, including whether environmental goals are consistent with economic and social ones.

Directly addressing the question of growth is important as well. While we can readily identify goals such as gender-equitable access to secure livelihoods as part of sustainable development, and are rightly critical of economic models of development that fail to measure outcomes by these and other principles of sustainability, there is much less analysis, in most discussions of sustainability, of growth processes and the global and macroeconomic policies that shape them. But ignoring the macroeconomic aspects of development cedes too much to narrow growth theorists and adherents of unfettered markets. Feminist economists working in the macroeconomics field have long been grappling with these questions from a gender perspective – an early example is the 1999 *World Survey on the Role of Women in Development* (UN, 1999). Integrating this work with the principles of sustainable development would mean progress for both perspectives. Such a combination would also strengthen the gender component of plans for green growth, which tend to ignore issues such as the environmental benefits of growing the care economy, or how achieving ecological goals will affect gender equality at work.

The chapter begins with some economic context, providing a summary review of neoliberal macroeconomic policy, and how the macroeconomic policy stances of the world's governments and financial institutions shape and constrain the employment-generating capacities of a variety of economies. This provides context for the discussion of globalization, growth and women's employment that follows, which considers the sustainability of its social, economic and environmental dimensions. Though the chapter considers employment overall, its focus is on the industrial sector because: (1) raising industrial value-added is the most-trodden pathway to growth and development; (2) industrial employment has been the main avenue by which both women and men have typically accessed the better paid and protected jobs associated with growth and development; and (3) efforts to make growth more environmentally sustainable have focused primarily on the industrial sector, where much environmental degradation is generated. In this, the chapter also complements Chapters 4 and 5 in this book, which have a more rural and agricultural focus to their discussions of gender equality and sustainable development.

The analysis begins with the potential for decent work and gender equality in industrial labour markets; then evaluates whether these structures are part of a larger sustainable model of economic growth; and concludes with a review of green growth, its gendered employment effects, and the role of the care economy in building sustainability.

The key arguments are that macroeconomic policy and growth trajectories are relevant for charting pathways of sustainable development, but that these need to be scrutinized for their capacity to generate opportunities for decent work, sustainable livelihoods, gender equality and environmental protection. The neoliberal macroeconomic policy agendas that dominated over the past three decades have not performed well on these counts: wage compression, debt accumulation and the primacy of finance, which have been concomitant aspects of dominant policy prescriptions, create conditions that undermine economic, social and environmental sustainability. By constraining quality employment generation, limiting the role of the state, and generating global imbalances, this pathway hinders growth in domestic aggregate demand and fosters macroeconomic fragility that is, ultimately, economically unsustainable. Furthermore, by relying on the undervaluation of women's work, care, and the natural environment, it further generates gender inequality and environmental degradation.

The chapter goes on to consider a range of alternative pathways that address these problems. In particular, wage-led and green growth approaches offer potential pathways of development that advance economic, social and ecological sustainability. However, the right to decent work and secure livelihoods, by enhancing women's knowledge, agency and decision-making capabilities, is key for gender equality in this context. Any alternative growth or macroeconomic policy framework must meaningfully address inequality, not only by gender, but also by class, race and ethnicity. Furthermore, pathways need fully to enumerate and internalize the incentives and consequences for care, social reproduction and the natural environment. The chapter concludes with a discussion of potential pathways that integrate the care and green economies, as well as with examples of progressive women's movements and state policies that support innovative systems combining green production, sustainable livelihoods and gender-equal work.

The economic context

Neoliberal macroeconomic policy

Although the term 'Washington consensus', a policy perspective that relies largely on markets to deliver economic growth and development, may seem somewhat out of date, the core triad of its macro policy conventions – liberalization, privatization and macro stability – is rarely critiqued as a failure in need of a new macroeconomic paradigm. The 'augmented' or 'post' Washington consensus, which adds to the standard triad a number of institutional reforms and some points about the proper sequencing of reform, reflects an acknowledgement among international financial institutions (IFIs) that the original list of reforms was not sufficient to deliver substantial improvements in economic growth. This shift happened on the heels of IFI missteps during the Asian financial crisis and the growth failures of the 1980s and 1990s, and continues to evolve today (Rodrik, 2006; Stiglitz, 2008). But the original triad is still central to the variety of idealized policy lists that have been generated, becoming a sort of conventional wisdom that is so settled as to be almost invisible. We pause to consider this macroeconomic policy stance because it has fundamentally shaped the growth and employment challenges that most countries face today, moving through a brief discussion of each component (see Braunstein, 2012 for further detail).

Liberalization refers to liberalizing domestic markets, including labour and product markets, as well as liberalizing international trade and investment. Policies have included gradually doing away with import controls, opening capital accounts, promoting free purchase and sale of domestic currency, and emphasizing the promise of export promotion as a development strategy and employment generator. Macro stability is widely understood to mean simply price stability (as opposed to, for instance, employment stability or financial stability). In combination with the commitment to open capital accounts, maintaining price stability necessitates a distinctly 'market-friendly' monetary regime. This regime has been shown to restrict economic growth and the employment-generating capacities of the economy, while creating instability that necessitates further contractionary fiscal and monetary policy responses (Pollin et al, 2009). The push for privatization and limits to government action frame the relationship between public and private expenditure as competitive, as opposed to cooperative. It reflects the dominant economic narrative that government spending is not just inflationary, but also tends to 'crowd out' private investment that is presumed to be more efficient than public investment. It ignores the likely possibility, especially in developing economies where market imperfections are extensive, that public investment can 'crowd in', or encourage, private investment.

Taken together, the neoliberal macro policy conventions of liberalization, privatization and macro stability create an economic environment characterized by deflation, slow growth, limited public policy space and fiscal squeeze. The rise of global finance, partly as a result of the widespread adoption of these conventions, serves only to reinforce these dynamics. In such a context, it may appear that the best, or indeed the only, avenue for generating employment and raising incomes is to pursue an export-led growth strategy. But, in the past decade or so, two new economic developments have emerged that make pursuing such an externally oriented agenda even more complex: global imbalances and the rising dominance of global value chains in international trade.

Global imbalances refer to the distribution of large current account deficits and surpluses across a number of countries (UNCTAD, 2010; Bernanke, 2011). These imbalances reflect a set of economic systems that differ in their particular national circumstances, but all produced a trajectory of wage growth that lagged far behind productivity growth and resulted in rising levels of inequality across both North and South (Blecker, 2012). The collective result of these imbalances was a state of 'underconsumption' in some regions and 'overborrowing' in others, financed in part by global financial flows from current account surplus to deficit countries, but ultimately made possible by the rising tide of financialization and the shift in emphasis from production to financial profit-making (Cripps et al, 2011). Such terms of production and exchange, centred on wage compression, debt accumulation and the primacy of finance, are economically unsustainable. The financial crisis of 2007–08 reverberated throughout this system, and left sluggish growth and high unemployment in the developed world and the parts of the developing world with current account deficits (UNCTAD, 2010). The collapse of global trade and investment that followed undercut the demand that fuels export-led growth, and while it is true that emerging market economies have added to global demand, it is a long way from replacing the USA as the global engine of consumption growth. Furthermore, a shift away from demand in industrialized countries means a shift away from demand for manufactured goods to commodities such as raw materials, energy and food, with consequences for global commodity prices (they will increase) as well as terms of trade (labour-intensive manufactures will buy fewer imports) (UNCTAD, 2010). The take-away message is that the persistence of global imbalances, and their inherent fragility and dependence on keeping wages low, severely limit the prospects for export-led growth as a viable development model in the future.

Global value chains (GVCs) are defined as 'borderless production systems' involving either sequential or complex networks that span anywhere from just two countries to the entire globe (UNCTAD, 2013b, p122). The ascendancy of GVCs in global production is linked with the drivers of the modern era of globalization, including advances in technology that enable the close management of widely spun production networks, the ongoing push towards trade and investment liberalization and, more recently, a shift in corporate strategy to one that emphasizes the cost savings and flexibility afforded by outsourcing and focusing on 'core' activities such as design and branding (Milberg and Winkler, 2013). The recommendations for trade policy, given this context, tend to sound like an echo of the standard neoliberal variety, only with a new and commanding set of logics: trade should be liberalized because import barriers of any sort are an effective tax on exports, and with goods passing through so many countries, even very low trade taxes can become serious inhibitors of growth; the same goes for limits on foreign investment, which will only discourage the sorts of relationships with lead firms that are so essential for upgrading production (OECD 2013a; OECD et al, 2013).

Missing from this discussion, however, is whether participation in GVCs, and the policies designed to promote them, will generate decent employment. Given the state of global imbalances, and how far forces of globalization and financialization continue to drive them, one could reasonably argue the opposite: that the growing dominance of GVCs in global production will in fact produce more insecurity and less decent employment as it expands the global competitive stage. The rise of GVCs reinforces the need for export orientation coupled with the conventional policy menu: open trade and capital accounts, a finance-friendly monetary regime and a modest public sector. But from an economic sustainability perspective, there is a fundamental contradiction here: competing on price with lots of other producers constrains wage growth and domestic aggregate demand, and the state of global imbalances makes success on this challenging path even more elusive.

The failures of neoliberalism

It is useful at this point to pause and consider the failures of the neoliberal approach to growth and development, and how these are reflected in gendered employment outcomes and environmental degradation in the context of sustainability. While these issues are taken up in various ways throughout the chapter, a summary is provided here. Interestingly (and unfortunately), they tellingly reflect the critical predictions of the 1999 *World Survey* (UN, 1999), which long ago warned of the deflationary bias of macro policy, increasing risk and volatility, and the diminishing role of the state associated with the neoliberal approach to development.

Under the neoliberal approach, employment generation is inadequate, in terms of both quantity (the right to work) and quality (rights at work). Furthermore, greater instability and volatility from globalization, trade liberalization and financialization is reflected in rising insecurity, not just in export-oriented employment, but in employment overall. This has strong implications for gender equality. While trade liberalization has raised the relative demand for female labour in industry and services, these patterns are typically reversed as industries upgrade.

Moreover, the export-led growth model is based on keeping wages low, and there is little evidence of social upgrading, a prospect made more remote with the rise of global value chains and the persistence of global imbalances. The consequences for the care economy are an issue as well, as the combination of post-crisis austerity and longer work days for women compromise capabilities and threaten both gender equality and the terms of social reproduction (cf. Bahçe and Memiş, 2013).

This pathway also heightens the dominance of capital over labour. The evolving terms of work in the context of increasing global capital mobility, magnified by the rise of outsourcing and the prominence of finance in profit-making, have disembedded global corporate interests from local economies and led to increasing inequality in both North and South. One of the manifestations of these dynamics is a declining share of labour income (versus the share going to profits), which has been empirically associated with financialization, globalization, and the retrenchment of the welfare state (Stockhammer, 2013). As women's share of the industrial labour force is negatively associated with the labour share of income, women's poor fortunes in industrial labour markets can serve as a sort of proxy for these dynamics.

The low wages associated with maintaining a global competitive edge and the rising dominance of capital over labour are also associated with deficient aggregate demand, in terms of both the market for global exports and domestic demand. As noted in the discussion of global imbalances, efforts to maintain consumption in the context of low wages have been linked with the incidence and spread of financial crises, and thus represent another source of instability and unsustainability in this system.

To make matters worse, the neoliberal approach effectively delegitimizes the state, resulting in fiscal constraints that not only limit the state's capacity to engage in counter-cyclical macro policy in response to crises, but also limit its participation in the provision of public goods. The emphasis on privatization undermines state capacity by portraying government spending as not only inflationary, but also compromising to private investment. The resultant cuts and constraints of public expenditure often have disproportionately negative impacts on children and women, partly because their status and the content of their work is so closely linked with the care economy and the extent of public supports for it (Ortiz and Cummins, 2013).

The dominant growth paradigm has also created environmental mis-incentives (see Leach et al, Chapter 1 in this book). By understanding the environment as external to the traditional market sphere, it overexploits nature as both a source and a sink. That is, the environment is a source of natural resources and ecosystem services that are merely inputs into the productive system. Because they are external to the market, they are often undervalued and therefore overexploited. Furthermore, treating nature as a sink, the environmental degradation that results from production and exchange is discounted as well. This is true on the global scale, too, where prominent global relations of production and consumption emphasize production for Northern consumer markets, promoting growth based on a model of extraction rather than the principles of sustainability. The shift of production processes to developing countries also relocates the ecological and health costs of polluting production processes to countries with less stringent environmental regulations and more vulnerable populations (UNCTAD, 2013b). Furthermore, the constrained state discussed above produces and reinforces vulnerability to environmental hazards by limiting the provision of infrastructure, services and social protection crucial to adaptive efforts (UN, 2014a).

Taken together, the macro policy conventions of liberalization, privatization and macro stability create an economic context characterized by reduced capacity to generate employment, fiscal squeeze and limited public policy space, with implications for the achievement of social and environmental sustainability, and gender equality. These outcomes have led to prescriptions for green growth, but unless we grapple with these issues in the context of gender relations, care and social reproduction, the results for sustainability will be disappointing. This chapter goes on to consider these interactions further – first considering diverse pathways through which economic growth and decent work for women might be linked; then addressing the prospects for green growth and economies; and finally addressing the potential for pathways that combine greening and gender equality – including through re-valuing care.

Socially and economically sustainable pathways? Industrial production and decent work from a gender perspective

In this section, we consider sustainability from the perspective of women's employment status and gender inequality in industrial labour markets, and the potential for decent work and social upgrading. Furthermore, this section examines whether the structure of employment generated by the global economic system is part of a sustainable model in economic terms. Here the aim is to link these features with the rising dominance of GVCs and the limits posed by global imbalances, ultimately situating them in a wider context of sustainability.

Employment and wages

Globalization and trade liberalization underlie the nearly universal increase in women's share of the industrial labour force among high-growth or semi-industrialized economies (SIEs) in the past few decades, a result of the tremendous growth in manufacturing trade and export processing from the developing world (Standing, 1989, 1999; Wood, 1991; UN, 1999; Nordas, 2003; De Hoyos, 2006; Berik and Rodgers, 2009; Barrientos and Evers, 2013). The relative increase in the demand for female labour is not just a matter of expanding the available labour force when male labour is in short supply. With labour costs such a crucial part of international competitiveness in these industries, labour-intensive exporters prefer to hire women both because women's wages are typically lower than men's, and because employers perceive women as more productive in these types of jobs

(Elson and Pearson, 1981). Foreign investors and firms looking for low-cost outsourcing platforms conform to the same pattern, at least on the lower rungs of the value-added ladder.

However, this positive association between trade liberalization and female employment is strongest in labour-abundant semi-industrialized countries. In primarily agricultural economies where women are concentrated in food production, some (but not all) of which compete with imports, men are better situated to take advantage of export opportunities in cash crops or natural resource extraction, and women may lose employment and income as a result of trade liberalization (Fontana, 2007; Bussolo and De Hoyos, 2009). Alternatively, in agricultural economies where horticulture exports have taken off, women constitute a significant proportion of seasonal employees (Bamber and Fernandez-Stark, 2013). These countervailing forces come in the context of an overall feminization of agriculture, especially in Asia and Africa, a phenomenon associated not with trade liberalization but with a number of other factors, including greater male rural–urban mobility in response to structural change, conflict, and the consequences of HIV/AIDS (FAO, 2010; see also Fukuda-Parr, Chapter 4 in this book). Finally, in developing economies with less globally competitive manufacturing sectors, tariff reductions on labour-intensive imports have resulted in higher job losses for women than for men (Adhikari and Yamamoto, 2006; Seguino and Grown, 2006).

Extending these dynamics to wages, the standard theoretical prediction is that trade liberalization should increase female wages and lower the gender wage gap, for two reasons. First, increased competition introduced by trade liberalization makes it more costly for domestic firms to discriminate thereby diminishing gender wage discrimination; and second, when developing countries open to trade, the exports of labour-intensive goods produced by 'unskilled' labour will increase. Presuming that women constitute a disproportionate share of the 'unskilled' labour force, trade liberalization should bring about convergence in male and female wages because it raises the relative demand for female labour.

A number of empirical studies support these predictions, finding female wages increasing relative to male wages in a variety of country contexts and cross-sectionally as well (Wood, 1991; Milner and Wright, 1998; Tzannatos, 1999; World Bank, 2001; Paul-Mazumdar and Begum, 2002; Nicita and Razzaz, 2003; Black and Brainerd, 2004; Oostendorp, 2009; Chen et al, 2013; Juhn et al, 2014).

However, there is also substantial evidence that the gender wage gap – both absolute measures of the gap and the proportion of the gap attributable to discrimination – has either persisted or widened as a result of trade and investment liberalization (Standing, 1989, 1999; Mehra and Gammage, 1999; Artecona and Cunningham, 2002; Berik et al, 2004; UNRISD, 2005; Busse and Spielmann, 2006; Braunstein and Brenner, 2007; Menon and Rodgers, 2009; Dominguez-Villalobos and Brown-Grossman, 2010). These contradictory findings may have to do with the fact that women seem to lose their 'comparative advantage' (i.e. providing low-paid labour) as industries upgrade and search for 'skilled' and better paid labour. This leads to a process of de-feminization of industrial employment (Elson, 1996; Ghosh, 2007; Berik and Rodgers, 2009; Tejani and Milberg, 2010; UNRISD, 2010).

Taken together with the rise in more capital-intensive outsourcing among expanding networks of GVCs, the defeminization effects in industry help explain why trade and investment liberalization have raised the skilled–unskilled wage gap in both developed and developing countries, creating a positive association between trade and income inequality (Feenstra and Hanson, 1997; Rodrik, 1997; Harrison and Hanson, 1999; Goldberg and Pavcnik, 2007; Bacchetta et al, 2009).

Production at the low end of the value chain in a developed economy that is consequently outsourced to a developing economy is actually at the higher end of the value chain from the perspective of the developing economy. Hence the growing reach of higher value-added GVCs is likely to speed up defeminization of the industrial labour force to the extent that women in export sectors are confined to the least skill-intensive parts of GVCs (Staritz and Guiherme Reis, 2013). There is also evidence that links trade-related increases in the gender wage gap with the increase in rewards to skill (Artecona and Cunningham, 2002; Black and Brainerd, 2004) or, alternatively, a decline in the manufacturing gender wage gap because of disproportionate job loss among women who are concentrated in low-wage production (Kongar, 2007).

In summary, women's employment is positively associated with trade liberalization, a relationship that is strongest in semi-industrialized export-oriented economies, and commonly reversed as industries upgrade and increase value-added. The net result for relative wages is mixed, though the rising dominance of GVCs in global production, and the wage compression encouraged by the system of global imbalances, cast strong doubt on globalization as a force for gender wage equality – at least via upward harmonization (as opposed to lower male wages). The literature on social upgrading in GVCs provides a good venue for considering these processes in more detail.

Decent work? Social and economic upgrading

The four strategic objectives of the International Labour Organization's decent work agenda are a good way to understand what a labour market characterized by social upgrading includes: high quality employment generation; workers' rights, including freedom from discrimination; access to social protection; and ongoing social dialogue among a variety of economic and civil society organizations (ILO, 2008). Looking to women's trade-related employment in the context of global production networks and GVCs, however, the evidence on trajectories towards decent work is limited and contradictory. Part of this is because studies on GVCs and the changing relations of global production have very little to say about social upgrading, as the focus has been on governance structures and the potential for economic upgrading (Staritz, 2013). And because it is widely acknowledged that economic upgrading does not necessarily lead to social upgrading in global production networks, studies that infer the latter from the former are misleading (Barrientos et al, 2011).

Some are decidedly optimistic about the potential for global production networks and GVCs to generate decent work. GVCs have been credited with reducing poverty and creating more formal job opportunities characterized by better working conditions (OECD, 2013a; UNCTAD, 2013b). In addition to being conduits for export market access and technological upgrading, GVCs also help spread social norms about responsible business conduct, not just towards labour but also towards the environment. These sorts of 'reputation effects' offer potentially powerful sources of leverage for host country governments engaged with multinational coordinated GVCs, especially among first-tier suppliers that have established publicly visible relationships with lead firms (OECD et al, 2013).

From a policy perspective, there is indeed a lot of optimism about the potential for globally coordinated efforts to raise labour standards and encourage socially responsible business conduct. For instance, the ILO's Core Labour Standards, the UN Guiding Principles on Business and Human Rights, and the OECD Guidelines on Multinational Enterprises help guide multinational behaviour in GVCs and have become a part of some company codes of conduct (OECD et al, 2013; UNCTAD, 2013b). However, these standards and others like them are of course *voluntary* (unlike trade agreements), and there is a sense that they do not have much effect beyond the first tier of suppliers, and what reputation effects exist are not very large (Hoang and Jones, 2012; UNCTAD, 2013b). Experience varies across countries and settings. Thus Berik and Rodgers (2010) find that in Bangladesh there is a persistence of low wages and poor working conditions, despite its passing a number of ILO Conventions and having its own set of national labour laws. In Cambodia, however, there has been an improvement in labour standards, which they link with a trade agreement with the USA that provides trade incentives for improving labour standards.

This points to the challenges that the changing relations of global production pose for social upgrading. In one of the few studies to take up the question of GVCs and social upgrading directly, Bernhardt and Milberg (2011) find that social upgrading (defined as experiencing both employment and real wage gains) is less common than social downgrading. Considering the structure and complexity of GVC production, this conclusion is not surprising. Because so much of the spread of GVC production is linked with the drive for cost savings, there is substantial cost pressure on suppliers, creating strong incentives to cut labour costs and, in many cases, inducing further subcontracting and increasing dependence on temporary or casual workers (Barrientos, 2007; UNCTAD, 2013b).

The consequence is significant variation among different sorts of chains and different parts of chains: pay can be low, working conditions poor, and insecurity high in those that are most exposed to the ups and downs of external demand and competition, an increasingly large share of global production networks as the scope of outsourcing expands (UNCTAD, 2013b). For instance, a study of the Moroccan garment industry showed that in order to deal with short lead times, last-minute changes and demands for high quality, firms employed two types of workers: regular workers who were highly skilled and on permanent contracts to ensure quality; and irregular workers working on less skill-intensive tasks for little pay under poor working conditions (Barrientos et al, 2011). Unskilled and casual workers were more likely to be young women, a finding that is reflected in the more general conclusion that, consistent with gender segregation in industry overall, women tend to be concentrated in the lowest value-added parts of particular GVCs as well, and therefore in the least promising segments for social upgrading (Barrientos, 2007; Staritz and Guiherme Reis, 2013).

Furthermore, while the expanding reach of industrial sector GVCs may proffer new employment opportunities for women, especially in the lower value-added production processes most accessible to developing economies, the relative increase in demand for female labour is largely structurally transitory, and the evidence on wages is decidedly mixed. Social upgrading is not an automatic consequence of GVC participation (or even climbing up the chain), especially among the more female-dominated segments of GVCs. Considering the state of global imbalances, and the constraints on export expansion that these dynamics pose, capturing the bargaining power that is required to push a social upgrading agenda seems remote for all but the very top tier of suppliers (Heintz, 2006).

The prospect of economic upgrading is also a concern in this context. How to incorporate GVCs into a wider development strategy is a challenging question, and cannot be reduced to the usual platitudes about the benefits of trade. Climbing the value-added ladder in this context requires industrial policy that is more exacting and fine-tuned, as doing so is no longer about targeting a final good or service, or picking a particular winner, but rather about how to embed production in a highly complex globalized network with a terribly high concentration of pricing power at the top and intense competition everywhere else (UNCTAD, 2013b). Low- and middle-income countries also need to be wary of success in lower parts of the chain because of the low-wage low-productivity trap, a risk that certainly preceded the rise of GVCs but has only become more intense in their ascendancy (UNCTAD, 2013b). Successfully fielding these challenges, particularly in light of the ongoing problems of global imbalances and the limits on industrial policy posed by global trade and financial institutions, is a tall order. Expanding domestic aggregate demand may offer a potentially more promising path.

Demand-led growth from a gender perspective

UNCTAD has called for a shift away from the export-led industrialization paradigm and towards cultivating domestic aggregate demand to generate employment and sustainable development. This pathway involves active industrial policies that raise investment in fixed capital and induce increases in productivity (UNCTAD, 2010, 2013a). Subsequent wage increases in line with productivity gains support higher domestic aggregate demand, leading to a virtuous cycle of growth coupled with social upgrading in employment. Turning instead towards expanding domestic sources of aggregate demand enables a rise in female wages and a decline in the gender wage gap without sacrificing economic growth (Blecker and Seguino, 2002; Seguino and Grown, 2006). Furthermore, given the association between women's incomes and spending on basic needs, there may be positive ripple effects for domestic production to the extent that demand shifts away from imports (Benería and Roldan, 1987; Blumberg, 1991; Hoddinott et al, 1998). The issue of the balance of payments constraint remains, however. It is possible that improvements in capabilities that are a consequence of higher incomes for women more than compensate for the loss in foreign exchange, a scenario that is more likely in low-income agricultural economies than in semi-industrialized ones (Seguino, 2010).

A related question is how the turn away from production for export and/or productivity growth in industry induced by industrial policies that raise capital investment will affect the relative demand for female labour. Given persistent gender segregation in labour markets, and the evidence that increasing capital intensity is associated with a defeminization of industry discussed above, raising industrial productivity, is likely to result in a decline in industrial sector demand for female labour.

One alternative source of demand for female labour is expanding employment in services, the largest employer of both women and men among high-income countries, and an increasingly important contributor to productivity growth in emerging economies such as China and India. The service sector, however, is highly uneven. Higher value-added services (e.g. information and communication technologies) tend to generate very little employment relative to their value-added in emerging economies (UNCTAD, 2010). Alternatively, care-related services, which are both labour-intensive and traditional sources of employment for women, commonly exact what is termed a 'care penalty' in pay, with systematically lower wages than other jobs that require similar levels of skill (England et al, 2002; Budig and Misra, 2010). Ultimately, the terms and conditions of employment for care sector workers are closely connected with wider labour market structures and the role of the state, a point that should certainly be incorporated in visioning for wage-led growth with gender equality (Razavi and Staab, 2010). But in highlighting the potential of service sector employment for women, there needs to be caution against blueprints for raising investment and industrial transformation that (albeit unintentionally) marginalize women from industrial employment opportunities and, effectively, consign them to lower wage, seemingly less developmentally 'significant' service sector employment.

The question of the (un)sustainability of the prevailing model is thereby rooted at the intersection of its social and economic dimensions, and it is here that considering social reproduction and the care economy become essential for establishing an alternative pathway. Moreover, any alternative pathway must address the failings of the prevailing model with respect to the environment. Hence we turn to a discussion on the potential of a green economy, before expanding upon the prospects of revaluing care and social reproduction. Ultimately, the intersection of all three dimensions – social, economic and environmental – is what will offer pathways to sustainability and gender equality.

Environmentally sustainable pathways? Green economies from a gender perspective

Green growth

The prevailing economic model is also an environmentally unsustainable one, resulting in patterns and relations of consumption and production that fail to adequately recognize and value their environmental impacts. The consequent environmental costs motivate the green growth agenda, where the so-called 'greening' of investment and public policy in both developing and developed countries is designed to enhance environmental protection while also raising economic growth (ILO, 2012; UNCTAD, 2013a). This particular agenda is gaining prominence in both national and international policy debates. However, there are many versions of the approach which vary in their recognition of gender perspectives and thus warrant a detailed examination.

The concepts of green growth and sustainable development are not interchangeable (see Leach et al, Chapter 1 in this book). Green growth is premised on growth as essential for sustained improvements in wellbeing. The central question then becomes how to shape growth processes in ways that are environmentally sustainable. Conversely, the concept of sustainable development, as it emerged from the environmental movement, maintains a deserved scepticism of the promise of growth and – with growing alarm about the social and environmental consequences of unregulated growth, production and consumption – its necessity (Jacobs, 2012). In its most common usage, sustainable development conveys that development need not occur at the expense of people and nature.

At an institutional level, green growth is most often treated as a pathway to sustainable development rather than an end in and of itself (see, for instance, UNEP, 2011; World Bank, 2012a; OECD, 2013b). Yet green growth is firmly situated in the standard growth lexicon. Its earliest appearances are associated with a concern that environmental degradation would impose significant costs on growth in the long-run (Jacobs, 2012). More recent elaborations emphasize the costs of greenhouse gas emissions and climate change for growth, and command significant intellectual terrain in the environmental macroeconomics literature. Beyond concerns over climate change and the environmental limits to business-as-usual growth scenarios, a number of growth theorists argue that environmental protection can actually boost economic growth. So it is about seeing environmental preservation not as a constraint, but rather as an opportunity.

These green growth advocacies are based on different causal pathways and policy scopes. For instance, Green Keynesianism, alternatively proffered in the guise of 'green stimulus' or a 'global green new deal', promotes directing government spending towards technology and employment generation in ways that enhance environmental protection and raise efficiency, for instance by retrofitting energy-inefficient buildings or infrastructure (e.g. UNEP, 2009). These sorts of green investments were a much discussed and promoted part of counter-cyclical macro policies adopted in the wake of the recent global recession in both the global North and South.

A second category of green growth proponents emphasize how markets fail to price natural assets and ecosystem services, which are ultimately factors of production like capital and labour. The result is that this 'natural capital' is overexploited relative to what is socially or economically optimal. In this context, where negative externalities render market outcomes socially inefficient, market interventions such as taxing carbon, or legislating that forest management rights be given to local communities, are about properly pricing natural assets and defining property rights, thereby making market-determined growth processes more in line with environmental values (World Bank, 2012a). These approaches are consonant with a neoliberal perspective in that interventions are about perfecting market processes.

A third approach to green growth emphasizes how environmental policy can actually raise rates of technological innovation in ways that promote growth (Acemoglu et al, 2009; OECD, 2009). There is a market failure to address in this literature as well. Since the social returns to these innovations are higher than the private returns – there are positive externalities to environmentally enhancing innovation – government policy becomes central to ensuring that such research and development takes place. While such interventions are clearly desirable from a strictly environmental perspective, they also conform to the tenets of standard economic growth frameworks.

One problem with extant visions of green growth is that they do not deal adequately with issues of inequality. In an important sense, there is not enough integration of the principles of sustainable development in green growth. A good counter to consider is the work of economist James Boyce and others linked with the environmental justice movement, who see environmental preservation as an opportunity to understand and redress inequality. For example, maintaining crop biodiversity enables future food producers to deal with new pests and diseases that threaten the food supply. Today, crop biodiversity is sustained largely by farmers in the global South, but they receive no compensation for this tremendously valuable social and ecological service (Boyce, 2011). Compensating them for their contributions to long-term food security should appeal to green growth advocates, but it also directly addresses questions of development and sustainability in economically just and pro-poor ways. Explicitly incorporating women's traditional work in agriculture – for example, in seed selection and preservation to maintain crop biodiversity – is extremely important in these analyses as well. Moreover, gender inequality in land rights and access to resources poses substantial barriers to greening agriculture in sustainable and pro-poor ways (Herren et al, 2011; see also Fukuda-Parr, Chapter 4 and Levien, Chapter 5 in this book).

Of the approaches to green growth, Green Keynesianism goes the furthest in addressing inequality via its focus on using environmental policy as a way to generate high-quality employment. This emphasis is also reflected in many of the treatments of environmental policy among international development institutions. The next section evaluates these employment claims from a gender perspective.

Gendering green jobs

A part of the green growth agenda targets the expansion of 'green jobs', which are understood primarily in terms of their environmental impact, but are also linked with the ILO's notion of decent work (UNEP et al, 2008; ILFSD, 2009; ILO, 2012). Focusing the discussion on industry, where it is estimated that 80 per cent of green jobs will be located, it is notable that a small number of manufacturing industries are responsible for a large share of resource and energy use as well as greenhouse gas emissions and other pollutants (ILFSD, 2009, p8). These include energy, construction, transportation and, among basic industries, aluminium, iron and steel (ILO, 2012). Most of the projected employment gains are expected to come from activities involved in transitioning to a low-carbon economy, including renewable energy resource development, producing more fuel-efficient vehicles, constructing and retrofitting buildings, transport and infrastructure, and waste management and recycling. In manufacturing, the emphasis is on introducing clean processing techniques and controlling pollution, with less of an apparent total employment effect (ILFSD, 2009). Green jobs are also generally seen as middle-skill jobs, and expanding sectors as more skill- and knowledge-intensive than their counterparts in conventional industry; the concomitant pay and benefits are also higher (Muro et al, 2011; Chan and Lam, 2012). These features make the association between green jobs and decent work a seemingly natural one, but the connection is closer in some industries than others. For the remainder of this section, we consider the green jobs agenda from a gender perspective, focusing on problems and prospects for women in industry.

Given the extent of gender segregation in labour markets generally, and industry in particular, there is a risk that efforts to green industry will not only bypass women, but may actually marginalize them. Sectors targeted for green employment expansion, such as energy, construction and basic industry, are very male-dominated. Among green jobs that already exist, women tend to have low representation and/or occupy the lower value-added rungs. For instance, in the OECD, where women earn more than half of university degrees, only 30 per cent of degrees in science and technology (key majors for green jobs) go to women, and just 12 per cent in countries such as Japan and South Korea (Strietska-Ilina et al, 2011, p127). In developing economies, women are highly concentrated in low value-added green jobs, for instance as informal workers in waste collection and recycling (Strietska-Ilina et al, 2011). Although the goals of greening jobs are certainly laudable, the potential impacts on women's employment require explicit consideration.

This is already happening in some public policy discussions. Relative to prescriptions for demand-led growth, the green jobs dialogue pays more targeted attention to gender issues. Visions of environmentally sustainable industrial transformation often acknowledge the need to target specific skill development and education for women and other disadvantaged groups, as well as the need to incorporate principles of pay equity and ensure freedom from discrimination, echoing the principles of decent work (see, for instance, UNEP et al, 2008; ILFSD, 2009; Strietska-Ilina et al, 2011; ILO, 2012). The shift to green jobs is sometimes lauded as an opportunity to draw women into non-traditional, more highly paid sectors because they are perceived as freer from the limits of entrenched gender stereotypes (ILFSD, 2009). But breaking down these stereotypes requires more than creating new types of work. Traditional cultural frames defining gender are often used to manage changes in social and economic organization (Ridgeway, 2011), so integrating women into green employment requires specific effort.

For example, in the 'Working for Water' project in South Africa, a part of its expanded public works programme that trained people to remove invasive alien plants to enhance water security, ultimately successful efforts were made specifically to recruit women, youth and people with disabilities into the training programme (Strietska-Ilina et al, 2011, p83). In Bangladesh, as part of a larger project to extend electricity to rural areas by installing solar home systems, women were trained to install and repair solar panels and electrical outlets, serving as 'rural electricians' in ways that are revolutionary by traditional labour market standards (Sidner, 2011; ILO, 2012). In the USA, a number of programmes aim to draw women into green jobs through skill development and networking, including the Women in Apprenticeship and Nontraditional Occupations (WANTO) programme. This gives grants to community-based organizations that provide pathways for women into non-traditional occupations, such as pre-apprenticeship programmes, with recent rounds emphasizing green jobs. The project has been deemed a success, but it is woefully underfunded, garnering just US$1 million a year from the federal budget (WOW, 2012). Via the Women in Renewable Energy Sector (WiRES) project, organizations representing labour and business collaborate with academics to study women's employment and working conditions in Europe's renewable energy sector, with the aim of expanding their representation in this highly male-dominated sector. In addition to calls for promoting skill-specific education and training for women, WiRES also emphasizes the need for reconsidering traditional occupational requirements that effectively act as barriers to women, such as requiring international mobility and prior experience in the electricity sector, as well as thinking creatively about how work is organized (typically long hours and irregular shifts) to accommodate working parents (Rustico and Sperotti, 2012).

While these efforts are instructive and promising, they do not directly address the systemic challenges associated with the global production and institutional incentives discussed throughout this chapter. In particular, the increasing cost pressures associated with global competition, in the context of GVCs and global imbalances that make the turn towards demand-led growth seemingly so inevitable (albeit a turn that, in its current form, is not sufficiently gender-aware), should be a central part of the green growth and jobs logic. Some of this promise can be seen in the case of waste pickers, where efforts to green work have gone well beyond patchy skill development into addressing informality and marginalization in ways that are transformative and essential to accomplishing sustainable growth and development in today's globalized context.

In the developed world, the waste management and recycling industries are highly formalized and automated, as well as dominated by men. But in developing and emerging economies, an estimated 15–20 million waste pickers, many of them women and families driven into this work by poverty, claim reusable and recyclable materials from what others have discarded, providing an essential environmental service to areas experiencing rapid urbanization rates with limited public services (Samson, 2009; ILO, 2012). The work is largely informal, the earnings low and unstable, and it is typically associated with strong social stigma and very poor, even hazardous working conditions (ILO, 2012; WIEGO, 2014). However, the contributions waste pickers make to environmental sustainability are substantial: they improve public health and sanitation; divert materials from the waste stream; reduce the need to use new materials and for municipalities to fund full waste management systems; and provide livelihoods for the poor and most marginalized (WIEGO, 2014). And it is not just about picking up bits of plastic or paper. For example, 20–50 million tons of electronic waste containing valuable metals are discarded each year, with much of it exported to countries like China and India for dismantling. These materials often go to small, informal family workshops or other informal facilities to be dismantled, where knowledge is limited and dangers are high (ILO, 2012, p120).

Efforts to organize and enfranchise waste pickers worldwide, both among the waste pickers themselves and with help from global institutions such as the ILO, provide an excellent example of using green job strategies as pathways towards greater social inclusion (ILO, 2012). Examples of these efforts abound in all regions of the world, with most focused on expanding the social power and safety that comes with collective organization, legalization and formalizing relationships with municipalities, and getting greater access to social protections. Many also grapple with better incorporating waste pickers into waste management and recycling value chains, countering the push towards commercialization which is linked with adopting incineration and landfill-based technologies, and instead promoting zero waste strategies that maximize recycling and provide decent employment for the poor (ILO, 2013; WIEGO, 2014). Interestingly, women are more likely than men to participate in waste picker organizations, perhaps because women tend to be concentrated in lower-earning waste picking activities and, according to studies in Tanzania, Brazil and Chile, are paid lower rates than men for equivalent work (ILO, 2012, pp119–120).

Integrating care – new gender-aware pathways

The case of waste pickers brings us back to the question of equality and social justice, and illustrates the potential power of recognizing and formalizing work in ways that prioritize the goals of sustainability. Incorporating care in visions of greening growth and green economies offers one such avenue, as the primary responsibility that women have for providing care is a root cause of gender inequality. Sustainable and gender-equal pathways, whether in economic, social or environmental terms, will need to give serious attention to the care economy.

Part of the problem here is how economists and policymakers think about growth. By the standards of a typical growth model – which can itself be seen as a kind of narrative about change (see Leach et al, Chapter 1 in this book), the process of development is simply a process of capital accumulation and productivity growth. Although most contemporary growth models do incorporate some measure of human as well as physical capital, labour, like land or ecological services, is not produced but rather appears spontaneously (Elson, 1998). Human capital is rarely treated as a component of investment.[1] And while growth prescriptions almost always call for skill investment, such calls are limited to increasing formal education. This approach to growth and development completely ignores the tremendous amount of paid and unpaid care work, much of it done by women, that goes into the production and maintenance of the labour force – the process of social reproduction. Indeed, from an economic and social sustainability standpoint, one might argue that the biggest threat to the future of the current global capitalist system is how much it lowers incentives to invest in human beings, as the 'care penalty' can be applied to entire societies that prioritize social reproduction over gaining a competitive edge in the global economy (Folbre, 2012).

Feminist economics offers an alternative narrative that centres on the essential role of care in production. Unpaid work and care – the processes that underlie social reproduction – have been understood by feminist economists as highly gendered activities with gendered meanings, asymmetrically distributed between men and women in both the paid and unpaid sectors (Badgett and Folbre, 1999; Nelson and England, 2002). Thus analyses of unpaid work and care must be gender-aware, as these activities impact the economic lives of women and men differently. For instance, women's disproportionate share of unpaid work relative to men constitutes a stronger constraint on their participation in and gains from the market and the state. Women's lower incomes and relative lack of power over public finance decisions contribute to this inequality. The gendered care components of paid work also help to explain differences in male and female employment and wages. At the same time, the so-called 'care economy' is fundamental for maintaining wellbeing. So any alternative pathway must incorporate care directly to ensure sustainability and to redress gender inequality.

But the care economy is still largely marginalized from thinking on the green economy (van Heemstra, 2013). This is curious, as there are important parallels between threats to sustainability for environmental resources and care. Both exist primarily outside the traditional market sphere, and therefore their prices are far from an accurate portrayal of their social value. In a related sense, their provisioning roles both within and outside markets create public goods and positive externalities that benefit even those who do not directly utilize them, and thus make the market mechanism an economically inefficient arbiter of their use. As a result of these market failures, both human and natural resources are in danger of being used up, given the incentives produced by the prevailing global economic system.

These parallels, especially the 'public good' nature of ecological services and social reproduction, point to the need for state activism, both in terms of restructuring markets in ways that more equitably and accurately price the social value of these goods, and in social provisioning of and investment in infrastructure and services that reflect their nature as public goods. Barring such intervention, markets will result in shortages of ecological and care goods and services, shortages that ultimately press into the realm of crisis.

When care work is decently paid and protected, it can meet the interests of both care workers and users, as well as reduce the burden that is placed on women, girls and the environment. Shifting towards a more care- or social services-intensive economy would have environmental benefits, in that providing care does not generally entail intensive use of natural resources. Such a shift would have to be accompanied by changes in the typical terms of employment for care services, which not only exhibit a 'care penalty' in pay, partly as a consequence of gender norms and stereotypes, but are also structurally handicapped by labour intensity and low (as measured by the market) value-added. Green growth needs, in essence, also to be concerned with making care work decent work. This means that investment in the care sector needs to be accompanied by policies that reduce occupational and sectoral segregation and improve the pay and labour market conditions of such work.

However, lowering consumption and challenging the relentless push for growth is one thing in the North, where inequality and environmental degradation are primarily problems of value and distribution. But the question of growth in the South, where in many economies redistribution will be insufficient to adequately improve wellbeing and raise living standards, is still a pressing one. Increasing productivity and value-added in these contexts needs to play a part in pathways towards sustainable development. Growth itself is not the problem. For instance, even in the North, the paid care sector may need to expand as societies age, which will actually contribute to growth as typically defined (van Heemstra, 2013). It is, rather, certain types of growth that are unsustainable.

The state, however, is not the only actor needed to forward alternative pathways. In fact, activism at every scale is needed in the face of such challenges. In promoting social production, investment and consumption, there must be production by for-profit as well as non-profit institutions such as cooperatives and community enterprises, community management of forest and irrigation systems, as well as community kitchens and childcare centres. By strengthening the rights of users, and building links between producers and users, such hybrid systems are more responsive to the needs and demands of all, regardless of position or prosperity (Elson, 2011). In addition, social production and investment are vital to ensure a sufficient quantity of public goods – most notably, a sustainable climate and care system (Folbre, 2012; UN, 2014a). Though few in number, there are examples of such programmes in the South.

For instance, in the Republic of Korea, the government has significantly expanded social care provision in the form of universal long-term insurance schemes for the elderly, statutory parental leave, and publicly subsidized childcare since 2000. By redistributing care responsibilities more evenly between state, market, family and community, this public support of the care economy is seen as an engine for economic growth (Peng, 2012). Another example is Pakistan's 'Lady health worker' programme, which establishes a vital link between households and health services, particularly for women in rural areas whose mobility is restricted. The programme represents a major source of employment and predictable income for the women who bring their training back to their local communities (Khan, 2014). It is important to note, however, that these workers earn less than the national minimum wage and thus are still subject to the care penalty (UN, 2014a).

Promising cases are also found in the actions of grassroots and activist organizations that pursue economies based on the principles of sufficiency, care and an integration of people and nature. For instance, La Via Campesina[2] represents a collective movement, spanning from local to global scale, that promotes economic, social and environmental sustainability by recognizing and empowering farmers' rights to decent work and secure livelihoods. This empowerment includes the knowledge, action and agency of women. The National Association of Rural and Indigenous Women in Chile, for example, with its 10,000 members, is linked to La Via Campesina and is launching an agroecology institute to train women smallholder farmers in South America (UN, 2014a). Movements like this, that integrate both gender equality and sustainable development, are cause for much optimism. Often they represent the voices of those most marginalized by the dominant development models (for instance, women, care and informal workers, and the poor) and thus are powerful advocates and rich sources of alternative narratives and pathways.

Concluding thoughts

This chapter began by arguing for the relevance of macroeconomic policy and growth in visions for sustainable development, using the lens of women's employment to assess the record and potential of the global economic system to provide opportunities for decent work, gender equality and environmental sustainability. In an economic sense, neoliberal macroeconomic policy creates a deflationary growth environment and limits the role of the state in guiding development. Environmentally, such a framework devalues nature and inhibits the state's ability to build institutions that protect resources from overexploitation, and vulnerable populations from the consequences of environmental degradation.

The terms of production and exchange that underlie global imbalances are premised on wage compression, debt accumulation and the primacy of finance. The result is an economic fragility and susceptibility to crisis that does little to promote sustainable development, equitable growth or high-quality employment. While the rise of global value chains in international production eases access to global markets, it also intensifies competition, constrains wages and limits the expansion of domestic aggregate demand – magnifying the challenges posed by neoliberal macroeconomic policy and global imbalances. Furthermore, these global dynamics have amplified environmental pressures by intensifying the competition between countries, especially in the global South, with respect to environmental policy, raw materials markets and intensive resource extraction. The consequent increasing power of globalized capital relative to labour is thrown into starker relief when considering the challenges it poses for social, environmental and economic upgrading.

The dominant growth paradigm, along with the added pressures of global imbalances and GVCs, is especially troublesome when considering gender equality. Labour market segregation, especially in industry, often places women in the most vulnerable positions vis-à-vis global competitive pressures, leading to low pay, poor working conditions and insecurity. Promotion of wage-led growth is an appealing alternative in that it offers an economically sustainable vision for raising wages and creating decent work to advance social upgrading.

A plausible intersection, then, between social, economic and environmental sustainability, is the greening of growth. A domestic orientation, emphasis on innovation, and an expanded role of the state are prominent features of both wage-led and (the more progressive variants of) green growth. But while approaches founded on employment and decent work, and on green growth and green economies, offer potential alternatives, they are not always adequate from a gender perspective. To ensure sustainable development, any alternative growth or macroeconomic policy framework needs to address inequality meaningfully, not just by gender, but also class, race and ethnicity; create decent work and sustainable livelihoods for all, regardless of employment sector; and fully enumerate and internalize the incentives and consequences for care, social reproduction and the natural environment.

Feminist economists and others have done substantial work visioning along these lines (cf. Jain and Elson, 2011; Genanet, 2013). Such alternatives cannot just be about reforming economic relations, they must reconceptualize how we organize and evaluate economies and policy-making (Elson, 2011). For instance, one proposal is a 'purple economy', where care for human beings is the organizing principle and green economy concerns help guide macro policy formulation (Ilkkaracan, 2013). Likewise, this view advocates moving beyond growth to a broader array of goals, evaluating economic policies, for instance, based on the extent to which they lower and eventually eliminate inequality, raise economic mobility for low-income households, and address the unequal distribution of caring labour between women and men (Seguino, 2011). These alternative measures could be the subject of collective discussion and debate, one built around the principles of sustainable development. Thus there is a need for international collaboration to adequately address the linkages between gender and the environment, such as those between gender inequality and the food, water, energy and health crises generated by climate change (Castañeda and Gammage, 2011).

Overall, these alternatives highlight the fundamental role of care – for humans and ecological systems alike – in a sustainable future.

All of these alternatives require central roles for the state, and other public institutions, in social provisioning. Such roles directly contradict neoliberal edicts for limited public budgets and market liberalization, and challenge the practicality of finance-friendly monetary and fiscal policies. Still, global volatility and the strictures of prevailing models of macroeconomic management have affected state practice already, spurring the rise of what is alternatively termed the 'social investment state' or the 'new developmental welfare state'. Traditional models of social protection have been deemed insufficient effectively to counterbalance the negative impacts of new economic realities, and so a new model of state activism in managing social investment and building human capabilities emerged. Experiments in social policies in Latin America such as conditional cash transfers, as well as social welfare reforms in a number of European countries, reflect this new perspective. At the centre is a strong emphasis on providing care for children in ways that target the development of their capabilities, such as early childhood education (Jenson, 2010).

We need more than adaptive social (or environmental) policies to fundamentally change the future. We need to rethink the basic economic framework on which our social, economic and environmental systems operate; these include prevailing systems of growth, globalization and macroeconomic policy management. The prevailing system of market-led growth is unequal and unsustainable. But these dual problems also point to a dual solution: one that integrates feminist thinking with green economic thinking, and moves us towards pathways that more fundamentally integrate care and wellbeing, and thus sustainability as a whole.

Notes

1 Two important exceptions are the models presented by Braunstein et al (2011) and Seguino (2010).
2 Discussed in more detail in this book by Leach et al (Chapter 1) and Fukuda-Parr (Chapter 4); see Via Campesina (2014a).

3

POPULATION, SUSTAINABLE DEVELOPMENT AND GENDER EQUALITY

Betsy Hartmann, Anne Hendrixson and Jade Sasser

Introduction

The aim of this chapter is to rethink population so as to open up new socially just and gender-equitable pathways to sustainable development. Population is never an easy topic. It elicits contentious debates about the relationships between humans and nature, men and women, old and young, rich and poor. Population policies often centre on women's bodies,[1] with direct impacts on their health, reproduction and sexuality; individual bodily integrity and autonomy can be sacrificed in the name of the greater social, economic and environmental good.

At the heart of competing population ideas and policies are different, and often incompatible, value systems and visions of the future. Scholars have produced abundant research documenting the ways in which scientific knowledge production is reflective of social values, political priorities and disciplinary paradigms. Rather than simply representing observations about the world, scientific research is produced in the context of existing social and political orders, which it has an integral role in shaping (Jasanoff, 2004). In other words, knowledge of the world is inseparable from the context in which that knowledge is produced. The ability to produce, shape and circulate knowledge is deeply linked to notions of authority and expertise.

Making transparent the complex processes by which certain ideas about population have become dominant to the exclusion of others exposes the politics and power dynamics that contribute to their salience. It can also affirm alternative knowledges, such as those that emerged from the international women's health movement in response to population control abuses and problematic framings of the relationship between population and the environment.

Powerful conventional beliefs and narratives about overpopulation pervade popular media, environmental education, and policy debates and decisions in the health, conservation and security arenas. With long historical roots, they have recently gained renewed force in discourses about climate change and planetary boundaries. They deeply influence the ways current demographic dynamics are framed in relation to gender and sustainability. Although variations exist on the theme, the conventional wisdom on overpopulation runs like this:

Human population growth is overshooting the carrying capacity of the planet, pushing against limits to growth and planetary boundaries, enacting tragedies of the commons across the poorer regions of the globe. It is a root cause of poverty, environmental degradation, resource scarcity, migration, violent conflict and climate change. Increased funding for women's education, micro-credit schemes and family planning programmes will help bring birth rates down, but maybe we don't have time for them. Coercive measures, such as China's one-child policy, may be the only answer. At stake is the very survival of the planet.

This chapter challenges these narratives of overpopulation, and argues for the creation of a new sustainable development framework in which a comprehensive platform for sexual and reproductive health and rights (SRHR) is central.[2] Such a framework would be rooted in a non-negotiable commitment to bodily integrity, including freedom from all forms of violence, and equal access to decent work, secure livelihoods, a clean and safe environment, education, health, and other social services and public goods.

A first step towards this new sustainable development framework is to question thinking on overpopulation through a gendered, political ecology analysis. That critique challenges us to move beyond the limits of overpopulation thinking in order to better understand the complex interplay of contributors to global problems and to find effective solutions to them that strengthen gender equality. A second step is to explore how feminist understandings of the linkages between gender, population, poverty and sustainability enable more just and effective policies in the present, as well as a more positive, non-apocalyptic vision of the future.

The chapter is organized into three sections: on population and the environment; current demographic dynamics; and the strategic production and deployment of population and climate change narratives. It concludes with a call for new pathways and new politics of the future to redraw the landscape of population discourse in ways that expand, rather than constrict, the policy horizon. To open these pathways, we must examine entrenched ideas about overpopulation.

Population and the environment: Ideas and consequences

Today, concerns about overpopulation play a central role in the main discourses about sustainable development. They draw on old theories, models and narratives about the relationship between population, resources and the environment that have proved remarkably resilient. They carry with them problematic assumptions about gender and women's roles in development.

There are a number of reasons for the resilience of these views of population and their strategic reuse over time. First, even though they have been disproven by historical evidence, these overpopulation paradigms are able to escape the test of time by continually projecting population-induced scarcities into the future (Hildyard, 2010). Because sustainable development takes a long-term and future-oriented view, such projections are appealing because they seem to provide insight into what lies ahead for humanity.

Secondly, they serve to obscure power relations by making hunger, poverty, environmental degradation and even war seem like the inevitable consequence of too many people pressing up against too few resources. By eliding the politics of resource control, competition and conflict, they shift the blame away from powerful elites and vested interests onto the shoulders of the poor. As such, they have proved tremendously useful as tools of colonial, neo-colonial and post-colonial policy-making.

Thirdly, they draw on and reinforce dominant masculinities. In early paradigms, women matter only to the extent that they reproduce the population problem; biology is destiny. In later ones their agency is recognized, but only in a limited fashion as enlightened managers of their own fertility and local environments. Gender relations, as well as differences between women on the basis of race, class, ethnicity and sexuality, are conspicuous by their absence.

Fourthly, the implicit biases of these paradigms are made more explicit through negative metaphors and visual images, such as the population bomb, that employ racially charged and sexist stereotypes (Wilson, 2012). The visceral appeal of overpopulation propaganda is a key reason why many people are willing to suspend critical judgment when it comes to overpopulation paradigms.

The following critique of overpopulation paradigms is not intended to suggest that population growth has *no* impact on the natural environment, human society, or prospects for sustainable development. Rather, the relationship is context-specific and mediated by a host of other factors – economic, political, social and cultural. Research in historical and contemporary demography reveals just how complex demographic dynamics are, as explored in the second section of this chapter. The problem with the paradigms presented below is that they ignore this complexity and reduce demographic dynamics into the operation of abstract, universal, ahistorical laws. Dismantling them is a necessary first step to rethinking the relationships between population dynamics and the environment.

From Malthus to the degradation narrative: Creating knowledge about population

The idea that human population growth inexorably outstrips resources derives primarily from the work of the British political economist Thomas Robert Malthus (1766–1834). In his famous publication *An Essay on the Principle of Population*, Malthus maintained that, if left unchecked, human populations grow geometrically (exponentially), while food production at best follows an arithmetic (linear) path. This condemns humanity to a constant battle to provide sustenance for its growing numbers. Malthus originally maintained that only the ensuing miseries of hunger, poverty, disease and war keep human numbers in check by increasing death rates, along with some help from moral restraint and vice (infertility caused by venereal diseases) that keep birth rates down.

Malthus failed to foresee the social and technological innovations that would allow food production to outpace population growth, or the demographic transition to lower birth rates. Yet his principle of population and his pessimism continue to influence many environmentalists. The foundational concept of 'carrying capacity' is a case in point. The concept was initially used in the mid-1800s shipping industry in relation to cargo size; then employed several decades later in range and game management; and ultimately applied to human populations by ecologists in the United States beginning in the 1940s and 1950s (Sayre, 2008).

While there are variations on the concept, it suggests there is a direct relationship between the availability of resources, population size, and a corresponding demand for and depletion of resources (Höhler, 2005). William Vogt's 1948 bestseller *Road to Survival* used carrying capacity to paint an apocalyptic picture of population pressures outstripping food production, degrading the environment, and causing wars that would probably wipe out three-quarters of the human race (Vogt, 1948). This framing in turn came to naturalize international efforts to limit population growth in impoverished countries.

That population growth was exceeding, or on the verge of exceeding, the planet's carrying capacity became the rallying call of a next generation of Malthusian environmentalists. Bestsellers such as Paul Ehrlich's *The Population Bomb* and the Club of Rome's *Limits to Growth* spread messages of planetary crises – famine, resource depletion and environmental degradation – driven in large part by overpopulation (Ehrlich, 1968; Meadows et al, 1972). Likewise, one of the most widely read environmental essays ever, biologist Garrett Hardin's 'The tragedy of the commons', warns that 'Freedom in a commons brings ruin to all', advocating for the solutions of population control and private property rights (Hardin, 1968, p1244).[3]

These popular works discuss gender only indirectly, asserting the need for the reduction of women's fertility as an imperative. Hardin refers to 'breeders' as responsible for overpopulation. As political scientists Jane Jaquette and Kathleen Staudt observe, in Paul Ehrlich's early works women were present only in the sense of their dangerous sexuality. He suggested they used their year-long sexuality to entice men into staying in family groups, with the resulting uncontrolled biological urges leading to overbreeding (Jaquette and Staudt, 1985).

In international development circles, Malthusian policy narratives, commonly termed degradation narratives, gained increasing traction. Their basic premise is that in rural parts of the global South, population pressure coupled with poverty is the main cause of land degradation. In other words, the poor are primarily responsible for destroying their own environments. These narratives have their roots in colonial policies that justified land expropriation by blaming native agricultural practices and population pressures for soil erosion, deforestation and desertification (Hartmann, 2010). Later they came to be used by bilateral and multilateral development agencies to justify external interventions such as the top-down implementation of rural development projects and population control programmes (Roe, 1995; Williams, 1995). Over the course of the 1970s and 1980s they expanded to include a negative view of migration. After poor people deplete their immediate environments, the story line goes, many migrate to other marginal lands, setting in motion the same vicious downward spiral.

These troubling narratives linking population, poverty, environmental degradation and security had a deep impact on the emerging field of sustainable development in the late 1980s. While sustainable development advocates acknowledged the role of inequality, they still saw population pressure as the most important cause of both poverty and environmental degradation. British environmentalist Norman Myers claimed that the bottom billion of the world's people – the poorest of the poor – 'cause more environmental degradation than the other three billion developing-world people put together' (Myers, 1995, pp22–23).

The 1987 *Our Common Future: Report of the World Commission on Environment and Development* (known as the Brundtland Report), despite its many strengths, did little to challenge the conventional wisdom on population as a primary cause of environmental problems. On the contrary, it draws heavily on overpopulation paradigms, enshrining the degradation narrative as a centrepiece of sustainable development, and positioning women as agents of degradation, victims of environmental stress, potential contributors to environmental restoration, and culpable for alarming population growth rates. While the report suggests that improvements in health and education, the status of women, and women's self-determination will help reduce population growth, these efforts are secondary to an emergency prerogative to drive down birth rates. 'But time is short', it warns, 'and developing countries will also have to promote direct measures to reduce fertility, to avoid going radically beyond the productive potential to support their populations' (Brundtland, 1987, p51).

It may be a truism that ideas have consequences, but in the case of overpopulation paradigms, the statement is all too true. They raised the stakes on reducing women's fertility so high that coercive population control measures became justified.

Raising the stakes

In the heyday of population control, from the late 1960s to the end of the Cold War, reducing fertility in poor countries was a major component of bilateral and multilateral agencies' policies and programmes, and was vigorously pursued by national population planning in developing countries. So urgent was the imperative to drive down birth rates that coercive practices became routine. These included forced sterilization, and pressuring or bribing women to use higher-risk contraceptives without adequate informed consent or medical back-up. Divorced from primary health care, family planning became a weapon, sometimes deadly, in the war on population growth. The list of countries with coercive policies is a long one, with India and China having the most egregious practices, but many others – including Bangladesh, Indonesia, Brazil, Mexico, and the United States – targeted poor women and racial and ethnic minorities for population control (Hartmann, 1995; Connelly, 2008).

Framing the population issue in environmental terms was probably the single most important factor in building public consensus for population control interventions (Wilmoth and Ball, 1992). If people can be convinced that apocalypse looms, then they are more willing to endorse emergency measures to forestall it, and to bolster the power of experts who claim to know what is best for humanity and nature.

The one-child policy adopted in 1979 by the government of China followed policy debates about population in which natural scientists and systems modellers, influenced by the Club of Rome's *Limits to Growth*, won out over social scientists who advocated a voluntary and more humane approach to reducing population growth. Setting unrealistic targets, in 1983 the government launched a highly coercive population control campaign that forced millions of women to be sterilized or undergo abortions against their will (Greenhalgh, 2005).

Combined with son preference, the one-child policy has had terrible gender outcomes. Results from China's 2010 census show a sex ratio at birth of 119 males per 100 females, one of the worst in the world (Haub, 2011) – the normal sex ratio at birth is 105–107 males per 100 females. The policy has given rise to the widespread practice of sex selective abortion as well as the abandonment and hiding of female children. The policy has also had negative gender outcomes for men, especially poor peasants in rural areas who cannot find brides and who are stigmatized and discriminated against as 'bare branches' (Greenhalgh, 2012).

Although the Chinese government recently announced some relaxation of the one-child policy, it still remains very much in force (Johnson, 2014). In part this is due to political pressure from the huge birth planning bureaucracy whose employees benefit in terms of fines, salaries and prestige (Wong, 2013; Johnson, 2014). To justify continuing coercion, the government now claims that the policy has prevented the birth of 400 million Chinese. The prevention of these births, meanwhile, is framed as one of China's main contributions to mitigating climate change (Feng et al, 2013).

Increasingly, Chinese demographers are disputing these claims. Most of China's fertility transition was accomplished in the decade *before* the implementation of the one-child policy. The country's total fertility rate dropped from 5.8 in 1970 to 2.8 in 1979, and probably would have continued to decline even in the absence of the one-child policy due to mortality decline, increases in education, and rapid social and economic changes (Feng et al, 2013). History may also judge international population agencies harshly for their support of the one-child policy. For example, support from population agencies is implicated in the development and spread of sex selection technology in China and other parts of Asia (Connelly, 2008; Hvistendahl, 2011).

As feminist resistance to coercive population control policies mounted at both national and international levels, reaching its height in the 1980s and 1990s, population agencies began to develop softer approaches to reducing birth rates. Just as women as a category had been 'discovered' in the development field, so they became more present in the population field. In terms of sustainable development, instrumentalist views of women as managers of their own fertility merged with hopeful narratives about their potential as managers of environmental conservation and restoration. In other words, the degradation narrative might have a happy ending if you could harness women to the task.

Discovering women

The idea of women as environmental managers – not just as victims or agents of environmental degradation, as in earlier narratives – emerged from a shift in women, environment and development (WED) thinking. According to the new logic, women had a closer connection to nature, nurturing behaviours, and environmental knowledge that enabled them to take on an active role in environmental projects. Yet, as argued by Leach et al in Chapter 1 of this book, oversimplifying women's realities led to weak programming prescriptions that asked women to take on even more unpaid work, adding to their already considerable labour burdens.

The WED approach had a neo-Malthusian variant that became influential in population and sustainable development circles (UNFPA, 1992). This narrative puts women at the centre of a population–environment–development triangle because they determine population size through their reproductive behaviour; have an impact on the environment through their daily tasks of fetching water, wood, etc.; and affect development through their roles in family and society. Population growth, meanwhile, is still viewed as the main cause of both poverty and environmental degradation (Hartmann, 1997).

With the ascendency of neoliberalism, women's reproduction also became instrumentalized in terms of their integration into the market economy. Increasingly, international and national population policy discourses focused on how, through the correct 'choice' of modern contraceptive method, women could help themselves, their children and, by extension, the nation (Richey, 2008; Rao and Sexton, 2010). With fewer children, this new woman is a boon to the market economy: her self-regulation aids her in managing her family's adjustment to the instability and unpredictability of market forces.

Despite the many drawbacks of these approaches, they opened up political spaces for national and transnational feminist organizing to advance women's rights, and gave sympathetic feminists within the population establishment more room for manoeuvre. If women were suddenly so instrumental to solving population, environment and development crises, why weren't they fairly represented at the policy table?

The 1992 United Nations Conference on Environment and Development (UNCED) in Rio de Janeiro galvanized international coalitions of women's health and rights activists who were concerned about the ways in which population growth was being negatively linked to environmental destruction. These themes are highlighted in Agenda 21, UNCED's action plan for sustainable development, which emphasizes the vital role and knowledge of women for the conservation and sustainable use of biological diversity (UN, 1992). Feminist scholarship advanced new ways to look at the complex relationships between gender, demographic and environmental variables (Sen and Nayar, 2013).

Women's movements played a particularly important role at the 1994 UN International Conference on Population and Development (ICPD), popularly known as 'Cairo'. The conference represented a major international policy shift from population control to women's empowerment and a broader SRHR agenda. The conference's Programme of Action, or 'consensus', was endorsed by most of the world's governments and came out against the use of coercion, including incentives and disincentives in family planning provision. Instead it emphasized reproductive health services as a human right and promoted voluntary family planning, along with maternal care, sexuality education and prevention of sexually transmitted infections (UNFPA, 1995).

Many of these gains were the result of women's health advocates' participation in the Cairo process. Gita Sen and Anita Nayar suggest that women's groups successfully challenged the neo-Malthusian population paradigm through creating a consensus position on population policy that bridged the disparate politics and divides between women's groups from different regions of the world. This consensus gave women's movements the collective power to negotiate an alliance with family planning lobbies and challenge the growing bloc of religious conservatives spearheaded by the Vatican (Sen and Nayar, 2013). Others suggest that women's groups were able to forge a compromise with neo-Malthusian interests because the latter were worried about rising conservative opposition to birth control and abortion, and viewed the feminists as strategic allies against these forces (Hodgson and Watkins, 1997). Feminist reflections on Cairo also point to some of the serious fault lines between women's groups, particularly over the lack of sufficient critique of the impacts of structural adjustment and neoliberalism in the consensus position (Petchesky, 1995; Smyth, 1996).

Ultimately the ICPD's Programme of Action sent mixed messages. It maintained that rapid population growth was a major cause of poverty and environmental degradation, and that reduced fertility rates are necessary for sustainable development. At the same time, it advocated for a positive agenda of women's empowerment and broader reproductive health programmes as solutions to high birth rates, instead of the top-down, target-driven family planning programmes of the past. It challenged neither Malthusian views of environmental degradation nor neoliberal business as usual; instead of seriously addressing economic inequalities, it called for the vague formulation of 'sustained economic growth within the context of sustainable development' (Hartmann, 1995, p153).

Unfortunately, Cairo's SRHR commitments were not fully realized and were further watered down in the Millennium Development Goals (MDGs). The original MDGs did not include a specific target for advancing reproductive health and rights, and instead included Target 5 (now 5A), which called for reducing maternal mortality. Largely because of advocacy from the United Nations Population Fund (UNFPA) and others, MDG Target 5B was added in 2005 at the five-year review point, to promote universal access to reproductive health care. Yet Target 5, both A and B, narrows the Cairo Programme of Action from a broad SRHR agenda to an emphasis on pregnancy. With this narrowing of the agenda, women's roles shifted from 'agents of social change, and the subjects of rights' to 'child-bearers and caretakers' who are 'limited to their pregnancy status' (Yamin and Boulanger, 2013a, p80).

Following the emphasis on pregnancy, international funding streams have been channelled largely to maternal and child health provision, while other aspects of sexual and reproductive health, including contraception, experienced a decrease in funding. The upsurge in family planning aid since 2012 is in part due to concerns over sustainable development and economic growth, both in the Rio+20 outcome document and in popular and scholarly discussions (Yamin and Boulanger, 2013a, p77).

Current high-level agendas for sustainable development promise to include the Cairo commitments and a gendered lens to some degree. In the *Framework of Actions* from ICPD +10, UNFPA highlights a rights-based approach to sustainable development, and includes the strengthening of health systems for universal access to SRHR (UNFPA, 2014). Of the 17 proposed Sustainable Development Goals (SDGs), Goal 5 specifically aims to 'attain gender equality, empower women and girls everywhere' (UNDECA, 2015). Gender-responsive policies are seen as central for sustainable development, and the SDG technical paper on population gives nuanced attention to multiple demographic trends, such as population aging, as well as the role of SRHR in sustainable development. However, while promoting voluntary SRHR, it also promotes lowering birth rates to bolster economic development, reflecting the aforementioned neoliberal instrumentalization of women's reproduction for market gain (UN TST, 2014, p78). This echoes the mixed messages of the ICPD Programme of Action and the Brundtland Report by pitting the goals of comprehensive SRHR against sustainable development and economic goals, while assuming that they are aligned.

There are many challenges to successfully advancing SRHR in global agendas such as these. One challenge is finding alternative pathways to the two extremes that continue to limit the implementation of a broad and effective SRHR agenda: the neo-Malthusian approach that views family planning and contraception as tools to reduce population growth; and the conservative position that denies people the services they need to exercise reproductive and sexual rights. Another is positioning SRHR among often competing issues in broad agendas. Nevertheless, participating in these international policy fora presents an opportunity to reframe the linkages between population, gender and the environment. The way that population dynamics are understood within these agendas will have implications for not only SRHR, but also for approaches to climate change, poverty reduction, resource use and environmental management.

Interpreting demographic dynamics

Demographic realities today are very different from how they were even 50 years ago. Birth rates have declined more quickly than anticipated, while the overall global population is still growing. The differences in birth rates between countries have contributed not only to a polarized population age distribution – a youthful global South and an aging North – but to increased efforts to bring down birth rates among global South youth as a global imperative.

The previous section examined the limitations of conventional understandings of the relationship between population and environment, and how they instrumentalize notions of women and gender. This section looks at how current narratives of demographic dynamics are shaped by the values and assumptions of dominant neoliberal models of development, and also build on neo-Malthusian thinking. To respond to the very real challenges posed by demographic change – and work toward a sustainable development framework that integrates gender equity – requires thinking beyond these narratives.

This section examines the complexity of current population dynamics and narratives through a gendered lens. It starts with a summary of the present population picture and then moves on to critique the overly simplistic ways in which the demographic transition – ostensibly speeded by greater use of family planning to reduce fertility rates – is positioned as a process that will ensure economic development. The case of Nigeria shows us that overemphasis on family planning ignores the roles of inequality and privatization in keeping birth rates high. Finally, the narratives on youthful population dynamics not only reflect neo-Malthusian and neoliberal ideas about population and the economic benefits of slowing growth rates, but also promote gender stereotypes and deepen an old–young binary that runs counter to gender equity and sustainable development.

The present population picture

In the course of the twentieth century, the world population almost quadrupled – from 1.65 billion in 1900 to around 6.1 billion in 2000. But this so-called population explosion is fizzling out. The rate at which the world population is growing has been slowing down since the late 1960s, with birth rates declining more rapidly than anticipated. Smaller families are becoming the global norm.

Presently, the average number of children per woman (measured as the total fertility rate, TFR) is estimated to be 2.53 for the period 2005–10 according to the 2012 revisions of the World Population Prospects (UN, 2013a).[4] That figure masks differences between countries. Sub-Saharan Africa has 33 countries with a TFR over 4. Eight of these – Niger, Somalia, Chad, Mali, Burundi, Democratic Republic of the Congo, Angola and Uganda – have TFRs over 6. Nevertheless, fertility rates are declining in most of these countries as well, especially in urban areas. In other countries, mainly in East Asia and Eastern Europe, fertility rates have fallen well below replacement level fertility of roughly two children per woman. However, the population is not yet declining in most of these countries because of population momentum, except in countries such as Japan which are most advanced in the demographic transition (Fischer, 2014). In 2005–10, the 75 countries with below-replacement fertility made up 48 per cent of the world's population (UN, 2013a).

The result is a heterogeneity of demographic sub-trends around the world. As noted in the UNFPA's *Framework of Actions*, 'The demographic transition associated with declining fertility and mortality levels, together with the urban transition that has shifted the locus of human activity from rural to urban areas, have caused unprecedented changes in population size, age structures and spatial distribution' (UNFPA, 2014, p223). Children and young people are the majority of the population in the global South, with 1.7 billion children under age 15 and 1.1 billion young people aged 15–24, making up the largest global cohort of young people in history. Youthful populations predominate in countries that are considered to be the least developed, including Niger, Mali, Zambia and Somalia, which also have the highest population growth rates (UN, 2013a).

Population aging, when the number of older people in the population increases and the number of young decreases, is occurring throughout the world. It is most concentrated in the global North, in countries including Japan, Russia and Italy, where the number of older people exceeds the number of those under 15 years of age. *World Population Prospects: The 2012 Revision* reports that by 2050 there will be close to double the number of older people than children in developed countries (UN, 2013a).

Today there is renewed interest in overall population growth rates, propelled largely from upwardly revised estimates. *World Population Prospects: The 2012 Revision* estimates that the present world population of about 7.2 billion in 2014 will reach 8.1 billion in 2025, 9.6 billion in 2050, and 10.9 billion by 2100. These calculations are based on the medium-variant projection, the one most widely used. The projected global population total is higher than in the previous 2010 revision, which estimated a population of 10.1 billion in 2100. This is mainly because projected fertility levels have been adjusted upward in a number of countries, particularly in sub-Saharan Africa (UN, 2013a).

The new numbers require scrutiny. As noted in the first section, scientific knowledge is produced in the context of social and political orders. Likewise, demographic projections include weighted uncertainties which are not necessarily objective. A number of demographers, including the former director of the UN Population Division, believe that even the UN's 2010 projection of 10.1 billion people by 2100 is too high because it is based on a questionable projection. According to critics, the world population is likely to reach its highest peak at around 9 billion, not 10 (Pearce, 2011).

Whether or not the *2012 Revision* projections prove accurate, the idea that world population may grow to almost 11 billion people is being met with increasing alarm in population and environment circles, with the main response being to call for greater investments in family planning to reduce population growth and speed demographic transition to lower birth rates. The *2012 Revision* itself presents increased uptake of modern contraception in high-fertility countries as the key to preventing a grim scenario of the world population increasing by nearly six times more than is currently projected (UN, 2013a, p3).

Demographic transitions

The presentation of contraception and family planning as the key to reducing birth rates oversimplifies the complex interplay of social, economic and cultural factors in demographic transitions to lower birth rates. In re-wedding family planning to population reduction, it also threatens to undermine the positive gains of Cairo in situating family planning within a broader SRHR framework.

Demographer Tim Dyson describes the broad contours of demographic transition thus:

> The demographic transition is a global phenomenon – one that, at its heart, involves the movement of all human populations from experiencing high death and birth rates to experiencing very much lower death and birth rates. Essentially, these are the processes of *mortality decline* and *fertility decline*. As populations go through the transition, they always increase in *size*. That is, they experience a period of *population growth* due to natural increase. And they always undergo two fundamental changes in composition: they move from being predominantly rural to being predominantly urban (i.e. the process of *urbanization*); and they move from having young age structures to having old age structures (i.e. the process of *population ageing*). These are the five main processes of the transition.
>
> (Dyson, 2010, p3)

How important are contraceptives and family planning programmes in these processes? They can certainly play a role as one among many proximate factors that influence the timing and speed of fertility decline. Family planning, especially the provision of safe abortion services, can also play a positive role in mortality decline, particularly in reducing maternal mortality rates. Unsafe abortion, for example, causes 13 per cent of all maternal deaths (Global Health Watch, 2011).

The frequent claim that family planning is one of the most effective ways to reduce maternal mortality should be viewed with caution, however. In addition to unsafe abortion, the four other most immediate medical causes of maternal death are severe bleeding (26 per cent); infections (15 per cent), eclampsia (12 per cent) and obstructed labour (8 per cent). Indirect causes, accounting for 20 per cent of maternal mortality, are co-existing conditions of malaria, anaemia, jaundice and tuberculosis. These diseases are largely related to poverty and lack of access to health services. 'Maternal health needs to be addressed within the larger framework of collapsing health systems further burdened by repressive policies and programs, affecting the socio-political context of health', states the 2011 Global Health Watch report. 'This is especially important in a context where privatization, cutbacks in allocation to the social sector, shrinking wage structures, declining work opportunities, and dwindling food security are hitting women the hardest' (Global Health Watch, 2011, pp130–131).

The idea that family planning by itself will induce demographic transition is rooted in the politicization of demographic transition theory in the USA during the Cold War. Ideas like these had powerful backers. Private sector donors in the USA were central to the development of new knowledge about population trends, due in large part to their funding of demographic studies. In the 1940s and 1950s there was an unprecedented increase in the development of formal networks between government economic planners, foreign policy experts, professional demographers, corporate leaders and directors of philanthropic organizations, which – based on US geopolitical security interests newly outlined in Truman's Point Four Program of Technical Assistance to Developing Nations (Truman, 1949) – were particularly interested in the 'population problem' and its potential for promoting regional destabilization, especially in global South countries. Private donors and philanthropists came to play a key role in this process by subsidizing demographic research that underpinned demographic policy (Sharpless, 1997).

While initially demographers posited that Western-style industrialization would bring about mortality and fertility decline in the developing world, the spread of communism, especially the success of the Chinese revolution, led to a reformulation. Demographers began to identify rapid population growth in poor countries as a serious brake on capitalist development, and fertility decline as a prerequisite for, not a consequence of, successful industrialization (Hodgson, 1983; Szreter, 1993, Greenhalgh, 1996). In other words, rapid modernization was needed in poor countries to stave off the Communist threat, and for modernization to occur, birth rates had to come down. As the Cold War accelerated, that agenda was increasingly framed in crisis terms.

This new version of demographic transition theory provided an important rationale for US population control interventions overseas. US government and private foundation funding began to flow generously into the field of demography, so much so that, in the words of demographer Paul Demeny, the field began playing the role of 'handmaiden in family planning programs' (Demeny, 1988, p24). The industry generated a number of rationales for population control, including the view that investments in family planning were much more cost-effective than other development strategies (Connelly, 2008, p313). Of course, not all demographers shared these views, and historical demographers in particular complicated demographic transition theory, pointing to how economic, social and cultural differences between countries, even in the same region, influenced the shape and timing of mortality and fertility decline.

While demography as a field has grown much more heterodox, the idea that family planning is the best development investment survived, and is being resuscitated today in some powerful quarters. In fact, the parallels between the dominant population discourse of the Cold War and that of today are quite striking.

Both see high rates of population growth as an impediment to modernization, with family planning proffered as the solution.

The case of Nigeria

Such is the current view of sub-Saharan Africa, especially Nigeria because of its large population of 170 million. Reducing Nigeria's TFR of 6 through family planning programmes has become a global priority as international development agencies such as USAID and DFID, as well as private foundations such as the Bill & Melinda Gates Foundation, provide targeted funding and urge the Nigerian government to take a greater role in family planning provision. In 2012, Nigerian President Jonathan was quoted as saying that Nigerians are having 'too many children' and that birth control legislation could control future population growth rates (BBC News Africa, 2012).

This emphasis on fertility rates diverts attention from the country's poor performance in reducing mortality rates. Nigeria, like other high-fertility countries in sub-Saharan Africa, has low life expectancy and high infant and under-five mortality rates. It also has the dubious distinction of having the second worst maternal health statistics in the world, with one in 13 women dying in childbirth (Wakabi, 2013). Since mortality decline is the main impetus for demographic transition, shifting the policy spotlight to that side of the equation could yield a more holistic set of responses than the current narrow focus on family planning. For a start, it is worth exploring the power relations that shape who lives and who dies.

In the Nigerian case, slow mortality decline cannot be blamed on a shortage of resources. For decades the country was awash with oil money that could have funded health care and social development. Instead, that wealth was siphoned off by the elite; an estimated 80 per cent of Nigeria's oil wealth has gone to 1 per cent of the population (Maas, 2010). This has caused the paradox of a country with immense oil wealth having some of the world's worst human development indicators. Nigeria's oil-producing regions, meanwhile, have experienced a toxic combination of environmental degradation and suppression of political dissent, with transnational and state-based violent contestation over oil extraction (Obi, 2010).

In the 1980s and 1990s, World Bank-imposed structural adjustment programmes in Nigeria led to a serious decline in public health delivery. Privatization and the imposition of user fees put health services out of the reach of poorer sections of the population, including women seeking reproductive health care. Between 1986 and 1991, health costs increased between 400 and 600 per cent, while other structural adjustment measures, such as the retrenchment of formal sector workers, had negative impacts on employment and increased women's care burdens (Pearce, 2000). Today, lack of government commitment and the poor quality and effectiveness of health services underlie high rates of maternal mortality (Okonofua, 2010).

Nigeria's demographic dynamics then must be considered within the context of this troubling intersection between political repression, rising inequality, structural adjustment, oil development, and environmental degradation. Such an approach would position family planning not as the magic-bullet solution to high birth rates, but as a necessary part of a much needed expansion of universal primary health care including better SRHR services. It would ask what kinds of economic, social and environmental policies would best accommodate the pressures of a growing population, and how gender relations should figure into their design and implementation.

It would also look far more closely at the role of capital flight in Nigeria and elsewhere in Africa. Over the period 1970–2008, capital flight from 33 sub-Saharan African countries totalled a staggering US$735 billion (in 2008 dollars), far more than their combined external debts of US$177 billion. Nigeria has the most capital flight of any country in Africa (Boyce and Ndikumana, 2011). Capital flight plus the public burden of debt-servicing have robbed resources from Africa that could have funded mortality reduction. Sub-Saharan African governments as a whole spend roughly the same amount on debt service as they do on public health. Economists James Boyce and Léonce Ndikumana estimate that debt-fuelled capital flight resulted in 77,000 excess infant deaths in Africa per year from 2005 to 2007. Yet capital flight figures little in current discussions of demographic transition in Africa. What is hidden from view is often just as important, or even more important, as what is foregrounded.

Population politics of bonus and bomb

The narratives about large youthful populations in the global South most often characterize them as bonus or bomb. Two theories – the demographic dividend and youth bulge theories – dominate scholarly and policy discussions about how youth will influence economics, development and international security. The demographic dividend concept maintains that large youthful populations can create economic growth and development under the right conditions, including increased youth education and economic policies that support open trade (Bloom et al, 2003). This neoliberal conception of youth as economic drivers is widely promoted as central to development in many African countries (Hendrixson, 2014) and for sustainable development generally (UN TST, 2014, p78). It promotes population reduction as the key to realizing the benefits of dividends because it influences when demographic transition takes place, and creates a large proportion of working-age adults to dependent seniors and children (Bloom et al, 2003).

In contrast, the youth bulge theory predicts that large youth populations are prone to violence and unrest at a variety of levels and intensities. Political scientist Henrik Urdal suggests that youth bulge violence is not inevitable, but is due to a combination of population stress and lack of employment, resources and education for young people (Urdal, 2012). It is thought that states can mitigate or harness the impact of bulges through providing increased educational and employment opportunities (Fares et al, 2006).

This binary understanding of youth as dividend or bulge is common among proponents for development and family planning programmes aimed at young people. At a Rio+20 plenary on the subject, USAID Deputy Administrator Donald Steinberg stated, 'The youth bulge are the young people we didn't reach, the demographic dividend will be the ones we reached' (Markham, 2012). For many analysts, whether a cohort achieves dividend productivity or demonstrates youth bulge unrest depends largely on the role of family planning in precipitating falling birth rates, along with other interventions such as education, employment and civic participation. It means reducing birth rates and speeding demographic transition, particularly in Africa.

This 'bonus and bomb' thinking about young people is overly simplistic about the range of youth behaviours and possibilities, and treats the entire age group as homogeneous, often juxtaposed to a stereotypic stagnant, aging North. It distracts from the multiple realities and experiences of young (and aging) people and, in flattening out the range of youth sexualities and identities, can skew policy aimed at serving them, particularly approaches for SRHR (Hendrixson, 2014). At worst it propagates gendered stereotypes of youth violence and dysfunction. Popular images of the youth bulge portray an angry, young brown man from Africa, the Middle East, or parts of Asia or Latin America. The counterpart to this angry young man image is often a passive, veiled young woman, whose presence serves to accentuate the implied male violence and menace or, in the case of the demographic dividend, an empowered young woman who is able to freely access jobs and education opportunities (Hendrixson, 2004, 2014).

Aging in 'shrinking Europe' has led to considerable anxiety about the changing face and race of nations (Krause, 2006). Here the angry young man of the 'youth bulge' is seen as catalysing nationalistic responses in the global North as workers migrate in search of work. It is assumed that nations with dependent aging populations will require more working-age people to sustain national economies and also care for the elderly, which will mean increased immigration from the global South. Analysts doubt the ability of global North countries to 'accept large waves of culturally different immigrants without substantial tension (already visible in anti-immigrant right wing movements in both Europe and North America)' (Ness, 2001). While the potential for conflict exists – and certainly the tightening of international borders in the USA and countries in Europe is evidence of nationalistic anxiety about immigration flows from the global South – it is nonetheless important to challenge assumptions of friction based on migration. These intensify ethnic and religious prejudices against Muslim communities in particular.

Young SRHR and AIDS advocates interrupt dominant narratives of young people and population much in the same way that international women's health advocates have articulated feminist analyses of women, gender and SRHR. As such, they are producing knowledge on SRHR, gender and youth that offers insight into the scope of young people's experiences and multiple, intersectional identities, as well as the age-specific biases young people can face (Link Up, 2013). Recognizing and respecting the variation among young people is a proactive step toward addressing stigma and age discrimination in service design and provision. It can also break down the silos of sexual and reproductive health care and HIV care, and lead to a transformative integration of services. Emphasizing the range in genders and sexualities among young people dislodges the assumption that pregnancy prevention and fertility control should be the sole goal of sexual and reproductive health provision. It provides openings for more inclusive, integrated services.

In short, the emphasis on speeding demographic transition through family planning so prevalent in policy discussions runs counter to a full platform of SRHR and a broader rights and justice-centred approach to sustainable development. What is required is a new social contract that breaks free of the constraints of neoliberalism to advance a reinvented and reinvigorated role for the state and public policy in guaranteeing health, including SRHR, human rights and civil liberties; dramatically reducing social, economic, political and gender inequalities; assuring full employment; respecting the environment; and promoting peace and de-militarization. It means developing alternative approaches to understanding demographic dynamics that counter overpopulation alarmism. As the next section shows, there is a real danger that this alarmism could undermine not only SRHR but also sustainable development by strengthening the hand of national security and corporate interests.

The population, climate change, resources and security nexus

Malthusian concepts are presently being mobilized by powerful actors in relation to climate change, related resource scarcities and notions of security. Clearly, climate change is one of the most urgent global challenges of our time. We can ill afford to follow policy pathways that lead away from, rather than towards, effective and equitable solutions.

This section begins with an examination of current models of the relationship between population and climate change which aim to 'anticipate the future'. These anticipatory knowledges shape thinking and policy around carbon emissions, human activity, population growth and family planning. Much like the discourses of planetary boundaries and resource scarcity, discussed next, the anticipatory knowledges of climate and population promote family planning as a solution to environmental problems. This section concludes with a consideration of the emerging Malthusian Anticipatory Regime for Africa (MARA) as an example of how these linkages between population, resources, climate and migration serve powerful national security and economic interests.

Anticipating the future

Recently, knowledge production and policy advocacy on global population have turned toward a heavy emphasis on the future – specifically, the charts, graphs and other models that project possible futures in the realms of population and climate change. These tools can be described as anticipatory knowledges used 'to imagine possibilities, appreciate potentials, estimate probabilities, sketch trajectories, and frame choices' (Nelson et al, 2008, p546).

Many of these models project relentless global population growth, in direct contrast to data indicating a fragmented, contradictory picture of population growth in some regions, contrasted with a plateau or even decline in other regions. Nevertheless, the multiple possible futures represented in demographic projection models invoke the ideas of both promise and threat, much like narratives of youthful populations as bonus or bomb. Vincanne Adams, Michelle Murphy and Adele Clarke locate this affective dimension in their concept of anticipation, which creates 'the sense that the future is inevitably in some senses *already "here"* as a site for active intervention. It must not only be engaged, but also be engaged properly and effectively to avoid traumatic outcomes' (Adams et al, 2009, p249).

There is often an institutional intentionality in the production of such anticipatory knowledges, especially regarding the relationship between population and the environment. In the 1990s private foundations, especially in the USA, began approaching grantees to develop multi-sector development programmes focusing on population growth as a driver of environmental problems. In 1993, the Pew Charitable Trusts made a set of prospective grants to environmental organizations to draw them into addressing population issues from an environmental standpoint, at the very moment when this approach was losing its base of support from the public sector. Pew viewed this as a new, experimental approach to framing population–environment linkages through the lens of women's sexual and reproductive health, based on what staff saw as an emerging consensus view that improving quality and access to contraceptives was a synergistic approach to addressing issues of overpopulation, overconsumption and environmental degradation (Pew Global Stewardship Initiative, 1993).[5]

Today the emphasis has shifted to climate change. In 2009, a study on the future relationships between population growth and greenhouse gas emissions on a global scale was commissioned by a private foundation that has long been engaged in population stabilization projects (Sasser, 2012). Brian O'Neill and co-authors produced what they claimed to be the first study to 'explicitly investigate the separate effect of demographic influences on emissions' (O'Neill et al, 2010, p1). Working at a global level, they analysed an integrated set of projections focused on economic growth, energy use and emissions scenarios, disaggregated by world region. They then projected population growth and greenhouse gas emissions to the year 2100 in one integrated model, concluding that slowing population growth would reduce future emissions by 37–41 per cent.

The assumptions of the study were challenged by two alternative studies that emphasized differences in resource consumption between rich and poor countries and consumers. The first study analyses what it refers to as the 'carbon legacies' deriving from individual women's reproductive behaviour (Murtaugh and Schlax, 2009, p15). The study demonstrates that there is generally an inverse relationship between individual childbearing and per capita greenhouse gas emissions; in other words, countries where women bear the fewest children are most often those with the higher rates of per capita greenhouse gas emissions, and the highest carbon legacies.

The third study, 'The implications of population growth and urbanization for climate change', retrains the lens away from populations and toward resource consumers, demonstrating that 'it is not the growth in (urban or rural) populations that drives the growth in greenhouse gas emissions but rather, the growth in consumers and in their levels of consumption' (Satterthwaite, 2009, p545). The author argues that greenhouse gases are not emitted by 'people' in general, but by specific activities engaged in by particular groups of people, often determined along class lines. In global South countries with rapid population growth, those in more privileged classes are most able to consume resources such as fossil fuels for vehicles and household electricity, making high level per capita greenhouse gas emissions primarily the domain of the affluent. Ironically for population–environment advocates, these are most often the people whose fertility rates are relatively low.

Despite their divergent approaches, methods and conclusions, the first two studies in particular rely on a logic that transforms humans into potential humans, potentially averted humans, and ultimately potentially averted emissions. The logic of averted-humans-as-averted-emissions raises significant questions about the power dynamics of how value in human life is assigned, to/by whom, and at what scale. To borrow a phrase from feminist technoscience scholar Michelle Murphy, it reflects strategies of the economization of life, in which certain lives are deemed investable, others expendable and avertable (Murphy, 2009). In this case, avertable lives are only those in the global South.

When population is articulated as a driver of greenhouse gas emissions, population interventions focused on the most rapidly growing countries are a logical outcome. This approach is common in policy advocacy communities, where reducing complexity and uncertainty, as well as simplicity of approach, are key components of achieving policy success (Sasser, 2012, 2014a).

For example, family planning, climate change mitigation and adaptation are increasingly being promoted as naturally synergistic strategies, reminiscent of earlier WED approaches examined in the first section of this chapter. While there are scientific and ethical problems with this approach, it is gaining ground through its solution-oriented focus, for two key reasons. First, it frames population–climate interventions as socially just and woman-centred: a 'win–win' for women and the environment. Second, it ignores the complex and challenging social–structural forces that determine whether, when and how women access the tools available to support reproductive decision-making, by subsuming them into simplistic solution narratives. As a result, 'family-planning-as-climate-change-solution' is a framing that, in its simplicity, becomes broadly accessible, easily transformed into sound bites, and a rallying cry for new advocates (Sasser, 2014b).

Contraceptives thus come to serve as an important non-human actor, perhaps the most important one, as they represent the technological fix advocated by population–climate advocates, with the role of providing access to contraceptives to women around the world highlighted as the ultimate goal of population–climate advocacy. If only contraceptives can get into the hands of women who need them, so the argument goes, they will work to solve both population and environment problems. This theme continues in narratives about population, planetary boundaries and resource scarcity.

Rising demand for resources and planetary boundaries

While climate change is clearly a very serious problem that requires urgent action, this tendency to define everything in relation to it, to make it the grand, over-arching narrative, has encouraged a resurgence of planetary systems models in the tradition of *Limits to Growth*. The standard claim is that we have entered a new geophysical era, the Anthropocene, in which human-induced climate change as well as other negative human impacts on the environment threaten to exceed planetary boundaries and cross thresholds that will push natural systems over dangerous tipping points. The consequences for human wellbeing are potentially catastrophic.

The notion of planetary boundaries, as discussed by Leach et al in Chapter 1 of this book, has gained traction in international environmental circles. At the same time, it has come under criticism from numerous quarters, including the scientific community, about how the boundaries are defined and estimated, and their emphasis on global over local ecological processes. Many argue that addressing the problem of climate change is more about the politics of balancing trade-offs – economic, moral and aesthetic – than setting absolute geophysical limits. At least the trade-off approach allows for acknowledgement of power relations in the determination of policy. It also moves the discussion away from humanity writ large.

In fact, a basic problem with planetary boundaries and similar concepts is the lumping of humanity into one impossibly broad category, a legacy from not only *Limits to Growth* but also a number of the other population and environment paradigms discussed in the opening section of this chapter. The result is once again to reinforce Malthusian logic: since people are the problem, reducing their numbers is the prime solution. An article in *Nature* on the plausibility of a dangerous planetary-scale tipping point thus calls for reducing world population growth as its first recommendation (Barnosky et al, 2012).

There are very real pressures population growth can put on the availability of vital resources – food, water, sanitation, energy, housing, jobs and social services among them, especially in an era of rapid urbanization and climate change. For those following in Malthus' footsteps, scarcity is a foregone conclusion and population growth rates must be forced down. Technological and market enthusiasts are more optimistic. In the case of food, for example, they put their faith in genetically modified organisms (GMOs) and the expansion of industrial agriculture. Between these two poles, however, are a range of issues that get lost when the discussion focuses on abstract aggregates of per capita population and resource supply.

It is important to define the problem differently, first by moving away from Malthusian postulates of the inevitability of scarcity that have proven wrong for over two centuries now (Mehta, 2010). The question then becomes not *if* but *how* – and on the basis of what values – will enough food and other resources be produced and distributed to meet human needs *and* ensure ecological integrity. Here one re-enters the thornier territory of political, economic and environmental decision-making. What institutions have the power to decide the present and future course of agricultural and industrial development and employment creation? Who gets to sit at the table and set priorities? Whose knowledge and claims to resources count more?

Although in mainstream sustainable development circles attention is at times paid to the needs of the poor – who are typically lumped together in another broad sub-category – there is little critical analysis of the differentiated causes and effects of climate change and other environmental threats by class, race, gender, etc. A 2012 paper, *Environment and Development Challenges: The Imperative to Act*, by 18 winners of the Blue Planet Prize, including Gro Harlem Brundtland and Paul Ehrlich, calls for a more equal world, but then puts reducing population size and growth, and related consumption patterns, at the top of its list for solving global social and environmental problems. Instrumentalizing women once again, it advocates for their education and empowerment, along with modern contraceptives, as the way to bring birth rates down (Brundtland et al, 2012).

Questioning the political economy of resource production and distribution spotlights how neoliberalism has not proved up to the job of providing resources for a growing population, not because of aggregate scarcity, but because neoliberal policies lead to concentration of wealth, rising inequality and erosion of public services. When the rubber of neoliberalism meets the road of demographic necessity, it comes up short. This calls for re-imagining, re-inventing and re-energizing the role of the state, rather than a reduction in the number of people. As social scientist Andrew Fischer writes, strong state developmentalism and universalistic social policies are required: 'Developmentalism in this sense means state-led industrial policy rooted in nationally owned firms, regulated capital accounts to ensure that wealth remains national, and a bias towards generating employment rather than efficiency. This is the opposite of the neoliberal dictates that demand employment austerity in the name of (transnational) firm profitability' (Fischer, 2010). The arena of public policy – local, national, global – also provides a space where political participation by diverse actors and social movements is more possible than in corporate boardrooms.

Instead, there is a certain stasis and boundedness inherent in concepts like planetary boundaries, with its 'safe operating space', a desire to frame and constrain both ecological and social complexity, to wall it in, in order to make it *manageable* for business as usual. Ultimately, this kind of thinking could lead to population, migration and security policies that encourage violence and the violation of basic human rights. This is already happening in Africa.

The Malthusian Anticipatory Regime for Africa

Because Malthusianism is predicated on the threat of impending doom, it resonates particularly well with apocalyptic framings of climate change that paint a dismal future of famine, natural disasters and war. Today, Africa is the main focus of these fears. Not only do population agencies view high fertility in sub-Saharan Africa as distinctive and dangerous, but US and European defence interests see the African continent as the main locus of future climate conflicts. Their reasoning is largely based on Malthusian crisis narratives about population pressure on the environment causing migration and violent conflict.

Although these narratives may originate in separate, though not unrelated, institutional settings, together they conjure up a continent on the brink of disaster. They form a powerful Malthusian Anticipatory Regime for Africa (MARA).[6] The way MARA predicts disasters on multiple scales makes it useful to a wide variety of political actors, allowing for moving seamlessly between humanitarian imperatives (saving women), environmental imperatives (saving the planet), and security imperatives (saving ourselves from terrorists).

For population agencies, averting disaster means averting births by the most effective means possible, namely through the promotion of contraceptives like the injectable Depo-Provera. In July 2012, at the London Summit on Family Planning, a public–private partnership of the Bill & Melinda Gates Foundation, USAID, DFID, UNFPA, Pfizer and the medical non-profit PATH announced a new initiative to reach 3 million women in sub-Saharan Africa and South Asia over the next three years with 12 million doses of a new subcutaneous delivery form of Depo-Provera called the Sayana Press (PATH, 2012). The Gates Foundation is now the most influential private donor in the population field. Its family planning strategy is openly neo-Malthusian; it has claimed that population growth significantly contributes to 'the global burden of disease, environmental degradation, poverty and conflict' (Bill & Melinda Gates Foundation, 2012).

The decision to push Depo-Provera in HIV-endemic regions of Africa is happening despite the fact that medical studies have provided compelling evidence that the contraceptive may increase the risk of women and their partners becoming infected with HIV (Heffron et al, 2012; Ralph et al, 2015). Anticipatory regimes can be selective in terms of what they seek to avert, and in this case averting births is a higher priority than averting HIV/AIDS. It is not so much a medical calculation as a political choice influenced by other logics of MARA.

Initially, population actors raised the stakes with claims that averting African births was essential to mitigating climate change. However, over time this narrative was difficult to sustain. After all, many sub-Saharan African countries have the lowest carbon emissions per capita in the world (Dow and Downing, 2007; Satterthwaite, 2009). In the face of mounting criticism (Silliman, 2009), population agencies are now arguing that family planning is a vital component of climate change *adaptation* rather than mitigation in Africa (Dabelko, 2011; Mutunga et al, 2012).

The link between population and climate change also has a strong security dimension. Malthusian eco-logic, expressed through carrying capacity, the tragedy of the commons, crisis narratives and environmental conflict models, helped lay the ground for the concept of 'climate conflict' which garnered serious international attention starting in 2007.

Climate conflict narratives spread out from Darfur – where violence was attributed by international agencies to a combination of demographic pressures, resource scarcities and climate change – to encompass large swaths of Africa's drylands. At the same time fears also began to mount about a rising tide of 'climate refugees'.

Despite a wealth of scholarly critiques of climate conflict (e.g. Derman et al, 2007; Witsenburg and Roba, 2007) and climate refugees (e.g. Doyle and Chaturvedi, 2011; Tacoli, 2011), narratives about them are still widely accepted in policy circles, and in particular serve to legitimize growing Western military involvement in Africa. What makes MARA so effective in this regard is that it is predicated on not one, but two Malthusian streams that converge around the issue of climate change to create a forceful ideological current. On one hand, the female stream: the overpopulated continent that can be contained and/or saved by reducing its women's fertility, improving adaptability to climate change at the same time. On the other, the male stream: the population powder keg of poor African men set even more violently against each other by climate change. Women come to symbolize the humanitarian imperative, men the strategic threat, together creating a strong rationale for certain state and foreign interventions in the realms of national security and land appropriation.

The dominant view in US defence circles is that climate change is an important accelerant of instability and a 'threat-multiplier', particularly in Africa. A report on climate and security by the US Department of Defense Science Board identifies pastoral landscapes in Darfur, the margins of the Sahel, and southern Africa as threatening sites of future climate conflict (US Department of Defense Science Board, 2011). With the drawdown of troops from Afghanistan, Africa is fast becoming the Pentagon's new frontier. A 2013 investigative report by Nick Turse found evidence of US military involvement in 49 African nations (Turse, 2013). While the Pentagon has multiple reasons for intervening in Africa, preventing and responding to future climate conflicts serve as important rationales (US Department of Defense, 2014).

Some African states also find the climate-conflict framing useful. According to African studies scholar Harry Verhoeven, the Sudanese regime 'loves the climate war rhetoric' about Darfur since it obscures its own role in fomenting exclusion, patronage and violence in the region (Verhoeven, 2011, p695). In his book on climate change and migration, political scientist Gregory White points out how current threat projections around climate refugees serve the larger aim of building up borders in northern African transit states through the construction of fences, patrols and detention centres. In the case of Morocco, the securitization of migration from southern Africa suits both state interests and those of NATO, with increasing interoperability between their respective armed forces (White, 2011).

Also worthy of consideration, and more research, are the ways MARA functions in relation to the massive land grabs now occurring in Africa. While estimates differ, Africa is widely acknowledged as the region of the world most targeted by large land transfers (Anseeuw et al, 2012). Malthus himself wrote at a time when the enclosure of the commons in Britain was causing the increased pauperization of the peasantry. Rather than locate the roots of their distress in a specific political economy, Malthus naturalized it with his principle of population (Lohmann, 2005). MARA may play a similar ideological role in the new enclosures that are bringing about the dispossession of small African farmers.

Conclusion

Now is a critical moment to rethink the links between population, gender and the environment in order to create new socially just and gender-equitable pathways to sustainable development. As the high-level sustainable development agendas – such as the SDGs and post-2015 agenda – are developed and implemented, it opens the opportunity to reframe those linkages to reflect the environmental knowledges of feminist thinkers and activists and the gains of Cairo and beyond in SRHR advocacy. At the same time, as this chapter argues, it will be important to pay close attention to processes of knowledge production that privilege powerful actors, including private foundations, militaries and corporations, in setting goals and priorities. This includes following the money trail, making policy processes fully transparent, and asking who has the upper hand in public–private partnerships. In regard to SRHR, it also means standing up to conservative forces that seek to deny women the right to control their own bodies through denying them access to safe contraception, abortion and sexuality education.

A new sustainable development framework that integrates gender equality and social justice must be rooted in the following.

- A non-negotiable commitment to women's bodily integrity and autonomy, including freedom from all forms of violence; full support of sexual and reproductive health and rights (SRHR); and equal access to decent work, secure livelihoods, a clean and safe environment, education, health, and other social services and public goods.
- Recognition of and respect for the long history of women's national and transnational activism to reframe conventional understandings of the relationship between population, environment and development; disentangle family planning from population control and embed it instead in a broad SRHR and public health agenda; and defend reproductive rights from those who seek to restrict access to contraception and abortion.
- Women's agency, power, knowledge and voice at all levels of decision-making regarding population and sustainable development, with an understanding of the diversity of women's views and experiences shaped by class, race, ethnicity, age and other axes of difference.

- Policies that protect the commons and challenge the appropriation and exploitation of natural resources by powerful private and state interests, and that ensure gender-equitable control and governance of common resources, especially by poor women who depend on them for their sustainable livelihoods.
- Contextualization of demographic dynamics within broader social, economic, political and gender systems that not only shape family size, but help condition who lives and who dies, who prospers and who suffers. This includes supporting feminist critiques of science that provide the theoretical underpinnings to trace the biases about gender, race and place in purportedly neutral scientific knowledges.

It is important to recognize that, in the case of population policy, feminist movements – at the local, national, regional and transnational levels – broke through the Malthusian barrier long ago. Cairo was but one step in a much longer process that continues today. There is much to be learned from this rich history of feminist activism and political and theoretical innovation. That tradition is what can sustain us as we move forward and learn from the contributions of not only feminist thinkers and advocates, but young SRHR and AIDS activists, and those from other health, environment and social justice movements. Building from these knowledges, we can commit to women's bodily integrity and autonomy as a cornerstone of sustainable development policy. There is no easy road to a more peaceful and just future, but the new guides, signposts and maps highlighted in this book can help chart the way.

Notes

1 The authors use 'woman' and 'women', acknowledging that women have been disproportionately targeted by population control programmes. At the same time, we recognize that those terms do not represent the full range of ways in which people experience and perform sexuality and gender. Like new feminist political ecology theorists (see Leach et al, Chapter 1 in this book), we agree that gender is not a binary.

2 A comprehensive SRHR platform should include access to contraceptive and conceptive methods, along with complete information on their use and adverse effects, and follow-up care to address any contraindications and concerns. It includes access to safe and legal abortion, free of stigma, as well as maternal care. It means education and support on issues of sexuality, healthy relationships and gender. Comprehensive care includes full incorporation of HIV treatment and prevention, as well as screening and treatment for other sexually transmitted infections. SRHR services should be available and appropriate for people of all genders and sexualities, as well as all ages. Finally, it includes accessible and high-quality general health care, with practitioners who view sexual and reproductive health concerns in the context of overall health.

3 The real tragedy of 'The tragedy of the commons' is its enduring impact. It is still one of the most widely read environmental essays ever, influencing generations of students and policy-makers. Yet people have been managing common resources cooperatively for centuries and are able to negotiate successfully the tension between private gain and the public, and environmental, good. Such cooperation does not always occur, but it is more frequent than Hardin or his intellectual successors would admit. In 2009 the late Elinor

Ostrom became the first woman to win the Nobel Prize in economics on the basis of her work on common pool resources. She documented many cases where individuals create stable institutions of self-government that make and enforce rules that protect natural resources and provide mutual protection against risk (Ostrom, 2000). Gender relations are often critical in those processes (Agarwal, 2010).

4 According to the World Bank, total fertility rate 'represents the number of children that would be born to a woman if she were to live to the end of her childbearing years and bear children in accordance with current age-specific fertility rates' (http://data. worldbank.org/indicator/SP.DYN.TFRT.IN, accessed 22 February 2014). Faster fertility decline would lead to an earlier and smaller peak population, whereas slower fertility decline would lead to a later and larger peak.

5 It is important to note that, in addition to funding scientific research, private foundation donors are able to use their access to capital as a means of engaging in politics without public participation (Page and Valone, 2007). Private foundations are not subject to any formal measures of public accountability aside from legal codes and tax structures, and ultimately their bottom line of responsibility is to their boards and organizational missions (Dowie, 2001; Page and Valone, 2007). A crucial difference between projects funded by private foundations and public agencies, such as USAID, is that various publics have the opportunity to influence the policies that public donors are mandated to implement.

6 This discussion draws heavily on Betsy Hartmann (2014).

4

RE-FRAMING FOOD SECURITY AS IF GENDER EQUALITY AND SUSTAINABILITY MATTERED

Sakiko Fukuda-Parr

Introduction

Food security is an essential aspect of sustainable development because to be free of hunger is a fundamental human right, and to be adequately nourished is a basic capability without which many other opportunities for a fulfilling life would be closed. Though substantial progress has been made, current trends raise concerns: undernutrition and malnutrition persist in old forms while new forms are on the rise; the effects of climate change are projected to heighten vulnerability of the most food–insecure households; and global economic trends put pressure on small-scale farming, namely investments in biofuels and other foreign investments that compete for land and disrupt traditional land rights, and new global financial instruments that not only drive up world market prices for cereals but introduce volatility.

This chapter reviews the current international policy challenges and responses on food security from the perspectives of gender, human rights and capabilities, using Amartya Sen's entitlements approach that focuses on access. It aims to dislodge the productionist framing that currently dominates food security debates. In using the alternative paradigm of food security, the chapter highlights the structural factors – the institutional and power structures at all levels, from household to global – that drive food insecurity, and the policies to address these constraints as priorities for ending hunger.

The chapter starts with a brief introduction on the role of the framing of food security discourse in shaping policy approaches. The second section reviews recent trends in hunger and nutrition and the paradox of plenty; the third elaborates on the structural causes of food insecurity and the importance of gender inequality; and the fourth reviews the current policy responses and the turn to the productionist framing. The final section discusses alternative pathways and is followed by concluding remarks.

Framing food security – capabilities and rights perspective

Since the 2007 spikes in world food prices, food security has become a top political concern. Driving this concern is the question 'can we feed the world?' (Tomlinson, 2013). The current narrative that dominates popular and policy debates explains hunger as a problem of supply shortages – due to such factors as war and drought, to which climate change and biofuels are adding new pressures in the new century. Emblematic of such narratives are the captions of articles in a recent *Financial Times* special feature on global food security: 'Population growth in sub-Saharan Africa raises food supply alarm'; 'Climate change risks to food supplies'; and 'India tackles supply chains to cut food waste' (*Financial Times*, 2014).

Such Malthusian narratives have a long history (Chapter 3, this book), but have regained popularity in the post-2007 food crisis debates. In fact, for most of the early twentieth century, hunger was conceptualized as a problem of supply shortages at national and global levels; the 1974 World Food Conference defined food security as: 'Availability at all times of adequate world food *supplies* of basic foodstuffs to sustain a steady expansion of food consumption and to offset fluctuations in production and prices' (emphasis added, UN, 1975). However, over the 1980s and 1990s, as hunger persisted even as global production increased and food prices fell, this supply-centric view was challenged by many food security and policy experts (Sen, 1982; Maxwell and Frankenberger, 1992; Hoddinott, 1999; Maxwell, 2001; Longhurst, 2010) and hunger came to be understood increasingly as a problem of access rather than supply, and of distribution rather than aggregate production. The 1996 World Food Summit (WFS) adopted a new consensus definition focused on access: 'Food security exists when all people, at all times, have physical and economic access to sufficient safe and nutritious food that meets their dietary needs and food preferences for an active and healthy life' (FAO, 1996).

This definition overlaps with the concept of the human right to food, and with Sen's capability approach. Access to food is not a matter for individuals receiving food, but of the individual's capability – or the range of options that she has – to be nourished, and involves the agency of individuals. The Committee on Economic, Social and Cultural Rights' General Comment 12 makes clear that 'the *right to adequate food* shall therefore not be interpreted in a narrow or restrictive sense which equates it with a minimum package of calories, proteins and other specific nutrients' (CESCR, 1999, para. 6). While the right to food 'is *not* a right to a minimum ration of calories… or a right to be fed. It is about being guaranteed the right to feed oneself' (De Schutter, 2012).

A person's ability to acquire nutritious food is therefore closely related to other aspects of her capabilities and rights. This includes in particular the rights that affect access by production (equal access to land, credit, information and other resources) and by purchase (waged employment), and utilization (health especially of children and women in pregnancy, education, information). The normative content of the right to food includes not only the elements defined specifically for this right, but also the principles that apply to all rights, notably non-discrimination and particularly gender discrimination.

The emphasis on access does not imply that production and supply are not important. They are essential to food security. But in the perspective of the individual, production does not automatically lead to access which depends on entitlements.

Sen (1982) argued that famines occur even when there is plentiful supply, because individuals and households lose the means to acquire food ('entitlements'). He identified three means of access – or entitlement: production entitlement, exchange entitlement and social transfer entitlement. He further elaborated the social and economic conditions that would enhance these entitlements within the capability framework as applied to 'endemic' – or deeply rooted and persistent – hunger and undernutrition (Drèze and Sen, 1989). With Drèze he argued that capability to be well nourished depends not on only *access* to food but also on its *utilization*, and that in turn depends on being healthy, knowledgeable, having a say in household decision-making, and many other capabilities. This conception takes the framing of hunger and undernutrition to their social, economic and political determinants. Hunger and undernutrition then depend on a host of economic, social and political factors that affect the ability of a person to consume and utilize food that is adequate in quantity and quality.

While the supply perspective on food security focuses on means to increase production, such as technological innovations and investments, the entitlements and human rights perspectives' frames focus on the factors that shape ability to access food by production, exchange or claim to social transfers. In contrast to conventional economic analysis, the human rights and entitlement perspectives ask *who* is food insecure, and seek to understand the institutional sources of rights and entitlement failures such as lack of power and discrimination in the means to access and utilize food.

By shifting the unit of analysis to the individual and household, rather than the country and global aggregates, this perspective accommodates gendered analysis of determinants of hunger. It opens up enquiry into the intra-household dynamics in the allocation of food amongst members of the household by gender and age, the voice of women in decision-making, the role of women in household food production and management, and other issues that are central to the gendered analysis of the determinants of, and prospects for, food security (Razavi, 2009).

The focus on the individual and the household also draws attention to the root causes of food insecurity that go beyond the micro contexts of household and community to macro contexts of national and international economic structures. Such root causes are systemic in nature, related to the workings of social institutions and power dynamics. Food security studies, however, have been dominated by analysis of short-term production/supply and price trends and their drivers, such as crop failures due to droughts and other weather shifts, wars and conflicts, rising consumption patterns, and shifts in demand such as competition from biofuels (for example IFPRI, 2013a).[1]

Yet gender has been invisible in much of the current debates about priority investments to combat hunger and malnutrition. Why? Because these debates are too often framed as a problem of supply and production: population imbalances rather than the inability of individuals to acquire food adequate in quantity and quality, and on global aggregates rather than on countries and subnational groups. Current global narratives are shifting the focus back to the earlier conception of food insecurity as a problem of production and supply, and on the provision of adequate calories and nutrients rather than the ability of individuals and households to feed themselves adequately at all times as a basic human right.

Framing sets the boundaries of analysis for policy choices. Framing is a process that determines how problems are defined, causes are explained, and policy responses and priorities are justified. Framing shapes narratives that articulate policy strategies in public debates. Thus framing can have powerful effects in shaping policy choices with respect to priorities for allocation of resources, policy reforms, and in mobilizing support for implementation of policies. The implications are far-reaching in influencing policy directions in fundamental ways. Framing creates a hegemony of ideas about problems and solutions, keeping out radical ideas that are seemingly unthinkable (Bøås and McNeill, 2003). It is an exercise intended to ensure that problems are seen in a particular way, and 'an effective "frame" is one which makes favoured ideas seem like common sense, and unfavoured ideas as unthinkable' (Bøås and McNeill, 2003, p1).

Recent trends in hunger and malnutrition

High levels and persistence of hunger and malnutrition

Global narratives on hunger and malnutrition framed by the MDG relate a story of steady decline, from 23 to 14 per cent of the world population, and the 2015 goal of halving the proportion of undernourished being within reach (UN, 2013c, p9). This account understates the severity of the problem and the uneven progress across regions, countries within regions, and particularly groups within countries. FAO's caloric supply undernourishment indicator estimates hunger to affect one in eight people in the world, yet other metrics reveal a much more extensive problem. By the stunting indicator, one in four children suffer from severe, long-term undernutrition that compromises the mental and physical development of the child. Similarly, micronutrient deficiencies, such as in vitamin A, zinc and iron, affect 2 billion – one in four persons (IFPRI, 2013a).

Household surveys find high levels of insecure food access even in countries with relatively low levels of food insecurity according to standard national outcome indicators. For example, the 2012 household food security survey in the USA found that 15 per cent (17.6 million households) reported being food insecure and experienced difficulty providing enough food for all their members; 7 million out of the 17.6 million had reduced intake (see Box 4.1). In South Africa, 2012 household surveys found 22 per cent of households (26 per cent of population) had inadequate access to food (Statistics South Africa, 2013).

BOX 4.1 PARADOX OF PLENTY: GENDER, ETHNICITY AND RACE

Hunger is rooted in poverty, yet disparities in gender, ethnicity and race overlap in the persistence of hunger.

Hunger amidst affluence in the USA

In 2012, 14.9 per cent of households – nearly 49 million people – were food insecure in the USA. The hunger crisis is related to lack of income, but this is not the only factor; while low-income households, earning less than 185 per cent of the poverty threshold, accounted for as much as 34.3 per cent of all food insecure households, those with children are almost twice as likely to experience food insecurity as those without children. Single mothers and women of colour, in particular, are at an extreme disadvantage. Households with children headed by a single woman accounted for an astonishing 35.4 per cent of all food insecure households, while households headed by a single man accounted for only 23.6 per cent. Race also plays a substantial role, with African-American and Hispanic households representing 24.6 and 23.3 per cent of all food insecure households, respectively. While one in five American children is currently at risk of hunger, it is nearly one in three among Black and Hispanic children (USDA, 2014).

Poverty intersects with discrimination – Women and indigenous groups in Guatemala

A middle-income country that has experienced steady growth, averaging about 4 per cent over the past two decades (World Bank, 2014), Guatemala has the highest child malnutrition rate in Latin America and the fourth highest rate in the world: one in two children under five years of age in the country is chronically malnourished (FAO, 2014). Stunting figures are almost twice as high among indigenous children under five years (65.9 per cent) compared with non-indigenous children (36.2 per cent). In predominantly indigenous areas, such as Totonicapán, chronic malnutrition affects 80 per cent of children under five years, while 36.3 per cent of pregnant women in rural areas are anaemic (MSPAS et al, 2010). Gender inequalities intersect with ethnic and geographical divides, and are reflected not only in malnutrition but across other important capabilities; just 14 per cent of indigenous girls and 36 per cent of non-indigenous girls in rural areas complete primary school, while indigenous women are three times more likely to die during pregnancy and childbirth than non-indigenous women. Despite being one of the 22 countries with a constitutional commitment to the right to food (CESR, 2008), food security indicators show worsening trends, with an increase of proportion of the population undernourished from 20 to 30.5 per cent between 1990/92 and 2011/13 (FAO et al, 2013, table A1.1a).

India – Hunger persists over two decades of rapid economic growth

India is home to 35 per cent of the world's undernourished children with a staggering 48 per cent of children under five stunted, indicating chronic malnutrition (IFPRI, 2013a, p29). Micronutrient deficiencies are extensive among both children and adults. Most alarmingly, many of these indicators have not improved over the past two decades of increasing prosperity. While undernutrition is highest among the poorest sectors of society, nearly half the children in the middle quintile and a quarter in the wealthiest quintile are stunted, suggesting that the problem is rooted in systemic factors that essentially affect the entire population (Gillespie et al, 2012, pp1–2). In fact, during the past two decades, while per capita income in India has more than tripled, the minimum dietary intake decreased (FAO et al, 2013). Child malnutrition has persisted regardless of the family's income or education level. Women are particularly vulnerable to undernourishment and micronutrient deficiencies. More than a third of all Indian women have a body mass index below 18.5 (IFPRI, 2013a, p29), while 56 per cent suffer from anaemia compared with only 24 per cent of men (Gillespie et al, 2012, p2). Girls are less likely than boys to receive full immunization as children, and more likely to be malnourished and underweight as they get older. Female mortality rates are higher than male for both infants and adults (World Bank, 2014). Hunger and malnutrition are even more severe for uneducated women, women from rural provinces, women from scheduled tribes or castes, and women belonging to the bottom two wealth quintiles (FAO, 2011, p98).

In response to this grim hunger epidemic, the Indian government passed the National Food Security Act in September 2013. This ambitious Act guarantees 5 kilograms of heavily subsidized grains per capita every month to roughly two-thirds of India's 1.2 billion people in one of the world's largest welfare programmes (IFPRI, 2013a, p29).

Moreover, obesity, a new form of malnutrition, has emerged as an urgent challenge. The proportion of population who are overweight has increased in almost all regions of the world, and now totals 47 million people or 7 per cent, an increase from 30 million or 5 per cent in 1990 (IFPRI, 2013a). Obesity raises risks of cardiovascular diseases and many cancers, and is a form of malnutrition that often co-exists with undernutrition in households resulting from shifts in diets that are increasingly heavy in salts, sugars and fats characteristic of processed foods.

Where and who are the food insecure?

Hunger is concentrated in South Asia and sub-Saharan Africa, which together account for two-thirds of the world's undernourished (FAO et al, 2013) and one-third of stunted children (IFPRI, 2013a). While progress has been significant in South Asia, it has been slower in sub-Saharan Africa where the proportion of undernourished has declined but total numbers have grown. But several countries in Latin America (e.g. Guatemala, Haiti), South East Asia (e.g. Cambodia, Lao PDR, Timor Leste), and Central Asia (e.g. Tajikistan) figure among the 55 countries classified as having 'alarming' or 'extremely serious' situations by the 2013 IFPRI Global Hunger Index (IFPRI, 2013b).

The hungry are predominantly in rural areas – estimated at about 80 per cent – amongst small-scale farmers (50 per cent), landless labourers (20 per cent) and those who depend on herding, fishing and forest resources (10 per cent) (WFP, n.d.). Women are disproportionately affected. While some 60 per cent of the undernourished are female (ADB and FAO, 2013 citing ECOSOC, 2007), about 50 per cent of pregnant women worldwide suffer from anaemia (FAO et al, 2013), which is a principal cause of 315,000 annual deaths during childbirth and contributes to the high prevalence of low-birthweight babies. More than one-third of adult women in Bangladesh, India and Pakistan are underweight (IFPRI, 2013a, p97). Hunger overlaps with other forms of vulnerability and exclusion, and is concentrated among marginalized groups such as low-caste and scheduled tribes in India (see Box 4.1), indigenous groups in Guatemala (see Box 4.1), and minority ethnic groups elsewhere.

Structural determinants of food insecurity

Abundant production drives down prices for both domestic and imported supplies, facilitating household acquisition of food. Household incomes, national incomes and economic growth are important drivers of food security. Food accounts for around half or more of expenditure by households under the poverty income line. But these links are not automatic – in a paradox of plenty, hunger and malnutrition persist in contexts of plentiful and growing production and incomes. At play are important structural factors behind who is food insecure, amongst which gendered institutions play an important role.

The paradox of plenty

Evidence from food production and consumption trends show that the relationship between production and hunger is far from straightforward.

First, food production has more than kept pace with population growth in all regions;[2] between 1990/92 and 2011/13, the index of per capita food availability rose globally from 114 to 122, in South Asia from 106 to 108, and in sub-Saharan Africa from 100 to 111 (FAO et al, 2013, pp18–20). At the country level, the inadequacy of food supply is strongly correlated with the prevalence of undernourishment, but since the undernourishment indicator is an estimate modelled on caloric supply based on production data, the result is not surprising. However, other nutritional indicators including stunting are not correlated with supply (FAO et al, 2013, p26). Countries with adequate dietary energy supply can have high levels of stunting, such as Bangladesh, Ghana and Nepal. Countries with just adequate dietary energy supply can also achieve low levels of stunting, such as Senegal and Costa Rica. Such persistence of malnutrition is often attributed to the ineffective utilization of food that is consumed. But it could also reflect poor quality of food consumed, and unequal distribution of available food within the country and within the household.

Second, hunger persists and is on the rise in the form of obesity in rich countries such as the USA, and high middle-income countries such as South Africa, revealing gaps in households' ability to access adequate food with the prevailing distribution of income, price levels, social transfers and the physical availability of nutritious food whose supply is increasingly driven by the global food industries and supermarket chains. Diets are changing, with the spread of purchased processed foods displacing traditional diets richer in fibres, minerals and vitamins (Box 4.1 – USA).

Third, the decline in undernourishment since 1990 (10 percentage points from 28 to 18 per cent) has not kept pace with the decline in the incidence of income poverty (23 percentage points from 47 to 24 per cent). Moreover, cross-country analyses show higher levels of poverty linked to higher prevalence of undernourishment, but with wide variance (FAO et al, 2013, p27). The disconnect between incomes and hunger is more marked when considering stunting and micronutrient deficiencies. For example, Ghana has made rapid progress in reducing the incidence of household income poverty and of caloric undernourishment. But malnutrition persists with the prevalence of stunting that still affects nearly a quarter of children under five in 2011, though this is an improvement from a third in 1994 (FAO et al, 2013).

Middle-income countries such as Cambodia, Ghana, Guatemala and Namibia have some of the most serious problems of hunger that are much worse than countries with similar levels of income. The situation has stagnated in Guatemala, where the number of undernourished more than doubled from 1.5 million to 4.9 million from 1990/92 to 2011/13 (see Box 4.1). Such situations are often explained by the persistence of hunger along with other forms of poverty amongst specific identity groups – such as the indigenous rural populations in Guatemala, and the people of the Northern regions in Ghana.

The persistence of malnutrition in spite of improvements in household incomes is often attributed to poor utilization of food due to underlying health status, and environmental conditions such as lack of access to clean water and sanitation (FAO et al, 2013). But a gendered analysis of structural constraints might reveal other reasons, notably the distribution of nutritionally adequate food within countries and within households; and the lack of time that women have for care of children due to the high burden of other unpaid work (Drèze and Sen, 1989; Harris, 1995; Razavi, 2009). The next section examines these institutional constraints within the framework of food security as a question of individual access, capabilities and rights.

Gender as a central factor in food security

Gender matters to understanding the causes of hunger and malnutrition because women play a central role in the food system: its consumption, production, processing and distribution (FAO, 2010). In these roles they face discrimination and lack bargaining power on account of their sex, often reinforcing discrimination and marginalization based on ethnicity, and income poverty. Gender equality matters in developing a path to sustainable food security because gender relations within the household and wider society shape the distribution of access to food for consumption and to land and other resources for food production, allocation of household incomes on food, and other determinants of food security such as health. Gender relations also shape the consequences of changing market environment for food production and exchange – prices, supply, competition for land, access to inputs and markets – on both distribution and production. The costs of gender bias for production and nutrition have been amply documented over the past few decades, and there is broad agreement on the strategic importance of empowering women (see FAO, 2010; ADB and FAO, 2013). Yet policies have resisted change. Unequal access to land, inputs and services for women farmers persist (FAO, 2010), and unequal power relations within the household and community continue to undermine nutrition (FAO, 2010). These gendered constraints combine with discrimination due to class, race and ethnicity in eroding right to food through the three types of entitlements: production, wage exchange and social transfers.

Production entitlements are important for food security amongst small-scale farmers in many parts of the world. Agriculture still accounts for 47 per cent of total employment in South Asia (2010/12), and exceeds 50 per cent in most sub-Saharan African countries with data, though the sector contributes much less to the GDP (18 per cent in South Asia and 16 per cent in sub-Saharan Africa) (World Bank, 2013). The majority of farmers in developing countries operate small farms or are landless, often in marginal environments. Most of this farming is engaged in low-yield subsistence farming and is 'trapped in low productivity cycles' (Agarwal, 2014, p6). Small-scale farmers face both long-standing and new constraints to escaping this trap. Many are systemic in nature and related to the local policy environment, including withdrawal of state support in the 1980s and 1990s in access to improved technology, credit, inputs and access to markets (as discussed later in this chapter). They also relate to structures of society and power relations, including insecure rights to land, weak bargaining power within the household and constraints to accessing markets (World Bank, 2007; FAO, 2010).

Women play an important role as agricultural producers and their work is central to household entitlement through own production, while it also has a positive impact on national agricultural productivity. While the refrain that 'women produce 60–80 per cent of the world's food' cannot be empirically verified, as Cheryl Doss remarks, perhaps this statistical claim is a distraction as it 'obscures the complex underlying reality which is that women's labour in agriculture cannot be neatly separated from their other time uses; neither can it be separated from men's labour; nor can women's labour in agriculture be understood properly without also understanding the differential access to land, capital, assets, human capital and other productive resources' (Doss, 2011, p20).

Evidence from studies over the decades have clearly shown that women face unequal constraints as producers in access to assets including land, machinery and livestock, credit and other financial services and improved inputs (see FAO, 2010; Agarwal, 2011; ADB and FAO, 2013). Similarly, the positive link between education and health of women, women's wage earnings and control of household incomes, their role in household decision-making, and the nutritional health status of their children has been well established (see ADB and FAO, 2013). There is widespread agreement that closing the gender gap in these and other areas, and the overall empowerment of women, not only has intrinsic value as a social goal but is instrumental to achieving food security (FAO, 2010; ADB and FAO, 2013).

These constraints and inequalities result in large part from social institutions, particularly discriminatory laws such as those around inheritance of land; formal and informal rules such as registration of land or qualification for credit; gender division of labour that places unequal and heavy burdens for unpaid care work on women and girls; gender discrimination in labour markets that results in fewer work opportunities and lower remuneration to women; and unequal power structures between men and women. The systemic disadvantage of women overlaps with inequality and exclusion based on low income and on group identity (ethnic, indigenous, racial, linguistic) and rural isolated location. For example, women from indigenous groups living in rural areas are likely to be particularly disadvantaged. Thus disparities in food security depend not on supply and production, but on social and political structures, and help explain why hunger persists in the context of plenty.

The historically institutionalized bias against women's land ownership – through inheritance, purchase or land reform programmes – continues. Available data on gender disparities in land ownership show substantial gaps in diverse parts of the world, showing up in different forms: in Nepal, women own land in only 14 per cent of landowning rural households; in China, 70 per cent of farm operators without their own land are women; in Kenya, only 5 per cent of registered landowners are women; in Bangladesh, Ecuador and Pakistan, land holdings of male-headed households are more than twice the size of the holdings of female-headed households (Agarwal, 2011). Recent research from Ecuador, Ghana and Karnataka (India) suggests an association between women's land ownership and their degree of participation in key decision-making about the land (what to cultivate, how much to sell, inputs to use, etc) (Deere et al, 2013). Women are thus likely to have greater control over what they produce and whether they use it to meet their household's food needs when they own the land.

Yet labour is increasingly female. The proportion of women in the agricultural workforce has been growing over the past decades in all regions except in Europe, and has reached 42 per cent in Asia. We might conjecture that this results from men leaving agriculture. Of the total workforce in 2008, 57 per cent of women in Asia and 63 per cent in Africa were in agricultural related work (Agarwal, 2011). More specifically in terms of food production, time-use surveys for parts of sub-Saharan Africa, India and China suggest that women contribute a significant proportion of the labour input to bring food to the table, if we aggregate the time spent on food production, processing and preparation (Doss, 2011). Most women, however, engage in subsistence farming, and are 'trapped in low productivity cycles' (Agarwal, 2014, p6).

Exchange entitlements are important, even amongst producers, since no household can be entirely self-sufficient, and households obtain food from a combination of own production and wage earnings. For wage earners, the relationship between their wage earnings and food prices determines access. Extensive research has shown the inadequacy of women's own earnings, as well as their decision-making power over how their earnings are spent. Labour markets are strongly gender-segmented, and women are more likely than men to be working in sectors that are low-paid and do not provide adequate social protection measures, sometimes being driven to this type of work by 'distress' associated with rising levels of debt or the loss of earnings by other household members (FAO, 2010). Furthermore, women who engage in formal or semi-formal paid work are more likely than women who engage in informal work, or are economically inactive, to participate in household decision-making (Kabeer, 2011). Even in relatively new sectors, such as horticultural production for export, in several countries, including Chile and Mexico in Latin America and Kenya and Uganda in sub-Saharan Africa, women make up a disproportionate share of low-paid casual and temporary workers (Barrientos and Evers, 2013).

These conditions that characterize labour markets are a major constraint to household food security. Proactive labour market policy is not easy in the political context of most countries where labour unions have limited reach. But there are important experiences; women flower workers in Uganda, with the support of an international network, campaigned successfully for higher overtime pay, better working hours and freedom of association, even if their real wages remained low as a result of high inflation rates in 2010/11 (Barrientos and Evers, 2013). The other side of exchange entitlements is food markets and the increasingly unstable and rising prices in many countries, as discussed later in this chapter.

The third entitlement is social transfers. There has been an important expansion of safety nets through conditional cash programmes, pioneered in Brazil and Mexico. In many countries these programmes have had an important effect on household food security and nutrition (for example in South Africa; May, forthcoming). A key issue in these transfer programmes is how they affect the intra-household distribution of food. Easing pressures on food-insecure households, whether through general income support or food subsidies or school feeding programmes, can reduce the negative impact of intra-household bias. Conversely, when households cannot access sufficient food, this bias is likely to be reinforced, with dire consequences. Hence, in the context of current price rises, cuts to food subsidies as part of austerity programmes in many developing countries are of serious concern (Hossain et al, 2013). A broader agenda for government and civil society is to promote the awareness of women's and girls' right to food, and to empower them to claim that right by confronting gender bias and discrimination in the intra-household allocation of food.

Emerging challenges: The global food system and rural livelihoods

Long-standing gender and institutional constraints on food security (discussed in the previous section) persist, but these are now challenged by new threats, emerging from the changing context of the global food system, that have further gendered consequences. As producers or consumers, households acquire food within a biophysical, market and policy environment of food production and distribution. The environment of the twenty-first century is markedly different from that of the previous century (HLPE, 2011; von Braun, 2014), and poses new threats to food security, particularly for poor households in poor countries, often with gendered consequences.

World food markets: Volatile and higher prices, financialization and competition with biofuels

The world food market has dramatically shifted. While the 1970s, 80s and 90s were characterized by abundant production and low international food prices, the current context is marked by rising and volatile prices. After decades of stable, historically low prices since the 1970s, world food prices began to rise from the early 2000s and peaked sharply over 2007/08. Prices rose dramatically for major staple crops – rice, maize and wheat – which more than doubled. After a short decline, prices started to climb again, peaking again in 2011. These trends persist and now are considered to be characteristic of contemporary world food markets, and must be understood in the context of other related factors in world financial and commodity markets, notably financialization and biofuels (HLPE, 2011).

As a globally traded commodity, food has become integrated into a more complex financial market. The price spikes of 2007/08 were related to the fuel and financial crises of 2008. The role of futures markets, new instruments and actors such as institutional investors in the price hikes has been much debated and controversies continue (see HLPE, 2011). Though it is acknowledged that demand and supply shifts explain much of the upward pressure on world market prices, many argue that speculative activities played a role in driving the spikes for some of the commodities (Robles et al, 2009; UNCTAD, 2009; Ghosh, 2010; HLPE, 2011).

Food consumers now compete with the biofuel industry that has grown dramatically since the early 2000s. For example, between 2000/02 and 2007/09, ethanol production doubled in Brazil and increased more than eightfold in the USA, and almost fivefold in the EU. While the EU, US, Brazil, China and India are the largest consumers, production is dominated by the EU, which supplies 80 per cent of biodiesel, and by the USA and Brazil, which together account for 75 per cent of ethanol supply. The Committee for World Food Security's High Level Panel of Experts (HLPE) explains that this development was 'made possible only because of massive public support: subsidies, tax exemption and mandatory use in gasoline' that amounted to US$8 billion for biofuels in the EU and USA in 2009 (HLPE, 2011, p32). They remark with irony that 'In quite an incoherent way, the European Union and the United States have boosted demand for agricultural commodities, including food products, by their support for the biofuel industry, at the same time as they have reduced support for agricultural production, at home and in their overseas assistance to poor countries' (HLPE, 2011, p32). Investment in biofuels drives up not only food prices but the value of land, furthering land grabs, discussed later in this section.

Though domestic prices do not always mirror international price trends and levels, the 2007/08 price hikes led to a sharp rise in food prices in most developing countries (HLPE, 2011). World market price increases threaten food security for poor households; as von Braun explains 'the most relevant price for the poor is the price of grain... the price increase (in 2011) implies that a kilo for wheat in many developing countries costs about $0.30 instead of $0.15 – a critical difference for a person who lives on $1 a day' (2014, p163). In countries with data in Asia and Africa, food constituted over 50 per cent prior to the 2007 crisis (e.g. 76 per cent in Kenya, 75 per cent in Pakistan, 63 per cent in the Philippines) compared with a range of 10-25 per cent in Western Europe (e.g. for 2003, 24 per cent in France, 18 per cent in the USA, 11 per cent in the Netherlands) (FAO, 2014). In 2011, maize prices were higher by 105 per cent and wheat by 102 per cent compared with the previous year. Such price hikes have devastating consequences for food security of net purchasers, and have pushed millions into poverty. The 2008 cereals price hikes are estimated to have 105 million below the international poverty line (Agarwal, 2011).

Households adjust to such falls in wage exchange entitlements in a variety of ways, including shifting to less costly and less diverse diets that are inevitably deficient in essential nutrients particularly important for women in pregnancy and in early childhood. Studies of 11 countries with data available found that in eight of them malnutrition increased or improvements slowed during 2007/10 (von Braun, 2014). Women bear the brunt of coping in these situations, often reducing their own consumption in favour of other members, but also spending more time on preparation and processing, adding to their unpaid household work (Quisumbing et al, 2008). FAO estimates that 173 million were added to the number of undernourished people (HLPE, 2011, p11). Higher prices could increase incomes and stimulate production. Yet, as already noted, when farmers lack the necessary inputs and resources, they are less able to respond to the incentives.

Foreign investments in land

Stimulated by increasing volatility and rising prices in world food markets, investment in agricultural land has been growing rapidly since the 2007/08 food and other commodity price boom (Deininger et al, 2011). Investors include foreign financial entities such as hedge funds and pension funds diversifying their portfolios, but also governments aiming to secure food supply for their national populations. These investments have been an important factor behind the expansion of cultivated land that has totalled about 5.5 million hectares per year in developing countries over 1990–2007 (Deininger et al, 2011). These investments are creating pressure on marginalized farmers for access to land, and in many cases resulting in their dispossession. Such farmers, particularly women, have insecure rights on land that they have cultivated for generations due to lack of registration, or ambiguities about the nature of rights often interpreted as limited to usufruct (FAO, 2010).

These investments might have positive benefits for aggregate GDP growth, national food production and employment creation. They could also open up new markets and technologies for the agricultural sector that would have spillover effects on small-scale farmers (Deininger et al, 2011). Yet it is clear that their consequences for marginalized farmers who are dispossessed are likely to be negative, and as Levien shows in Chapter 5 of this book, such consequences are likely to be gender-biased. Women have been systematically excluded from decision-making in planning, from compensation and resettlement provisions that were invariably given to male heads of household, and most affected by the loss of access to common resources. These experiences imply the need for much greater attention to asymmetries in negotiating power involved in these processes. Reliance on 'voluntary guidelines' promises little.

Climate change

Climate change will have important impacts on productivity, production and prices, both negative and positive, depending on location. In the marginal and tropical environments where farmers are most food insecure, studies consistently point to overwhelmingly negative consequences (IFPRI, 2009). Rising temperatures, changing precipitation patterns and extreme weather events will increase the likelihood of crop failures, reduce yields and encourage pests and weeds. Scenario studies by IFPRI predict major yield and production losses for wheat, rice and maize in the most food-insecure regions: South Asia and sub-Saharan Africa (IFPRI, 2009). Assuming no adaptive investments, child malnutrition could increase by 20 per cent by 2050, erasing the gains made in previous decades (IFPRI, 2009).

The consequences are likely to be particularly severe for small-scale, and particularly female farmers who are least well equipped to adapt to changing conditions, in large part because of bias in access to resources such as credit, information and inputs that facilitate adaptive production strategies (Agarwal, 2011). Studies of supply response among women farmers in sub-Saharan Africa found women were unable to respond to incentives to expand production because they had less access to inputs such as land, seeds, fertilizer, credit, and technical information (Quisumbing et al, 2008).

Climate change overlaps with the institutional constraints that women face to erode food security. Climate change can mean less predictable rainfall, more frequent floods and droughts. These require adaptation by investments in new technologies and inputs. Agricultural extension services are notoriously ignoring women farmers while information is vital to adopt climate-resilient practices. With fewer assets to fall back on and limited access to alternative sources of income, the impacts of climate change on the most food-insecure populations, and on women in particular, are overwhelmingly negative, making it more difficult to escape the traps of low-productivity work, poverty and food insecurity (Skinner, 2011).

International and domestic policy environments

Policy shifts since the 1980s and the advent of neoliberal policy environments and international trade regimes have eroded the ability of governments to adopt food security measures. Over much of the twentieth century, producers the world over benefited from a supportive domestic policy environment including: public investments such as in research and development, extension services, credit facilities, infrastructure development; price supports for outputs; income support; marketing of inputs and outputs such as through marketing boards; and price stabilization measures including the holding of reserve stocks. However, since the 1980s the policy trend has been a withdrawal of the state, reducing public investments in agriculture, and implementation of liberalization reforms that dismantled many of the interventionist measures, particularly in developing countries. Disinvestment in agriculture was also driven by world market trends since the 1980s of low and stable food prices. Policy liberalization was particularly pronounced in developing countries where agricultural liberalization was part of structural adjustment programmes, and which also experienced a massive withdrawal of development aid financing of the agricultural sector.

An important driver of these trends in domestic policy is the World Trade Organization (WTO) Agreement on Agriculture (AoA) that restricts 'trade-distorting' measures such as support prices and subsidies.[3] The AoA has been vigorously contested by developing countries which argue that they conflict with the objectives of food security and poverty reduction, yet accommodate priorities of developed countries (see De Schutter, 2011). Among the issues, for example, is the way that the 'trade-distorting' impact of policy measures is calculated, allowing income support but not the use of administered prices. Thus, ironically, support to producers remains extensive in developed countries, taking the form of income support. Such subsidies depress prices in world markets and can have particularly harsh consequences for food security when they compete with poor farmers and poor countries. In 2005, the EU spent €40.1 billion (US$50 billion) for farm support; the USA spent US$18.9 billion; and Japan US$5.8 billion in 2006 (ICTSD, 2009).

Several other aspects of the trade regime constrain developing country agriculture, such as tariff peaks (extremely high tariffs imposed by developed countries on developing country exports, such as 129 per cent for sugar in the EU, or 1500 per cent for rice in Japan); tariff escalation (heavier duties imposed on processed products than on raw materials) that effectively discourages investment in manufacturing; and highly demanding sanitary and phytosanitary measures (ICTSD, 2009).

Apart from the overall negative effect of these measures on developing country producers, the more important question is whether it is acceptable for the international community to pursue free trade at the expense of hunger and malnutrition. There are clear inconsistencies between these trade measures and the objective of reducing the massive levels of hunger and malnutrition, driven in large part by the low productivity of small-scale farmers in developing countries, notably in sub-Saharan Africa and South Asia (ICTSD, 2009; De Schutter, 2011). A second important point is the inequity in these global trade rules that are pitched against developing country farmers – where income support to EU and US farmers does not face the same restrictions as subsidies to consumers in India. They accommodate the measures that were taken in developed countries to suppress production in an era of depressed prices and abundant production, and which need to be changed to meet the needs of the twenty-first century, in which the challenge is high prices and potential new pressures on production from climate change, polluting technology and competition for fuel (De Schutter, 2011).

Consequences for rural livelihoods

These global systemic changes combine with the historical constraints discussed earlier in this chapter to erode food security for poor and marginalized households. Small-scale family agriculture has come increasingly under pressure as a viable livelihood base, leading to high levels of rural poverty and out migration (De Schutter, 2014). Escaping the low productivity/poverty/food insecurity trap is particularly difficult for women in the context of the institutional constraints embedded in gendered power relations and weak bargaining positions within the household, labour markets, public services and assets.

These traps have pushed out migration but, as explained by Braunstein and Houston in Chapter 2 of this book, manufacturing is no longer able to absorb the surplus labour as part of the process of development through structural transformation as happened historically. In the context of environmental degradation, it is often the men who migrate in times of difficulty and the women who are left to labour on increasingly unproductive land, while being responsible for household and family welfare (Skinner, 2011). These consequences are particularly negative for women because the structures of constraint make it difficult for them to adapt to changing environments, making it more difficult to escape the low-productivity/poverty/food insecurity traps.

Small-scale farmers have not been silent. An important global social movement has emerged – La Via Campesina – that defends small scale sustainable agriculture as a way to promote social justice and dignity, also known as the food sovereignty movement. Defining itself as an international peasant movement that brings together the voices of 'peasants, small and medium-size farmers, landless people, women farmers, indigenous people, migrants and agricultural workers', it is comprised of 150 organizations from 70 countries including 200 million farmers (Via Campesina, 2014b). Its agenda – conceptualized as food sovereignty – is to promote a food system that would be an alternative to the 'corporate driven agriculture and transnational companies that are destroying people and nature' (Via Campesina, 2014b).

An important voice, they should not be seen as the only source of alternative thinking pathways. Their positions have been controversial amongst the critics of mainstream approaches. For example, critics challenge the viability of food self-sufficiency as a strategy; neglect of democratic choice to reject farming as a way of life; potential contradictions between individual and collective freedoms; and neglect of gendered institutions (see for example Agarwal, 2014).

Policy responses and their framing

Reversing the period of neglect and underinvestment since the late 1980s, food security has risen to a priority policy issue on the global agenda following the food crisis of 2007/08. In response to the widespread protests over price hikes, the international community took steps to develop coordinated, multi-stakeholder initiatives and to raise funding. For example, the G8 summit announced an Alliance for Food and Nutrition, while the Secretary-General set up the High Level Task Force and the Comprehensive Framework of Action. In an earlier paper co-authored with Orr (Fukuda-Parr and Orr, 2014), I have traced how these new initiatives reflect a decisive shift in framing global hunger discourse, and summarize the process here.

These new initiatives depart in design and concept from the approaches to food security of earlier decades; they are outcome-driven, short-term oriented, and emphasize the roles of technology and private sector actors as solutions. They are justified by a narrative framed by the Millennium Development Goals (MDGs); the urgent task is to achieve the 2015 global target of reducing the proportion of undernourished population by half. Defined by this outcome indicator, the very concept of food security is simplified and narrowed to the adequacy of caloric intake, stripped of the broad dimensions of human rights and capabilities necessary to be well nourished such as food availability, adequacy, utilization, stability, cultural appropriateness and forms of entitlements, principles of equality and participation. The new narrative contrasts with the food security discourse of the 1990s reflected in the agendas adopted at the 1994 WFS and the 1992 International Conference on Nutrition (ICN) that emphasized empowerment of people, and the inter-relationship between food security and other social conditions such as health and education, including gender equality. The narrative framed food security as a right to food, the ability of individuals and households to assure sustainable access to appropriate food, not mere delivery of a certain amount of calories (Fukuda-Parr and Orr, 2014). While the new narrative privileges targets as the driving framework, the 1990s agendas included targets as tools of public monitoring, to be used contextually and adapted by national governments and civil society. The leading role of the government and the need for public intervention, including investments in infrastructure and services, and in price incentives, was implicit and a central part of the strategy.

The design of the largest resourced international initiative to support agriculture, the Alliance for Green Revolution in Africa (AGRA),[4] is illustrative of the new trend. While its stated objective is to support small-scale farmers and food security, the majority of total commitments are allocated to investments in technological research aimed at developing higher-performing varieties, and at market reforms, many undertaken in US institutions. The 'policy and partnerships' programme is principally focused on relaxing government restrictions to allow for improved varieties, reducing transaction costs, facilitating open markets, and securing land and property rights (AGRA, 2013). 'Early success' stories noted in AGRA's policy programme review included liberalization of seed policies in Ghana and Tanzania, and the removal of the maize export ban in Malawi (AGRA, 2013).

Similarly, the target-driven, private sector oriented, technological approach also characterizes the leading initiative in nutrition, Scaling Up Nutrition (SUN), which was introduced as a mechanism for gathering stakeholder groups to work towards comprehensive policies that include businesses as well as governments, civil society, donors and international organizations (SUN, 2012). It too is heavily geared towards identifying quick solutions that achieve short-term results. It proposes 'specific nutrition interventions' such as fortification of foods and micronutrient supplementation, both of which may produce short-term solutions to acute malnutrition, but are unlikely to address the structural causes of such conditions.

These approaches pay little attention to the distributive consequences and the broad social and political determinants of hunger that have long been emphasized in research and debates of the 1980s and 1990s. Not surprisingly, the new initiatives have drawn controversy. Critics argue that technologically driven, simple-fix solutions are not the most effective way to improve diets and nutrition, and that there are alternatives to improving diets through better education and household choices, promotion of local diets, and reining in of corporate marketing of unhealthy foods. Civil society groups argue that many of the initiatives are motivated by private industry interests rather than food security. Wise and Murphy (2012) question the intentions of agricultural investments from governments and private donors alike (p17). GRAIN, an advocacy group for small-scale farmers, found that the large-scale African land purchases since 2008 have been used predominantly to produce export crops, leaving African farmers without land to grow food staples intended for domestic consumption (GRAIN, 2013).

GRAIN further argues that the G8's New Alliance for Food Security and Nutrition rationalized land grabs under the Principles for Responsible Agriculture Investment, which was drafted by the World Bank and supported by the G8 and

G20, but rejected by the Committee on Food Security and many international civil society groups for being exploitative and largely in favour of profit interests rather than developmental objectives. Similarly, the liberalization policies promoted by AGRA are aimed at increasing production, but do not address the distributional consequences and multi-dimensional causes of food insecurity. As a result of this approach, AGRA has received harsh and widespread criticism from advocates of food security (Patel, 2013).

These trends in international initiatives for global hunger also reflect a broader trend in the aid environment in the 2000s – when the donor community turned to greater involvement of the private sector, and away from support to national public sector institutions. Greater demand for accountability has meant bilateral donors and international agencies came under pressure to 'show results' and to follow 'results-based management' in a climate of scepticism about the effectiveness of, and funding for, aid. New actors that emerged outspent public investment initiatives, and introduced new approaches to project delivery involving the private sector, and methods such as social entrepreneurship and impact investing. The new thinking also emphasizes the important role of technological solutions that deliver visible results, fast. In the health sector, international support was provided to 'vertical programmes' around specific diseases, displacing support to 'horizontal programmes' aimed at building national health system capacity.

Taking this vertical approach to solving the problems of hunger and malnutrition may help meet the 2015 hunger target (and similar target set post-2015), but it probably will not address the structural causes of hunger. Even worse, without strong social support for the human rights principles of accountability and participation, and non-discrimination, the food security agenda is at risk of being co-opted by profit interests, notably the use of land to produce cash crops and benefit from the rapid rise in commodities market valuation. Although, from a production standpoint, this sort of activity may appear as 'achieving' the hunger target, it would have serious and grave effects on the most vulnerable groups whose access to food may be severely constrained by such motivations.

Current official policy documents that are shaping the post-2015 development agenda overwhelmingly frame the debate with supply-oriented narratives that sideline issues of systemic sources of food insecurity. For example, the report of the High Level Panel of Eminent Persons envisions a 'transformative, people-centred and planet-sensitive development agenda which is realised through the equal partnership of all stakeholders... based on principles of equity, sustainability, solidarity, respect for humanity and shared responsibilities in accordance with respective capabilities' (UN, 2013c, p3). But the targets for ending hunger emphasize increasing production and supply, neglecting the structural constraints to hunger and poor nutrition such as reducing price volatility; reducing gender discrimination in access to land and services; removing agricultural export subsidies in rich countries; trade reforms that accommodate national policy space for food security such as public food stocks and support to small-scale farmers; or regulating the marketing of foods with deleterious nutritional consequences.

Similarly, international agency reports, including FAO's (2013) report *The State of Food Insecurity in the World* and IFPRI's *Global Food Policy Report 2013* (IFPRI, 2013a), frame food security as an aggregate production issue. They propose strategies that emphasize productivity increases and sustainability management, focusing on proximate causes of hunger and malnutrition rather than the root causes. Outside the frame are questions of distribution within countries, and gender, and other inequalities that are at the root of the human outcomes reported. Gender issues are barely visible; a word count shows women mentioned ten times and gender mentioned three times in the 52-page FAO report, while the IFPRI report mentions gender three times and women 17 times in 142 pages.

FAO's two gender-focused reports, the 2010/11 issue of *State of Food and Agriculture* (FAO, 2010) and its joint report with ADB on gender (ADB and FAO, 2013), advance broader policy agendas that go beyond the productionist strategy of the more generic reports, but they stop short of addressing structural issues that present some of the most pressing threats to food security. Issues that are off the agenda include climate change, volatility in world food prices in the context of the fuel/food/financial markets, multilateral trade rules that constrain countries' ability to use policy tools such as administered prices to contain prices for consumers and assure markets for small-scale farmers, and competition for land from fuels and foreign investors. The reports do not adequately address the unequal constraints faced by women; indigenous and marginalized people have to adapt to these new threats and changing conditions which lie outside of the 'food and nutrition' sector strictly defined, but relate to inequalities in wages, education, and decision-making power, and to the governance of international trade and climate change.

The 'meeting the target' discourse that frames international development debates makes technology and private sector investments look like common-sense solutions. By the same token, addressing systemic issues in the world economy and food system, and institutional constraints to empowerment, looks unthinkably impractical and ideological.

Alternative pathways

Against these mainstream narratives, civil society voices frame food security in the human rights and capabilities perspectives and as issues related to the asymmetric governance of the global economy. For example, meetings organized by the Center for Women's Global Leadership (CWGL, 2013) and the UN Non-Government Liaison Service (UN-NGLS, 2013) raise a fundamental issue that the global economic system and policies should not sacrifice human concerns for financial interests, and raise critical issues for food security, including price volatility and national policy space in the context of WTO agreements.

Some national governments, too, are experimenting with measures that address systemic issues of food markets to strengthen production, exchange and transfer entitlements. While policies to strengthen transfer entitlements such as cash transfers have gained much support in international debates, those policies that aim to stabilize food markets and household access remain controversial. As already mentioned, measures such as input subsidies, price controls on essential food items, and public food stocks were considered to be sources of inefficiency in stimulating agricultural productivity and growth during the 1980s. However, a reverse trend has emerged to reconsider and redesign them to address weaknesses of the past instruments: 'smart' subsidies that are more targeted and could have broader social and economic benefits are being developed (Dorward, 2009; Brooks and Wiggins, 2010; Tiba, 2011). Countries such as Ghana, Kenya, Mali, Malawi, Nigeria, Rwanda, Senegal and Tanzania have recently introduced new input subsidy programmes.

Another policy approach that is gaining ground is public procurement from small-scale farmers that addresses institutional constraints they face (particularly women) in accessing markets and obtaining fair prices. It simultaneously provides better quality food products to social programmes such as schools, hospitals and public restaurants, helping to diversify diets with fresh produce. It is a major aspect of India's new food security policy, launched in 2013. Brazil has made extensive use of this approach as a major element of the country's comprehensive food security policy (Fome Zero) implemented since 2003 that has contributed to the sustained decline in hunger which is concentrated in rural areas, especially amongst female-headed households. 2010 household surveys show gaps in the incidence of severe food insecurity between female- and male-headed households in all five regions studied, ranging from 4 to 8 percentage points. Amongst the lowest-income households (one quarter of the minimum wage) with severe food insecurity, the gap was 8 percentage points (IBGE, 2010). The programme is being replicated in several countries in sub-Saharan Africa.

Public food reserves have been one of the major food security policies throughout the twentieth century. They have been largely dismantled in the 1980s in the context of structural adjustment reforms. Critics argue that they are inefficient and ineffective; expensive and complex to manage, and distorting incentives for private storage that can more effectively offset supply fluctuations (Gilbert, 2011). However, it is also acknowledged that food stocks have been effective in stabilizing prices as well as in stimulating agricultural growth (FAO et al, 2011; Oxfam, 2011). Many rice-producing countries in Asia have long used buffer stocks, as well as export and import monopolies and public procurement as complementary tools for price stabilization. More recently, Madagascar, Burkina Faso and Indonesia have implemented effective stock programmes (Oxfam, 2011). Moreover, proposals are being discussed for international food reserves as a mechanism to reduce the risks of price hikes in world food markets (Wright, 2012).

The experience of Brazil under the Fome Zero concept is instructive as a comprehensive programme that combines several policy instruments to bolster production, exchange and transfer entitlements simultaneously. It includes public procurement, but also a major programme to support access to credit, inputs and other resources for small-scale farmers; a large programme for cash transfers (Bolsa Familia); increases in social investments; and minimum wage that has more than doubled since 2003. Food security is a consistent priority across different social and economic policies, including in their trade policies and positions in multilateral policy fora.

Ironically, under the current global economic system, giving priority to food security can conflict with the norms of international trade (ICTSD, 2009; De Schutter, 2011). Many of the support measures fall into a 'grey zone' and countries face uncertainty as to the trade consequences of adopting them, and fear that the policies might lead to retribution or litigation (De Schutter, 2011, p3). Poor countries are particularly averse to taking such risks given their lack of technical capacity and bargaining power in international dispute negotiations. Food security is an urgent priority in the countries with high levels of hunger and malnutrition, and international trading arrangements should encourage, not discourage them from taking proactive policy measures.

Concluding remarks

Current pathways are unsustainable, leaving one eighth or even one quarter of the world population unable to obtain adequate food and be well nourished, a basic capability and a fundamental human right. The biophysical, market and institutional environments emerging in the twenty-first century are eroding rather than supporting the wage and production entitlements of food-insecure households. The current approaches to food security depend on a powerful narrative that is framed by the question 'can we feed the world?' and a strategy to achieve the global hunger goal. The narrative is target-driven, emphasizing solutions that achieve short-term productivity gains, the role of technology and the private sector. The narrative relies on a productionist concept of food security which obscures the institutional factors that inhibit individuals' access to food, particularly the role of women and the gendered institutional dynamics in such areas as access to local and global food markets, intra-household allocation of food, and production systems that drive hunger and malnutrition; and in the broader context of global, national and local food systems within which individuals acquire food to meet their nutritional needs.

Out of this frame are the systemic issues that erode production and exchange entitlements. Food-insecure households face increasing pressure from the long-standing constraints of unequal access to labour markets, resources and inputs, and the gendered division of work, that combine with the new forces of climate change, price volatility, competition for land, and a domestic policy environment that prioritizes economic and financial interests over human rights. Alternative pathways are possible that empower women and men to meet their food needs and strengthen their exchange and production entitlements, shown by the reform agendas and initiatives advocated and implemented by civil society and national governments. This alternative will need an equally powerful narrative that would serve to articulate and justify a reform agenda addressing gender inequality in such areas as access to land and resources; lack of policy space for proactive measures to stabilize food prices and maintain them at accessible levels for consumers; and many other local, national and global institutions that constrain food security. An important intellectual advance in understanding the problem of hunger as an issue of access needs to be recaptured for the twenty-first century debate. Hunger and malnutrition are failures of a fundamental human right and a basic capability that requires an empowerment-driven strategy that supports national government and civil society efforts to prioritize food security over economic and financial interests.

Notes

1 The IFPRI *Global Food Policy Report 2013* proposes a strategy for food security through building resilience to shocks due to natural disasters (floods, droughts) and civil unrest.
2 The food production index set at 100 for 2004/06 in 2011 was 117.6, against 75.3 in 1994.
3 The AoA treats national support measures for agriculture in several categories and sets minimum allowable levels of 'trade-distorting' measures, evaluated by a complex set of criteria. Overall, these provisions leave much broader policy scope for developed countries than for developing countries. The level of support to agriculture in these countries remains very high (Demeke et al, 2012) using a wide range of government subsidies, such as income support, that are not considered trade-distorting and are permitted. For developing countries, formulating a robust set of food security policies is more constrained, in part because the AoA was designed in the context of the 1980s and 1990s to address OECD agricultural policies intended to support incomes and provide insurance against the natural risks of agriculture, and when developing countries were being encouraged to liberalize the sector to stimulate production. Food security in poor countries, and of poor households in them, was not the major concern.
4 AGRA was initiated in 2006 by Kofi Anan, The Rockefeller Foundation and the Gates Foundation.

5

GENDER AND LAND GRABS IN COMPARATIVE PERSPECTIVE

Michael Levien

Introduction

Rural people across the global South are confronting increasing demands on their lands for a variety of economic purposes. Whether for Special Economic Zones (SEZs), dams, mining, industry, urban real estate or transnational agricultural investments, rural land dispossession is now a central feature of economic accumulation and political contestation in many countries. This chapter seeks to advance our understanding of the gendered implications of such dispossession. It does so through a comparative analysis of five cases of rural land dispossession driven by different purposes in diverse socio-historical contexts.

An adequate understanding of the implications of land dispossession, or 'land grabbing',[1] for gender and other dimensions of social inequality has never been more pressing. The fact that land grabs are now attracting unprecedented attention is no mere intellectual trend, but a belated response to concrete political–economic forces. While different economic sectors are driving land grabs in different regions, and there is great variation in the politics surrounding them, it seems possible to say three things about land grabs at the global level. First, they are increasing. While governments do not keep track of the numbers of people they uproot from their land, and recent attempts to quantify just agricultural 'land deals' have been controversial (cf. Edelman, 2013; Oya, 2013; Rulli et al, 2013; Scoones et al, 2013), few doubt that the neoliberal period – and perhaps particularly the first decade of the 2000s – has been accompanied by an increase in the numbers of people forcibly removed from their land.[2] Second, in addition to increasing, land grabs are changing in character. For most of the twentieth century, the majority of 'development-induced displacement' in the global South came from public sector infrastructure (e.g. dams), industry and extraction. As they have moved to economic models prioritizing growth through private investment, states have increasingly used their coercive powers to transfer land from farmers to private companies. In India and China, state-backed dispossession has, in recent years, been used primarily to facilitate private industry, real estate and mining, as well as public–private partnerships (PPP) in infrastructure (Hsing, 2010; Levien, 2012). In many parts of Africa, Latin America and Southeast Asia, meanwhile, governments have been handing over large swathes of land to international finance and agribusiness capital (and, to a lesser extent, sovereign states) for crop and biofuel plantations (cf. White et al, 2012; Fairbairn, 2014).[3] Third, this increasing scale and changing character of land grabs has been met with increasingly widespread opposition. Opposition to land grabs has not been explosive everywhere, but has been documented in many countries across Africa, Latin America and Southeast Asia (Borras and Franco, 2013), and has become particularly explosive in India (Levien, 2013a) and China (Hsing, 2010). Land struggles will undoubtedly be a central feature of the political economies of many developing countries in the twenty-first century.

If the growing significance of land dispossession makes understanding its gender implications all the more pressing, scholars have recently argued that we know very little about what those implications are (Chu, 2011; Behrman et al, 2012). Behrman et al (2012, p72) identify a 'current lack of empirical evidence on the differential effect that large-scale land deals have on men and women', and, more generally, 'limited information on how local populations are affected by eviction and resettlement'. Given this lack of information, they suggest, we should be agnostic about the implications of large-scale land deals for women. They remain optimistic that, 'If large-scale land investments are properly executed with appropriate attention to gender dimensions, land deals can provide transformative opportunities for both women and men through the introduction of new employment and income generation opportunities, new technologies, and new services' (Behrman et al, 2012, p71).

It is true that scholars have paid far more attention to the gendered dimensions of land tenure and land reform than land dispossession. But if we know a lot more about women's existing land rights than about the consequences of taking them away, we should not over-state our ignorance. While research on the gender implications of some of the newest forms of land dispossession – such as transnational agricultural deals or SEZs – remains slender (largely because they are so new), there already exists a range of important studies of the gender implications of land dispossession under earlier historical regimes, from the English enclosures to, more proximately, the large infrastructural and agricultural projects of state-led development. Such scholarship has already identified many of the gendered consequences of land dispossession that we are likely to observe today, and provide important points of comparison to illuminate what may in fact be new about contemporary forms of dispossession in the neoliberal era. To my knowledge, however, such a comparison has yet to be undertaken.

The purpose of this chapter, then, is to consolidate some of the main findings about the gendered implications of land dispossession and to interrogate them for comparative insights. It draws on five in-depth case studies of land dispossession in radically different socio-historical contexts – early capitalist England, state-led development in India and The Gambia, and contemporary neoliberalism in India and Indonesia. In each case, dispossession is driven by different forms of accumulation – capitalist farming and sheep-raising in England, large dams in India, intensive rice cultivation in The Gambia, oil palm plantations in Indonesia, and SEZs in India. While the first three cases represent dispossession under earlier periods of capitalist development (one distant, two near), the latter two are drawn from quite recent research on the newer forms of dispossession that are at the centre of contemporary controversies. While I draw from already published studies for the first four cases, the fifth draws on my own primary research on an SEZ in Rajasthan, India.

My goal in comparing these cases, which are so different in multiple respects (time period, type of project, agrarian social structure, gender relations), is twofold. First, I try to identify some of the very common gendered effects of dispossession that we observe across radically different contexts. This serves to show how much, in fact, we do know about the likely consequences of contemporary land grabs for women and gender equality. And what we do know is so overwhelmingly negative that we have far more reason to be critical than agnostic about the implications of contemporary land grabs for gender equality. My second aim, however, is to go beyond the generic formulation that women are disproportionately affected by land grabs, and to show how some gendered consequences of dispossession vary across forms of dispossession and socio-historical contexts. As different forms of dispossession refract through diverse agrarian social structures, including specific gendered forms of property ownership and divisions of labour, they produce qualitatively different patterns of inequality and forms of disadvantage. They also produce different outcomes within dispossessed populations as gender intersects with class, caste and other inequalities. Perhaps the most important of these outcomes is the effect of land loss on the gendered division of labour, which is generally deleterious but varies qualitatively across the cases examined. While this exploratory chapter hopes to identify only some of the most relevant differences across cases of dispossession, my hope is that it also contributes to a more explicitly comparative research programme within an engendered agrarian political economy (Razavi, 2009).

This chapter contributes to this book primarily by demonstrating the ways in which land dispossession under specific historical forms of capitalist accumulation chokes off pathways of sustainable and gender-equal development. It also demonstrates, however, the myriad ways that women have challenged such assaults on their lives and livelihoods. While such challenges have often been unsuccessful, I suggest that supporting them may be crucial to opening up more promising pathways of development and social change.

Case 1: The English enclosures

The English enclosure movement is often considered the 'classic' case of dispossessing peasantries for capitalist development. In a slow and uneven process that stretched from the fifteenth to the nineteenth centuries, the great mass of the

English peasantry (or 'commoners') were dispossessed as 'commons' were privatized and enclosed for 'improved agriculture' (Neeson, 1993). In its early phases, enclosure often occurred through the independent initiative of lords and was slowed down for several centuries by protective legislation. With the adoption of parliamentary enclosures in the mid-eighteenth century, the pace of expropriation vastly accelerated with full legal sanction – what Marx called the 'parliamentary form of robbery' (Marx, 1977, p885). By 1840, most of England's common land had been enclosed (Neeson, 1993, p5), and its peasantry all but eliminated.

While the consequences of this forcible transformation of England's rural property relations have long been debated (cf. Hammond and Hammond, 1913; Chambers, 1953), recent historiography has demonstrated that it was devastating for the rural poor. Firstly, through the process of enclosure, various classes of the agrarian poor – small farmers, cottagers, rural labourers and artisans – lost access to the 'commons'. While often dismissed by supporters of enclosure, historians such as K.D.M. Snell (1985), Jane Humphries (1990), J.M. Neeson (1993), and Silvia Federici (2004) have shown that the common rights available to the pre-enclosure rural poor (commoners) contributed very significantly to rural incomes, wellbeing and autonomy. These rights included pasturage (grazing rights), tillage (cultivation of open fields), turbary (digging of turf and peat), estovers (rights to cut wood), gleaning (grazing on the post-harvest stubble), quarry, and the collection of wild plants, fruits, herbs and shrubs (Humphries, 1990). Enclosure extinguished these rights, depriving commoners of means of livelihood and increasing their dependence on wage-labour. Secondly, enclosure also undermined the private arable holdings of small peasants, who could least afford the substantial costs associated with enclosure (tithe payments, fencing, etc.), and who were consequently replaced by a class of larger, commercially oriented tenant farmers (Neeson, 1993). In sum, the enclosures transformed the English peasantry into the English working class (Thompson, 1966).

What were the effects of the enclosures on women and gender relations? Historians such as Neeson, Snell, Humphries and Federici have persuasively shown that enclosure had a disproportionate impact on women and expanded existing gendered inequalities – in ways, moreover, that are strikingly similar to more contemporary experiences.

Our starting point – in each case – should be to ask: who decides whether people should relinquish their land for a given purpose? Typically, states justify forcibly taking land from people with the claim that it serves the 'public' or 'national' interest. But who determines that interest? What we see in the English enclosures – and across other cases – is that it is very rarely women. But it is also rarely the dispossessed, and the enclosures proceeded against the will of the majority of commoners in general. To receive parliamentary assent (we focus here on the later parliamentary enclosures), acts of enclosure informally required local approval in the form of petitions, but signees were weighted according to landholdings or tax contributions, giving greater say to the largest landowners (who typically supported enclosure) rather than the majority of land*holders*. When these petitions reached parliament, they fell on the sympathetic ears of fellow landlord parliamentarians. In its early stages, enclosure did not enjoy unanimous elite support and was widely debated – it was often feared that enclosure would create 'depopulation' and social 'disorder'. Consequently, commoners could occasionally find liberal sympathizers to advance their cause. But by the late eighteenth century, 'commoners no longer found anyone to speak for them at the centre of government' (Neeson, 1993, p46). Counter-petitions drafted by commoners were rarely successful, even when villagers could muster the resources to hire a lawyer. Although commoners resisted enclosures, as we will see, the intractable hostility of parliament towards their concerns channelled this resistance into informal and extra-parliamentary forms.

A second question we will want to ask of all of our cases is how (if at all) states decide to compensate the dispossessed. In general, the enclosure of commons went un- or under-compensated; calls to provide proper compensation to dispossessed commoners went unheeded (Neeson, 1993, p46). What compensation did exist usually took the form of leaving aside small pieces of waste land, or establishing small funds that parish 'guardians' could distribute on a discretionary basis to the 'deserving poor' (Humphries, 1990, p20). Only a minority with legal property rights received any cash compensation, and often this compensation went to covering the costs associated with enclosure, which prompted many smallholders to sell out before enclosure proceedings even began (Neeson, 1993). Nevertheless, men were likely to control any monetary compensation that did exist; Humphries (1990, p20) suggests that it was sometimes drunk away at the alehouse. This can only be considered a minor aspect of the tragedy of the enclosures, as most families received no compensation at all. However, we will see that male control over – and misuse of – cash compensation is a common feature of land dispossession in many times and places. In the absence of explicit policies to prevent it, it is a ubiquitous outcome of the intersection between dispossession and patriarchy.

Since lack of deliberation and poor compensation were fairly generalized, however, the central issue is how the enclosure of commons disproportionately affected the livelihood and autonomy of women, and had dramatically deleterious consequences for the gendered division of labour. Women were centrally involved in most of the livelihood activities supported by the commons in early modern England. Women not only participated in cultivation, harvesting and grazing, but were the principal gatherers of fuel, wild produce and raw materials for household production; they prepared peat; and they gleaned after the harvest. Humphries argues that this work offered significant returns compared with the low wages women received as hired workers (one-half to two-thirds of men's wages), and that 'many gathering, scavenging, and processing activities were relatively rewarding' (Humphries, 1990, pp37–39). Self-employment was easier to combine with child-rearing than waged employment, and cow-keeping on the commons served as social insurance for widows (Humphries, 1990, pp37–38). Federici underscores the social and economic importance of commons for women, arguing that 'The social function of the common was especially important for women, who, having less title to land and less social power, were more dependent on them for their subsistence, autonomy, and sociality' (2004, p71).

Loss of the commons entailed a dramatic transformation in the gendered division of labour. First and foremost, enclosing the commons made women increasingly dependent on men's wages. Humphries argues that 'Since women and children were the primary exploiters of common rights, their loss led to changes in women's economic position within the family and more generally to increased dependence of whole families on wages and wage earners' (1990, p21). Snell's meticulous study of seasonable employment patterns before and after enclosure in the late eighteenth century demonstrates that enclosure generated a 'long-term reduction in female work' in agriculture, and that the waged female work that did exist was increasingly seasonal and differentiated from men's (Snell, 1985, p155). Snell concludes, 'Enclosure accelerated changes in the sexual division of labour, leaving women more precariously positioned on the labour market, their real wages falling' (1985, p218). Such findings lead Federici (2004) to argue that enclosure was the key historical moment through which productive and reproductive work became divorced: the first became male and socially valued, the latter female and devalued.

The particular significance of commons for women is attested by the large-scale participation of women in anti-enclosure protests. Resistance to enclosure began as early as the fifteenth century, and included large-scale peasant rebellions – such as Kett's Rebellion of 1549 – as well as the ubiquitous practice of levelling hedges and ditches used to enclose fields.[4] In 1607, 37 women led by 'Captain Dorothy' attacked coal miners working on village commons; in 1608, 40 women 'caste down the fences and hedges' of an enclosure in Waddingham; and, in 1609, a group of 15 women assembled at night to destroy the hedges and ditches on a manor in Dunchurch (Manning, 1988; Federici, 2004, p73). Resistance to the parliamentary enclosures of the eighteenth and nineteenth centuries was also widespread. Commoners 'contested enclosure Bills with petitions, threats, foot-dragging, the theft of new landmarks, surveys and field books; with riotous assemblies to destroy gates, posts and rails; and with more covert thefts and arson' (Neeson, 2003, p321). While men may have been largely responsible for writing formal petitions, women played major roles in the more common – and effective – informal methods of opposition. In Wilbartson, 'three hundred men and women tried to prevent the fencing of the common' after failing to prevent enclosure with a counter-petition (Neeson, 2003, p278). In Raunds, 'led by the village women and some shoemakers they pulled down fences, dismantled gates, lit huge bonfires and celebrated long into the night' (Neeson, 2003, p278). Women evidently felt strongly enough about enclosure that they participated in militant struggles against it over the course of several centuries.

Although remote in time and geography from present 'land grabs', the case of the English enclosures helpfully illustrates many of the gendered aspects of dispossession that continue under more contemporary guises. First, women were excluded from decision-making or consultation over land acquisition, something which stands out more sharply in circumstances – perhaps still rare – in which male landholders or users are themselves consulted. Second, patriarchal control over economic resources within the household was intensified by channelling compensation to men – something which becomes more gender-specific in subsequent cases when compensation is more significant. Third, women lost access to resources that enabled them to earn livelihoods, undertake meaningful work, and maintain some autonomy. These gender-specific and gender-intensified (Kabeer and Murthy, 1999, p179) consequences of expropriating common resources are repeated in almost all the examples that follow. In the English case, dispossession was accompanied by a simultaneous exclusion of women from much of the waged work that 'improved' agriculture generated – which was, anyway, less than supporters claimed for it (Snell, 1985). Marginalized or employed on discriminatory terms, women were forced by enclosure into a subordinate position in a deepening gendered division of labour. While we will see that dispossession transforms gendered divisions of labour differently depending on the pre-existing social structure and the ensuing form of economic activity, these transformations are usually deleterious. We thus find in the English enclosures many of the reasons why land dispossession is almost always particularly harmful to women, even if that harm takes socially and historically specific forms. This is undoubtedly the reason why we often see women centrally and even militantly involved in opposing dispossession. Our next four cases illustrate variations on these basic themes. We now move forward 100 years after the end of enclosure to the autumn of British colonialism in Africa.

Case 2: Wetland rice projects in The Gambia

While large-scale 'land grabs' for transnational agricultural investments are currently attracting much attention across Africa, there are to date few detailed empirical studies of these newer projects and their gendered effects on dispossessed populations. We can, however, turn to existing studies from previous phases of land dispossession as a starting point for anticipating the likely consequences of this current phase. The long and regionally diverse histories of land dispossession on the African continent dating back to European colonialism make selecting 'representative' cases chimerical. So while it involves overlooking many forms and periods of European land expropriation, I turn to one of the most exhaustive and sophisticated analyses of land dispossession from an explicit gender perspective: Judith Carney and Michael Watts' excellent study of late-colonial and post-independence projects to expand irrigated rice production in The Gambia (Carney and Watts, 1990; Carney, 2004).

The Gambia is a fertile river valley whose agro-ecological and social context is important for understanding the gendered consequences and overall fate of these projects. There are roughly two major agro-ecological zones: highlands suitable for growing cereals and groundnuts; and riverine wetlands used for rice production. Peasant households cultivate land in both zones, and this cultivation is imbricated in a gendered land tenure system and household division of labour. Members of extended polygamous households have access to lands that are classified either as *kumanyango* or *maruo* – the first refers to individual land that entitles the family member to cultivate it on their own account; the second refers to household land whose proceeds accrue to the extended patrilineal family unit (controlled by male household heads). Under the pre-colonial division of labour, it appears that there was a less clear gendered division of labour between upland and lowland production: men applied labour on wetland rice plots, and women also worked on the upland cereal plots. It was only with the commercialization of groundnut production in the highlands – forced on peasants by colonial taxation – that men focused their labour on upland groundnut production, while women were left responsible for raising subsistence crops in the wetlands. While forced commercialization intensified the gendered division of labour, women significantly held on to *kumanyango* rights to wetland rice plots (in addition to cultivating rice on *maruo* fields), providing them with discretionary income and security within extended kinship units (Carney and Watts, 1990, p220; Carney, 2004).

The shift to commercial groundnut production resulted in rice shortages, which provided the first impetus for expanding irrigated rice production in the Gambian wetlands. Under the auspices of the British Colonial Development Corporation, the colonial authorities sought to expand smallholder rice productivity by draining mangroves, building irrigation canals, and distributing improved seeds and technology. But expanding rice production through double cropping required an intensification of labour, and colonial authorities soon realized that men were unwilling to work in lowland rice production. Intensifying rice production would thus require intensifying women's labour. Appropriating women's wetland rice plots allowed the authorities to capture that labour in the next phase of the project in the 1940s. The project was, however, an 'expensive disaster' plagued with design flaws and mismanagement; it was brought to its knees by peasant resistance, which involved among other things the widespread pilferage of rice (Carney and Watts, 1990, p212). It was said that the peasants 'were taking the rice because the whites had taken their land' (Carney and Watts, 1990, p212).

After independence in 1965, the Gambian government continued efforts to increase wetland rice productivity with the support of foreign donors including Taiwan, the People's Republic of China and the World Bank. The Jahaly–Pacharr project studied by Carney and Watts in the 1980s was the latest in this series of – less than successful – projects. Financed by the International Fund for Agricultural Development (IFAD), its purpose was to expand irrigated rice production by peasant households in the Mandinka region, again transforming women's subsistence wetland rice cultivation into double-cropped commercial production. Carney and Watts provide a detailed micro-sociological account of the gendered effects of this endeavour.

The Jahaly–Pacharr project involved appropriating the land rights women held to the wetland rice plots and then renting the land back to their households through long-term leases. While women had previously controlled some of these rice plots under *kumanyango* tenure, under the project 'the control of land rights was centralised through a thirty-year state appropriation; use rights were subsequently distributed to growers in the form of long-term tenancies' (Carney and Watts, 1990, p215). Peasants were not displaced, but dispossessed of land rights *in situ* and turned into tenants on their own land. Their land rights were now contingent on serving as contact growers under the scheme, cultivating rice 'under conditions rigorously specified and regulated by the project management' (Carney and Watts, 1990, p215). In the absence of a local landless class, Carney and Watts explain, this arrangement effectively controlled the labour and labour process of Mandinka peasant households (Carney and Watts, 1990, pp215–216).

As in the early phases of irrigated rice expansion, this labour would come from women. Men still refused to apply their labour in rice production, and double-cropping thus required a doubling of female labour. Carney and Watts explain, 'The production strategy strikes to the heart of family relations because it imposes new and demanding claims on household labour; skilled female family labour in particular is critical to fulfilling production targets' (Carney and Watts, 1990, p223). They found that after the project began, men's agricultural work in the wet season decreased while women's total agricultural work increased (Carney and Watts, 1990, p223). The result was that 'Women naturally experience mechanised rice production as radically new claims on their bodies and the imposition of enormously demanding work routines' (Carney and Watts, 1990, p223).

Increased demands on their labour were accompanied by diminished control over the product of that labour. Men resisted having plots registered in the names of women, arguing that this would alienate family land in the case of divorce, and were successful in convincing authorities to classify the wetland rice plots as belonging to the household (*maruo*). This allowed men to exert control over the income derived from female labour on the rice plots. As Carney and Watts explain, 'The naming of the project's plots as household fields thus enabled the household head to make claims to women's unpaid labour when in practice the plot functions in part as his individual field capable of generating investment surpluses for personal accumulation' (Carney and Watts, 1990, p223). By transferring land rights from women to men, the state thus dispossessed women of their means of production and effectively turned them into proletariat within the household.

Women resisted this dispossession of their land rights and intensified intra-household exploitation of their labour in several ways. First, they opposed the classification of the wetland rice plots as *maruo* and asserted their *kumanyango* rights. In some cases, they demanded *kumanyango* plots in the highlands in exchange. Where these efforts proved unsuccessful, women demanded remuneration (in rice) from their husbands for work on the rice plots, using their structural bargaining power as the project's labour force to challenge patriarchal family relations (Carney and Watts, 1990, p226). Second, in some instances, they withdrew their labour altogether, refusing to work on the scheme during periods of high labour demand, reducing the productivity of the plots and the project as a whole. In some instances, this forced men to increase their labour in rice cultivation (Carney and Watts, 1990, p229). Finally, they organized into collective work groups to provide the labour on a cash basis, using their leverage to bargain up wages. Carney and Watts show how the project thus 'manufactured dissent', unleashing a gendered struggle over the conjugal contract and household division of labour. This dissent, in turn, undermined the aims of the project on its own terms.

The Gambia case has commonalities with several other cases in our sample. First, in keeping with the universal trend, women were in no way consulted in the initial stages of the project, which was experienced as an imposition by state authorities with the compliance of men. Second, the project was experienced as a diminution of women's land rights, with deleterious consequences for their independent control over household income.

What makes the case somewhat different is the *in situ* nature of the land dispossession, which did not transfer land and commons wholesale from peasants to outside actors, but redistributed superordinate rights to the state and subordinate rights to men within the household. The consequence was that men did not substantially lose from dispossession, as is often the case. While women often experience dispossession in *gender-intensified* ways, dispossession in this case was *gender-specific* (Kabeer and Murthy, 1999, p179) as men benefited from the project with increased incomes relative to their work. So while the project involved subsuming peasants to agro-commercial capital and its production regimes, conflicting gender interests channelled dispossession politics within the household. Instead of peasants fighting state encroachment on their land rights, members of households fought each other over the remaining rights. What further distinguishes this case is the tenacity and variety of forms with which women resisted their expropriation and exploitation.

Although the Gambia case may be unique in certain respects, it also illustrates some of the modalities of gender inequality that we can expect from today's large-scale 'land deals', which also often involve transferring rights to customary land and incorporating dispossessed peasants as contract growers. These findings will be reinforced in our fourth case, which examines land grabs for Indonesian oil palm plantations. But first we turn to probably the largest source of dispossession in the twentieth century: large dams.

Case 3: Large dams in India

In comparison with other forms of dispossession, the social and ecological effects of large dams are fairly well studied. This is undoubtedly due to their central role in twentieth century 'modernization' efforts, the fact that they were the single largest source of land dispossession in most countries (cf. WCD, 2000; Fernandes, 2008), and to their being at the centre of political conflict and public debate over involuntary displacement since the 1980s. While powerful social movement resistance to large dams made them a central focus of the growing policy literature on 'development-induced displacement' (cf. Fernandes and Thukral, 1989; Fernandes and Paranjpye, 1997; Cernea, 1999; Cernea and McDowell, 2000; Fernandes, 2004; Singh, 2008), their specifically gendered consequences were long neglected (Thukral, 1996; Mehta and Srinivasan, 2000; Mehta, 2009b). That is no longer the case, and in this section I draw primarily on research conducted on dams in India, where the literature is particularly rich.

Large river valley projects were cornerstones of national development efforts in the twentieth century. While many were initiated under late colonial rule, their execution by post-colonial governments became politically potent symbols of national progress. Dams promised to generate power and food, raise incomes and create employment, and contribute to national self-sufficiency and, indeed, to national security. But dams also involved submerging entire river valleys under human-made reservoirs. This made dams by far the largest source of dispossession in post-independence India (Fernandes, 2008, p91) and throughout the developing world: large dams displaced between 40 and 80 million people in the twentieth century (WCD, 2000, p104).[5]

A plethora of studies have demonstrated the devastating economic, social, cultural and health effects of large-scale displacement for dams in India (and elsewhere). While dams delivered the benefits of irrigation and electricity to farmers in the plains and to urban consumers (cf. Dwivedi, 2006; Nilsen, 2010), they disproportionately displaced *adivasis* and Dalits, the most marginalized groups in Indian society (Fernandes, 2008, pp91–92). Because the Indian government did not recognize customary land rights, thousands of families were displaced from land their families had cultivated for generations without compensation. Even with formal land rights, compensation was kept extremely low[6] and was usually not enough to allow the displaced to buy alternative land. Displaced people's demands of 'land for land' compensation was rarely forthcoming (Banerji et al, 2000, p222), and the dispossessed were rarely compensated for common pool resources such as forests, grazing lands and water bodies that are central to rural livelihoods (Banerji et al, 2000, p220; Fernandes, 2009). Beyond compensation, there was hardly any framework in place at this time for 'resettlement and rehabilitation', the first term referring to the mere provision of an alternative living site, and the second to a more substantial effort to restore the dispossessed to their previous quality of life (Fernandes and Thukral, 1989; Fernandes and Paranjpye, 1997; Cernea, 1999; Fernandes, 2004; Singh, 2008). Banerji et al (2000, pp221–222) found that fewer than a quarter of dam projects offered the displaced replacement land for housing, and less than half provided for basic amenities such as water, schools, health clinics, road access or electricity. Resettlement sites were often in the midst of culturally alien environments and hostile villagers (Singh and Samantray, 1992, p72). In some cases, farmers refused to move to unviable resettlement sites, preferring to shift their homes to marginal hill land above reservoirs, as in the Narmada Valley and the Hirakud Dam (Viegas, 1992, p49). In other cases, they simply migrated to urban slums to join India's informal proletariat. Studies almost unanimously show that the dispossessed wound up with less income and food security, and that they were reduced to landless labourers in large numbers. Aggregate poverty increased in dam-affected districts (Duflo and Pande, 2007), and the physical and mental health of the displaced often worsened (Kedia, 2008). Added to this was the violence often inflicted by the state on recalcitrant villagers, including assault, murder, rape, pillaging of homes, and the sudden flooding of villages without warning (Bhanot and Singh, 1992, p101; Singh and Samantray, 1992, p66; Thukral, 1992, p15; Viegas, 1992, pp45–46; Sangvai, 2002; Khagram, 2004, p51; Palit, 2009; Ramkuwar, 2009). What Nehru called the 'temples of modern India' were, in sum, experienced as impoverishment and brutal state violence by millions of people they dispossessed.

As universally traumatic as they were, however, the negative effects of large dams were experienced by women in gender-intensified and gender-specific ways. As the World Commission on Dams concluded, 'The general impoverishment of communities and the social disruption, trauma and health impacts resulting from displacement have typically had more severe impacts on women' (WCD, 2000, p115). The elements of these gendered consequences are well studied.

First, women have in almost all instances been excluded from formal decision-making over displacement and resettlement for large dams (Mehta and Srinivasan, 2000; Mehta, 2009b). While such exclusion is often general, as Dewan notes, 'even in the few instances where participation does occur, women are generally left out of the entire debate' (2008, p137). In India, state laws and policies regarding land acquisition and resettlement and rehabilitation treat 'project affected families' as adequately represented by male 'heads of household' (Thukral, 1996; Mehta and Srinivasan, 2000; Mehta, 2009b). India's Land Acquisition Act even prevents government officials from delivering acquisition notices to anyone but male members of the household (Dewan, 2008, p136). Such gender-discriminatory laws and policies marginalize women from decision-making over whether to accept compensation, and from negotiations over the terms of resettlement. As Mehta describes the process of identifying relocation sites for the Sardar Sarovar project, women 'were consulted neither by officials nor by their husbands in the process of land allocation and selection' (2009b, p17).[7] This marginalization of women by both the state and male family members has impacted attempts by villages to resist their dispossession. For example, Ramkuwar, a woman displaced for the Man Dam in the Narmada Valley, describes the village *sarpanch* (elected head), who was co-opted by the government, trying to prohibit the participation of female family members in the anti-dam movement (Ramkuwar, 2009, p271).[8]

Once decisions are made and projects move forward, the tangible result is to reproduce women's lack of land rights, or reverse them where they exist. Compensation – whether cash, replacement land, housing, or jobs when available – is inevitably allocated to male household heads. Even when women do have independent land rights, there are cases in which the government has registered compensation plots in the name of their husband, as with the Tehri Dam in Uttarakhand (Thukral, 1995, p25; Dewan, 2008, p137; Bisht, 2009, pp313–314). As one widow displaced for the Tehri Dam put it, 'When we got displaced, I did not get any compensation. Two of my sons have got land. If tomorrow they refuse to take care of me, where will I go?' (Bisht, 2009, p314). For the purposes of deciding who constitutes an independent family entitled to their own compensation, state governments typically only include the families of 'major sons' and not daughters. In the Rengali, Subarnarekha and Sardar Sarovar Dams, for example, only adult sons were entitled to separate compensation, with no mention of adult daughters (Dewan, 2008, p136; Mehta, 2009b, pp17–18).

While facing institutional discrimination in the allocation of compensation and resettlement, women have been disproportionately hurt by the loss of common resources submerged by large dams (WCD, 2000, p114). As we saw with the English enclosures, in many agrarian societies common lands are particularly important sources of income, autonomy and sociality for women. As Dewan argues, 'It is around these common property resources that women interact, exchange information, get employment, develop solidarity structures, and also gain access to resources required for own sustenance and that of their families' (2008, p130). As women are often primarily responsible for livestock rearing, and have a greater chance of controlling income from it, they are particularly hurt by the large-scale loss of animals that usually results from land dispossession and the resulting loss of fodder (Pandey and Rout, 2004, p21; Dewan, 2008, p130). Resettlement sites usually lack grazing and forest land, making the re-establishment of livestock economies difficult or impossible. Women also lose income-generating activities from minor forest products, and raw materials for craft production. In the Narmada Valley, many women derived independent income from processing leaves for *beedis* (country cigarettes), collecting gum, and rope-making (Mehta, 2009b, pp19–20). In addition to losing access to these sources of income, women also have to cope with diminished access to fuel, water and other resources, which makes their reproductive work more challenging.

While losing access to previous forms of work and income, women are often disadvantaged in the labour markets they face after displacement. In the Gujarat resettlement sites for the Sardar Sarovar project, Mehta (2009b, p5) found that women were increasingly dependent on male wages and had lost significant control over household income. In the Korba Dam project in Chhattisgarh however, Thukral found the reverse: men were unwilling to move into wage labour, putting the burden of low-waged and dangerous work onto women (1996, p1502). In other contexts, men leave for migrant labour, placing the entire household burden onto women (Thukral, 1996, p1502). Summarizing several studies, Dewan concludes that women rarely received employment from dam projects, and that what they did receive was usually low-paying and irregular.[9] However, there is a class–caste difference: while upper-caste women are often confined to the household as they lose agricultural work but face *purdah* restrictions on labour force participation, lower-caste poor women are often forced into waged (sometimes migrant) labour (Dewan, 2008, pp128–129). In sum, whether women are unemployed, confined to the household, or forced to work at low-waged jobs seems to vary across locations and across class and caste. What we might say in general about dams is that, while they are premised on the dispossession of resources that support remunerative activities by women, they themselves do not replace them, leaving women at the mercy of the patriarchal power relations that structure labour markets.

Ultimately, existing research suggests that being displaced for large dams has very serious and disproportionate effects on women's food security, health and nutrition (for a review see Dewan, 2008, p133; Mehta, 2009b, pp21–23). It is a common finding that alcoholism and domestic abuse increase in the wake of displacement (cf. Thukral, 1996, p1502, 2009, p86; Dewan, 2008, p135; Fernandes, 2009, p124). This increased vulnerability to male violence is compounded by the fact that displacement often results in women being resettled far from natal villages, removing the security and exit option this provides (Mehta, 2009b, p25; Palit, 2009, p285). In addition to domestic violence, the establishment of dams has often been accompanied by extreme state violence against women, including rape, beatings and mass jailings (Baviskar, 1995; Sangvai, 2002; Dwivedi, 2006; Palit, 2009). Appalling sexual violence and human rights violations, repeatedly tolerated by multi-lateral lenders like the World Bank, have accompanied displacement for large dams not just in India but throughout the world.[10]

While there is a great deal of evidence that displacement for dams has been particularly harmful for women, this does not rule out that it can have some positive effects on gender inequality. In her study of the Sardar Sarovar project, Srinivasan argues that women did gain some new freedoms in the resettlement sites and that their access to education increased (2007). Thukral similarly argues that more girls started going to school after displacement for the Tehri Dam and that *purdah* declined (1996, p1502). In a more recent study of those displaced for the Tehri Dam, however, Bisht found that women were increasingly marginalized from economic activities and confined within the home (2009, p311). What I think we can extract from this mixed evidence is that, under some circumstances, displacement might lead to some increased freedoms for women, especially when it leads to greater educational access or relative urbanization. However, the evidence for women becoming empowered through dispossession for large dams remains extremely scant compared with evidence for the contrary.

The significant threats to women posed by large dams help to explain why women have often been in the forefront of social movements opposing them. In India, there have been a number of well organized social movements opposing large dams, most famously the *Narmada Bachao Andolan* (Save the Narmada Movement). Women have played a key role in these movements as both leaders and rank-and-file participants (see Baviskar, 1995; Sangvai, 2002; Palit, 2009; Ramkuwar, 2009). Indeed, women leaders of the *Narmada Bachao Andolan* have been instrumental in bringing together anti-dispossession movements across India into the National Alliance of People's Movements (NAPM). If the social effects of large dams have been particularly disastrous for women, they have also propelled women into the forefront of national politics on these issues.

Such movements against large dams were the first to politicize 'development-induced displacement' and put it on the agenda of development agencies and scholars. Land grabs for large-scale agricultural investments have recently rekindled the issue in international policy circles. We now turn to the case of oil palm plantations in Indonesia for insight into the gender implications of this recent 'farmland rush'.

Case 4: Oil palm plantations in West Kalimantan

Since the 1980s, the expansion of oil palm plantations has been a major cause of land dispossession and deforestation in many Southeast Asian countries. This process has greatly accelerated in the past decade with the biofuels boom, in which palm oil has figured centrally (Borras et al, 2010). Indonesia is the world's largest producer of palm oil, for which it has been rapidly clearing forest. These forests are mostly held under customary tenure and cultivated by rural populations who depend on it for their livelihoods, but whose claims are legally unrecognized by the state. The gendered consequences of dispossession for oil palm cultivation have been studied most carefully by Julia and Ben White (Julia and White, 2012) in an ethnographic case study of a village in West Kalimantan. Their important study helps to illustrate the multiple ways in which land dispossession can disproportionately affect women, and actually expand gender inequalities.

Julia and White studied a village of 240 households from the Hibun Dayak community in West Kalimantan, which they call Anbera Hamlet. One-third of Anbera's land had been expropriated for oil palm plantations. The provincial government granted long-term land-use concessions (*Hak Guna Usaha*, HGU) for the village's land, previously held in customary tenure, to private companies for establishing oil palm plantations. The concessions were granted for 35 years with the option of extension; upon their termination, the land will revert back to the state rather than local villagers (Julia and White, 2012, p999). The government instituted several compensation schemes for dispossessed villagers, the most common of which involved incorporating them into oil palm production as contract growers on small plots surrounding the 'nuclear' plantation, which is cultivated using hired labour. Under this scheme, farmers who agree to be 'outgrowers' surrender their customary tenure land in exchange for land planted with palm oil, on either a 2:5 or 2:7 ratio (Julia and White, 2012, p999). The farmers receive these plots on credit, with payments deducted from their monthly income. In addition to these deductions for the (re)purchase of their land, farmers pay deductions for infrastructure, transportation, and input costs. They must sell their produce through the company. Under a second scheme, farmers can become non-cultivating partners with a 30 per cent share of the income from similar plots cultivated with hired labour (Julia and White, 2012, p1000).

Understanding the consequences of this project requires, as always, an understanding of the pre-existing agrarian social structure. While a national highway had brought migrants to the area, the majority of the village consisted of members of the Hibun Dayak community, the largest ethnic group of the area. Previous to the oil palm plantations, local livelihoods came from 'rubber, upland rice farming and other local agricultural products grown in sustainable mixed-farming systems' (Julia and White, 2012, p1001). There are three categories of land tenure: (1) collective land, which includes forests, honey trees, mixed-crop areas used for fruit and dry rice cultivation, rivers, cemeteries and sacred places; (2) ancestral land, which belongs to entire lineages descended from the same ancestors; and (3) individual land, which is inheritable and includes rice fields, orchards and houses. Under this system, 'Hibun women inherit land rights from their parents, and according to customary leaders there is no gender differentiation in land inheritance' (Julia and White, 2012, p1001). Whichever child cares for the parents inherits the most land. Despite having land rights, however, women are excluded from formal politics – an exclusion that became consequential with the arrival of oil palm plantations.

In Anbera, as in our other cases, the process of dispossession began with negotiations in which women played no part:

> When establishing the plantation, the company approached community leaders, customary leaders and other figures (teachers, religious leaders, etc.) who were all male, to do the public relations or information dissemination to the other community members. Usually, these formal and informal leaders received incentives (cash, promise of a smallholder plot, etc.) for this work, or for the number of community members who sign up as smallholders.
>
> (Julia and White, 2012, p1000)

The exclusion of women from local decision-making structures thus helped to preclude substantive deliberation among the affected population, and made it easier for the government to co-opt leaders and divide the village (Julia and White, 2012, p1014).

The state's compensation system not only reinforced existing patriarchal norms, but actually reversed the property rights that Hibun women had previously enjoyed. Ignoring women's independent land rights, the government registered only household heads as smallholders in the palm oil outgrower scheme. Except in a few cases of divorced or widowed women, husbands were declared the household head: only six of 98 registered smallholders were women (Julia and White, 2012, p1002). The consequence was that mostly men owned the new plots, controlled the credit made available to plot-holders, and were members of the smallholder cooperatives.

The effects on the gendered division of labour were pernicious. Julia and White argue that before the plantations, there was a relatively balanced gendered division of labour in subsistence and cash crop production. After the plantations, women became responsible for the most-labour intensive work on the smallholder oil palm plots, such as maintaining the trees (Julia and White, 2012, p1003). Similarly to the Gambia case analysed by Carney and Watts, the project thus intensified women's labour while attenuating their land rights. Women now had to work harder on land, which the project placed in the control of men. This led to escalating domestic conflict and violence over the control of oil palm income (Julia and White, 2012, p1010).

Women – and particularly older women – continued to do most of the labour on subsistence plots (Julia and White, 2012, p1003). Jobs created by the plantations were, in general, scarce relative to the local population. But while both men and women were absorbed to a limited degree as a casual plantation labour force, men (especially migrant men) received the better paying formal jobs. Women were most involved in hazardous work such as spraying and fertilizing fields without safety equipment (Julia and White, 2012, p1006). One of the main ways many women interacted with the palm oil plantations was informally, through *berondol* scavenging – the gleaning of fallen oil palm fruit. Women earned income by collecting the fallen fruit and selling it at a discounted price. This livelihood strategy was, however, ultimately prohibited by the companies, whose security guards harassed and abused *berondol* scavengers (Julia and White, 2012, p1007).

Women's reproductive work was also placed under strain by the enclosure of common property resources. Various kinds of local fruit and vegetables that were part of the local diet became scarce. Raw materials for craft production were lost due to forest destruction (Julia and White, 2012, p1011). As often happens when common property resources are dispossessed, reproductive activities typically undertaken by women became more difficult.

Anbera village did mount a political response. According to Julia and White, grievances mounted in the villages, particularly over the fact that it took decades for many families to have their rights to compensation plots recognized. Villagers blockaded and harvested part of the plantation, and filed a court case. While women were excluded from formal political arenas (such as the local union), they were informally active in asserting their rights. These efforts have resulted in a number of villages receiving their compensation plots, but apparently little more.

While the project brought some benefits to local people, such as increased access to wages, there were many costs and these were disproportionately borne by women. In Julia and White's summation, 'formalisation [of land tenure] has been accompanied by masculinisation (of oil palm plot ownership, of membership in producers' organizations, and of access to credit sources linked to land titles) undermining the position and livelihoods of women in this already patriarchal society' (Julia and White, 2012, p1015). They thus conclude that 'Oil palm plantation expansion has strengthened the patriarchal system of the state and the Hibun Dayak community' (Julia and White, 2012, p1014).

Dispossession for oil palm in Indonesia not only reproduced patriarchal social relations among the Hibun Dayak, but undermined more gender-equal ones – significantly, women's independent land rights. We now turn to rural north India to examine the intersection of another contentious mode of neoliberal dispossession – SEZs – with an arguably more severe 'regional patriarchy' (Kandiyoti, 1988; Sangari, 1995).

Case 5: The Mahindra World City SEZ, India

While large dams were once synonymous with 'development-induced displacement' in India, the shift to a neoliberal economic model over the past two decades has led to increasingly privatized forms of dispossession. Since the mid-2000s, SEZs have become the cutting edge of such dispossession, and the epicentre of so-called 'land wars'. Catalysed by a policy in 2000 and a parliamentary act in 2005, SEZs marked an important departure from previous forms of industrial infrastructure. First, they were much larger, some of them requiring up to 10,000 acres of land. Second, they could be developed by private companies and not just government agencies. And third, only half of their land had to be used for export-oriented production, which meant that SEZs would not be old-fashioned industrial zones but satellite cities with lucrative high-end housing. The opportunity they created for obtaining cheap land in the midst of a real estate boom generated an SEZ rush: almost 600 SEZs were approved between 2005 and 2008. State governments began acquiring land for these zones using India's Land Acquisition Act, which empowers the government to acquire private property for a 'public purpose'. This generated widespread farmer protests against land acquisition, which were surprisingly successful in stalling and cancelling many of India's largest proposed SEZs (Sampat, 2010; Levien, 2011, 2012, 2013b; Jenkins et al, 2014).

In part because so many SEZs were defeated or delayed by farmer opposition, there are to date few available studies of functioning ones that allow for an in-depth assessment of their consequences. Beginning in 2009, I studied one of the first large private SEZs to be established in north India – the Mahindra World City (MWC) outside Jaipur, Rajasthan. Developed by the real estate subsidiary of the US$16 billion Mahindra and Mahindra Company, this 3000-acre 'multi-purpose' SEZ was designed to include five sector-specific zones for information technology and services (IT/ITES), light engineering, gems and jewellery, handicrafts, and apparel. The 700-acre IT/ITES zone, supposed to be the largest in India, was the heart of the project, and Bangalore-based Infosys was the anchor investor. For most of my fieldwork, the only operational businesses in the zone were Infosys and Deutsche Bank, both running business process outsourcing (BPO) hubs that were employing mostly educated urban youth to do back-office work from glass and steel campuses carved out of local villages' grazing land. While slowed by the global financial crisis, Mahindra was preparing to use 1000 acres to build a 'Lifestyle Zone' with upscale residential colonies, shopping malls, schools, hospitals and recreational space.

Establishing the MWC involved acquiring 2000 acres of private farmland and 1000 acres of public grazing land from nine Rajasthani villages approximately 25 km from Jaipur. These mixed-caste, majority Hindu villages were highly dependent on rainfed agriculture and livestock rearing – especially for milk production – supplemented by wage labour in Jaipur and surrounding towns. Under the Rajasthan government's compensation package, families with land acquired were given the option of receiving small commercial–residential plots adjacent to the SEZ that were one-fourth the size of their previous land. While analogous to the palm oil plots we encountered in the Indonesia case, these plots had no agricultural value. The idea was that these 'developed' plots would have far more value as real estate or plots for small businesses than the original agricultural land, and thus incorporate farmers into the land or business opportunities generated by the project. This compensation policy did not produce consent, but divided the affected villages by individualizing people's relationship to the project. Instead of facing the state as a collectivity, they were thrust into land markets as individuals. Given the highly class- and caste-stratified nature of the villages, individual families came to different initial calculations about their ability to benefit from the compensation – and many lacked essential information about the project (including what an SEZ was) and the compensation package. The result was that the MWC did not generate the sort of 'land war' that accompanied SEZs elsewhere in India. Between 2009 and 2011 (with several subsequent follow-up visits), I conducted over one year of ethnographic fieldwork concentrated in a village I call Rajpura, a large multi-caste village that had the most land acquired for the SEZ. I also interviewed SEZ developers and government officials, analysed village land records, and conducted a random sample survey of 94 families in four affected villages.

I have detailed elsewhere the highly unequal developmental consequences of land acquisition for different classes and castes in these villages (Levien, 2011, 2012). In brief, land acquisition deprived these villages of private farmland and common grazing land, destroying agricultural incomes and food security. The SEZ, meanwhile, failed to generate significant employment for local people – only 18 per cent of dispossessed families had one member receive a job in the SEZ, and this was almost universally low-waged and temporary positions as gardeners, janitors or security guards, or in labour gangs for construction (survey by author). As a high-end service and IT enclave, the SEZ also generated few productive linkages and little ancillary industrialization within the surrounding villages. While the government committed to providing the SEZ with its substantial water needs (projected to eventually reach half a million gallons per day), villagers lost wells to the SEZ and were increasingly forced to purchase water of dubious quality from tankers. According to my random sample survey of 94 families in four villages, 65 per cent of displaced families reported having less income after the SEZ, 50 per cent reported having less food, and 75 per cent felt they had lost more than gained. However, things were much worse for the land-poor lower castes, called scheduled castes and tribes (SC/STs) in India, who, compelled by debts, lured by misinformation and cheated by brokers, often sold their compensation plots quickly and cheaply. At the time of my survey in 2011, 82 per cent of SC/ST families had sold their plots compared with only 18 per cent of general (upper) castes (most of whom were Brahmins). When they did sell, SC/ST families received on average US$12,000 less per hectare. They were consequently much less likely to come out of the process with productive assets and alternative livelihoods. A full 88 per cent of SC/ST families reported having less income, 75 per cent reported having less food, and 88 per cent felt they had lost more than gained.

Dispossession for the SEZ and the economic changes that followed had particularly deleterious consequences for women, especially lower-caste women, and worsened already extreme gender inequalities. Understanding these consequences requires outlining some dimensions of the 'regional patriarchy' that pre-dated the SEZ in this area of Rajasthan. First, as in many regions of India, Rajasthani villages are organized into patrilocal familial units in which women move to their husband's village after marriage and rarely have independent land rights. Women's lack of inheritance rights is ostensibly compensated by their dowries, but as scholars have observed, these resources are typically controlled by in-laws and husbands and do not provide women with independent economic assets (Agarwal, 1988, 1994). Even as widows, women's inherited land rights are vulnerable and likely to be *de facto* controlled by male relatives (Agarwal, 1988, 1994). Second, women are excluded in most ways from the public sphere of political and economic decision-making. They are sparsely represented in the *panchayat bhavan* where village meetings (*gram sabhas*) occur, and when elected to office on a seat 'reserved' for women, they are often controlled by male relatives or patrons. Women seldom even venture to the market unaccompanied by men, and are absent from the informal village spaces where men discuss business and politics. But the gendered segregation of space, along with the gendered division of labour, varies by caste. Upper-caste men confine women to the home as a mark of distinction; as do those who aspire to upper-caste status and can afford to forego women's wages. Lower-caste men usually cannot afford this distinction, poverty forcing both women and men of these households to do waged labour.

In all castes, women perform the vast majority of all household and reproductive work – gathering fuel, fodder and wood; preparing food; and caring for children. They also contribute the most labour to household agriculture, specializing in the most labour-intensive tasks of planting, weeding and harvesting. When women work outside agriculture, they are largely confined to the most arduous forms of work – construction and other forms of hard manual labour – and are paid less than men. Female literacy rates are very low: 29 per cent compared with 56 per cent among men. Rajasthan, finally, ranks below the national average in most indicators of gender disparity including sex ratio (World Bank, 2006, p11). In Rajpura, there are 897 women for every 1000 men (Census of India, 2001), which is even lower than the Rajasthan-wide figure of 906 (World Bank, 2006, p11).

The economic changes unleashed by land dispossession and speculation for the SEZ intersected with this patriarchal social structure in tragic but predictable ways. To start, it would be misleading to say that women within the villages were particularly excluded from the decision-making process: there were *no* public negotiations or consultations. A few village political leaders (all men) were in the know – as was the case with the arrival of the oil palm plantation in Anbera. But most villagers learned of the SEZ only indirectly as brokers and outside investors started pouring into the village to buy up farmland in 2004 (one year before the project was officially announced).[11] These brokers spread misinformation, deliberately sowing fear to persuade people to sell cheaply. By the time the land was officially acquired for the SEZ, a significant fraction of it – disproportionately that of lower-caste families – had already been alienated through brokers at retrospectively low prices.

If the decision-making process for the SEZ was universally exclusionary, the compensation system and the resulting real estate speculation had deeply gendered consequences. As landowners, men received the rights to most of the compensation plots allocated by the Rajasthan government. Women's informal influence over the disposition of these plots varied by household; but ultimately the decision of whether or not to sell one's compensation rested with men. It was men who negotiated land deals, served as intermediaries as brokers, went to the block (*tehsil*) headquarters to register land sales, and who ultimately received the cash from such sales. I was able to observe several land negotiations during my fieldwork, one of which included a widowed woman selling her compensation plots: she sat on the ground outside with women from the broker's household while male relatives negotiated the sale on cots inside (field notes, 8 July 2010). The process of forcible land acquisition thrust these villages into a real estate economy from which women were almost entirely excluded by virtue of their lack of formal property rights and patriarchal norms that relegated them from the public sphere.

While excluded from compensation and the real estate economy, women acutely felt the loss of farmland and common grazing land. The strongest and most ubiquitous complaint of women in the villages was of the loss of food and fodder following land acquisition, and the consequent need to buy everything on the market. Women – as well as many men – constantly spoke with regret of the grain, vegetables, lentils, milk, buttermilk, curd and butter that they no longer received from fields and livestock, and which they could not afford to buy in similar quantities – much less quality – from the market. This was made worse by the drastic food price inflation that was squeezing incomes in India and globally.

While women universally regretted the loss of agricultural products, the effects of dispossession on the gendered division of labour were complex, and varied significantly by class and caste (which closely align in these villages). For some items (such as fuel) that used to be obtained from the grazing land, women's domestic burden increased as they had to go farther afield to collect sufficient quantities, except for those (few) who could afford gas stoves. Other items simply became unavailable, thus reducing the work burdens associated with them – but with deleterious consequences for household consumption for families who could not purchase substitutes. Losing agricultural land in one sense unburdened women of their disproportionate share of agricultural work; however, most did not rejoice in this, but bemoaned the loss of grain and dairy products that fed their families, and repeatedly complained that they were now 'unemployed' (*berozghar*) (for similar findings, see Mehta, 2009b, p24). Puneeta, a Brahmin woman in her twenties, remarked that, 'Since they closed off the grazing land, it's gotten more difficult to get fodder or wood.' Her mother-in-law concurred, 'This has been a huge loss.' As for the loss of farmland, Puneeta ruefully observed, 'We've become unemployed.' When I asked whether there was any benefit from being relieved of agricultural work, she said, 'There is both loss and benefit. We've gotten some rest, but it's a bigger loss. We used to get grain, fodder, everything else from the fields' (field notes, 16 February 2010). Puneeta's family was quite well off by village standards, with several male family members running a dairy business in Jaipur. Matters were less ambivalent for most lower-caste women. When I asked Kamla Devi, a lower-caste woman whose family lost all their modest land holdings to the SEZ whether they had 'gotten some rest', as Puneeta had suggested, she replied, 'What rest? We carry stones under the hot sun (*dhup*)' (field notes, 10 March 2010). She worked with hundreds of other women from the *panchayat* on the National Rural Employment Guarantee Scheme (NREGA), which guarantees every rural family 100 days of work at Rs100 (less than the minimum wage). Many other lower-caste women combined work on NREGA (when it was functional) with waged labour on private construction gangs, for which they are paid Rs10–30 less than men. So, although the loss of common land was universally detrimental, it was unevenly so: wealthier families could purchase market substitutes for fodder, fuel and food. And while the loss of agricultural land turned many upper-caste women into unemployed 'housewives', it left lower-caste women increasingly proletarianized. Dispossession initiated caste- and class-inflected changes to the gendered division of labour.

The sale of land and plots further put unprecedented sums of cash in the hands of men who were often, at the same time, rendered unemployed. The predictable outcome, which appears with depressing frequency in many studies of displacement (e.g. Colson, 1999; Mehta and Srinivasan, 2000), was that many men misspent these earnings in a variety of ways, including on large quantities of alcohol. While alcoholism and domestic abuse were prevalent before the SEZ, it was an extremely common source of complaint among women in the villages that men were drinking more, and that this drinking was leading to greater domestic violence. Lada Bhunker, a Dalit woman explained: 'Before they drank, but not that much. Money has come, and now they drink morning and night' (field notes, 12 October 2010). Kamla Devi, a Nayak women, explained: 'Before they were doing work... it was better... [now] if they make Rs100, it's only with a fight that they give Rs50' (field notes, 6 April 2010). I heard numerous stories of men drinking away women's wages, and rampant domestic violence was hardly a secret in the close confines of the village.

The infusion of cash from land sales also, incidentally, drastically ratcheted up dowry levels and wedding expenses. One Dalit family spent Rs3.5 *lakh* (US$7000) on their daughter's wedding while I was there; a relatively poor Brahmin family spent Rs10 *lakh* (US$20,000). These lavish weddings – involving more elaborate food and sweets, larger guest lists, and much more expensive dowry – put a squeeze on the 'losers' from the SEZ, who had little savings and income, but felt compelled to take massive loans from moneylenders to maintain status. As one Dalit man explained, 'Before people would pay Rs20,000 to 30,000 (US$400–600) for an excellent wedding. Now it's at least 10 *lakhs* (US$20,000). They'll want a four-wheeler, cooler, gold and silver. The boy will want a motorcycle. Before dowry was five kitchen utensils (*barthan*) and some clothes... For the poor man, marrying [one's children] has become difficult. If there are three or four girls, he'll die' (field notes, 20 December 2010). As the last comment indicates, escalating dowry levels increase the financial cost of girls, a worrying development in a region that already had one 'missing' woman for every ten men – and whose gender ratio worsened over the 2000s (Census of India, 2001, 2011).

It is possible that, as urbanization in these villages progresses, some forms of patriarchal social relations might attenuate. So far I have found no evidence to support this. Instead of eroding rural Rajasthan's notoriously rigid gender relations in a tide of modernization, the arrival of an SEZ containing the most advanced sectors of India's 'new economy' has, if anything, reproduced these patriarchal relations, reduced women's autonomy and wellbeing (particularly in lower-caste families), and widened gender inequalities in important respects. The MWC's sponsoring of a 'self-help' group for village women – in which they would receive small loans and be taught how to sew and make soap – is a farcical footnote to these profoundly negative transformations, particularly in the lives and livelihoods of poor lower-caste women.

While the Rajasthan government's market-based compensation model divided the village and prevented organized opposition, women were involved in the resistance that did occur. In Rajpura's one holdout family, women physically clashed with police and government officials when they tried to forcibly fence their land. On another occasion, the women let their cattle loose into their field as assembled dignitaries tried to inaugurate a State Bank of India office upon it. More broadly, women participated in forms of 'everyday resistance' (Scott, 1985) such as grazing livestock within SEZ boundaries through breaches in the perimeter fencing. Poor women also engaged in the proverbial 'war of words', what Scott (1985) calls the 'small arms fire' of class struggle, expressing their dissatisfaction with expanding class inequalities by slandering or 'cutting' those – like the village brokers and village *sarpanch* – who had profited from the project at the expense of their poorer fellow villagers.

Nevertheless, like men, the women of Rajpura did not organize collectively to oppose the SEZ or demand concessions from its developers or the government. Aside from one brief protest organized by village leaders and brokers to demand timely delivery of compensation plots, and principally involving men, Rajpura's residents were not able to form a collective organization to advance their interests despite the majority harbouring significant grievances. Incorporation into speculative land markets individualized and fractured the interests of women along with men, transforming potential solidarity into internecine feuds and jealousies over compensation money, land proceeds, and the magnified inequalities these generated not just between castes, but within castes and even families. Many women mentioned the decline of unity (*ekta*) and relations (*rishta*) not just within the village, but among women specifically. Their solidarities were fractured along with men's, and this further undermined their capacity to stem the regressive social transformations unleashed by the SEZ.

Conclusion

Together, the five cases presented above paint a sobering picture of the implications of 'land grabs' for rural women. We encountered, to be sure, ambiguous and even positive changes for women in the wake of some of these projects: oil palm plantations created some income opportunities for the Hibun Dayak women; displacement for dams sometimes led to women having greater educational opportunities in the regions where they resettled; upper-caste women in Rajasthan saw their domestic burden reduced somewhat after the SEZ consumed their land. Nevertheless, these rare and limited gains were overwhelmed by a confluence of gendered exclusions and inequalities that shaped the process and outcome of dispossession. Several of these regressive consequences recur with remarkable regularity across project type and social context.

Commonalities

First, in none of our cases did women have any decision-making power in the planning of projects or in negotiating the details of resettlement and rehabilitation. Second, discriminatory compensation and resettlement almost universally reproduced women's lack of land rights (e.g. in early modern England and India) or undermined them where they actually existed (among the Mandinka in The Gambia and the Hibun Dayak in Kalimantan). Third, given their greater dependence on common resources for work and income, women were disproportionately hurt by the enclosure of commons and resulting losses of livestock. Given what we know about the relationship between control over income and intra-household welfare disparities (Kabeer, 1994), such articulation of patriarchal social relations and discriminatory state policies – what Mehta (2009b) calls the 'double bind' – ensure that women experience the impoverishment following dispossession in gender-intensified ways. Fourth, while the causal link between land dispossession and domestic violence and alcoholism remains underspecified – male control over compensation and the socio-psychological consequences of male unemployment are plausible intervening variables – the increase of both has been observed in innumerable studies of displaced populations. Fifth, since dispossession entails removing people from land against their will, states often resort to violence to push projects through, creating situations in which women's physical security becomes particularly compromised. The record of 'development-induced displacement' is replete with examples of sexual violence and other human rights abuses perpetrated by police, army or hired thugs. Finally, in all cases, we saw how women widely recognized the threats dispossession posed or ultimately created for their wellbeing, and played important roles in both overt opposition – as in the English enclosures, The Gambia rice project, and large dam projects in India – and in more 'everyday' forms of resistance (Scott, 1985; Hart, 1991) such as the gleaning of fallen palm nuts in Kalimantan (considered poaching by the company), 'trespassing' within the SEZ boundaries to graze animals in Rajasthan, and vehement participation (in probably all of our cases) in the everyday 'war of words' (Scott, 1985).

Variation

We also observed several dimensions in which the experience of dispossession varied for women. The most dramatic variation appears to be the consequences of dispossession for the gendered division of labour. This variation turns on at least two axes. The first is the type of economic activity driving dispossession, and whether it absorbs the labour of dispossessed women. We saw that in the cases of the English enclosures, large dams and SEZs, dispossession created little to no employment for women. In our agricultural cases – rice cultivation in The Gambia and oil palm plantations in Indonesia – women's labour was absorbed to some extent in the resulting project. This was particularly true for The Gambia project, where the dispossession of women's land rights was instrumental to capturing their labour for double-cropped (household) rice production. Following the loss of their independent land rights, women experienced this intensification of work as an intensification of intra-household exploitation. The Indonesian case was more ambiguous: some women did receive paid wage labour on the plantations, although this was limited and lower-paying than what men received. Men, moreover, controlled the outgrower plots of oil palm while women saw their land rights reversed, lost income-generating activities, and were subject to a greater work burden. Nevertheless, agricultural plantations do absorb more labour than the IT and real estate economy driving India's SEZs, creating a better chance that dispossessed women will be exploited rather than simply marginalized.

We also saw, however, that dispossession created different changes in the household division of labour for women of different classes and castes. This was particularly clear in our India cases, in which we saw a marked divergence between outcomes for upper- and lower-caste/class women. While dispossession of agricultural land prompted upper-caste men to further confine women to the home (*purdah*), lower-caste women were often proletarianized and forced to find work, even if the projects themselves could not employ them. This underscores the importance of examining how class, caste and gender intersect in shaping the outcomes of land dispossession. Neither 'peasants' nor 'women' are homogeneous categories, and it is imperative to understand how the process of dispossession refracts through the specific class and gender relations of different agrarian milieus.

The evidence of these case studies does, however, suggest one conclusion about land dispossession and the gender division of labour. While it may be the case that decent-paying and organized work can have positive effects on women's position within the household (Kabeer, 1994, pp152–153), none of the forms of accumulation examined here made such work available. This may reflect not only gendered exclusions, but the structural limitations of late industrialization in large parts of the global South (cf. Bernstein, 2004, p204; Razavi, 2009, p215; Li, 2011). But regardless of whether women's labour was marginalized or increasingly exploited after dispossession, in none of our cases was women's wellbeing and social position improved by the 'development projects' for which they gave their land. Indeed, the diverse patriarchal social relations that structure women's work within and outside the household were arguably strengthened in each case. This suggests that the implications of land grabs for the gendered division of labour should be at the centre of contemporary debates.

Implications: The gendered politics and policies of dispossession

What political and policy conclusions should we draw from these findings? First, while women fared particularly poorly in all cases of dispossession analysed here, it is important to recognize that the consequences were also typically poor for men. Only in the Gambia case, and to a lesser extent the Indonesian case, did a majority of men accrue significant benefits from the projects that dispossessed their land. The answer, then, cannot be simply to make dispossession gender-equal, which would amount to equalizing proletarianization and impoverishment. While some policy analysts suggest that resettlement and rehabilitation provisions can prevent impoverishment (Cernea and Mathur, 2008), the cases analysed here provided little evidence of that possibility – especially among the poor and marginalized. This suggests that, in the common formulation of 'development-induced displacement', it is the first term that needs further interrogation.

Since the English enclosures, governments have justified the forcible dispossession of rural producers as serving the public or national good; in the past century this has been expressed through the language of development. But development is a political and not a technical concept, and the utilitarian calculations typically used to justify dispossession for large-scale capital projects beg the question of rights and distributional justice (cf. Dwivedi, 2006). Who determines what development is, and who gets to use the state to redistribute society's resources? These are questions that the opponents of enclosure, the Mandinka women, anti-dam movements, and the protagonists of today's 'land wars' have all raised in their own ways. Asking these questions only takes on greater urgency in the neoliberal era, as states increasingly dispossess land for the use of private corporations in the name of the 'public good'. This study thus points to the need for maintaining narrow and democratically determined definitions of the 'public good', limiting forcible acquisition to public projects with widespread benefits to poor households and to women within those households, and making 'prior and informed consent' a prerequisite for private projects that require land. It goes without saying that such consent should be obtained by all members of affected populations (including those without formal land rights) and not simply 'household heads': this would also help to ensure that only those projects from which women can expect to benefit would move forward.

Although forcible land dispossession would decrease under a more rigorous determination of the public interest, there is still a pressing need to make national compensation and resettlement and rehabilitation policies gender-equal (Thukral, 1996; Mehta, 2009b). Resettlement and rehabilitation should be used as an opportunity to correct women's lack of land rights where they do not exist, and should protect them where they do. This can be accomplished simply by giving women joint and preferably independent rights in any land or plots allocated as compensation. Other forms of compensation – whether cash or jobs – must also be distributed to women on an equal or preferential basis. Probably the best possible outcome of dispossession for women would be to receive secure, good-paying, formal sector jobs. While this may be utopian in the context of neoliberal growth trajectories, resettlement and rehabilitation policies should at least ensure the jobs that do exist are distributed fairly.

These changes will have to be achieved through political struggle at the national level. Even if multi-lateral lending agencies were not losing relevance to private capital in financing land-consuming projects, the dreadful track record of institutions such as the World Bank in supporting projects opposed by local communities, and in utterly failing to ensure adequate resettlement and rehabilitation of displaced populations, disqualifies them as a force for change. Proposals such as voluntary international guidelines to 'govern' land grabs (FAO et al, 2010) – euphemistically called transnational agricultural investments – are also misplaced on at least three levels. First, they are of limited relevance since they are intended to apply only to cases of foreign investment in farmland – neglecting both other kinds of land grabs and those financed domestically. Second, and more importantly, 'voluntary guidelines' beg the fundamental question of who gets to decide whether people are dispossessed for a given project, and promise little more than involuntary dispossession with gestural corporate social responsibility. Third, to give rural women the power to make decisions about the disposition of their land, and to ensure they are fairly compensated when they are dispossessed, requires challenging the interests of corporations, states and, to some extent, men in general. To think that such a powerful nexus of interests could be checked by 'voluntary' guidelines is at best naïve.

With bleak prospects for 'reform from above', we should instead look to 'pressure from below', and particularly the collective organization of rural people. Such organization is not difficult to find as anti-dispossession struggles are now proliferating across many countries of the global South. Women have often been in the forefront of such movements, putting themselves at great personal risk to defend their land and homes. It is undoubtedly the case that patriarchal social relations pervade such movements, and that women may often be used for protests and encounters while being excluded from negotiations and strategic discussions (Campbell, 1996). But there are also many cases of women taking leadership roles in anti-dispossession struggles. Where this is not the case, feminist groups can play an important role in pushing anti-dispossession movements to become more gender-equal in their organization and demands. It is also true that securing land rights for women is no panacea (Jackson, 2003; Razavi, 2003), and that stopping dispossession will not in itself transform the patriarchal social relations that structure the everyday lives of rural women. But the cases above suggest that forced dispossession rarely makes things better for rural women, and in most cases makes things worse. Defensive struggles against dispossession may, consequently, be a pre-condition for more offensive struggles to generate pathways of gender-equal development and social change.

Notes

1   I use 'land grab' and 'land dispossession' synonymously, and restrict both to instances in which *states* make people leave their land *involuntarily*. This definition includes instances in which people are dispossessed of landed resources they own or use irrespective of whether the land is under formal or informal tenure (including customary land and

commons). It interprets any land acquisition undertaken without prior and informed consent to be involuntary, whether or not the dispossessed receive compensation. It excludes, however, incidences in which land is voluntarily sold on the market. Admittedly, the line between voluntary sale and coercion is not always clear; sales can be forced not only by states but also by decentralized or 'intimate' actors in ways that fall beneath the radar (Hall et al, 2011; Hall, 2012; Li, 2014). While blurred at their edges, these categories are nevertheless important for distinguishing between the large number of cases that clearly involve coercive acquisition (often exercised through *eminent domain*) and those that involve willing sellers. This definition corresponds with how most policy-makers and scholars have historically operationalized 'development-induced displacement'.

2 While most attempts to measure the scale of land grabs have focused on agricultural projects that are primarily located in Africa and Latin America, it is probably in India and China, which together contain 45 per cent of the world's rural population (World Bank, 2012b), that the majority of the world's land dispossession is occurring. While we should also treat these numbers with caution, scholars estimate that in China between 50 and 66 million people were dispossessed for various kinds of development projects between 1980 and 2002 (Hsing, 2010), and that over 43 per cent of Chinese villages have experienced compulsory land acquisition since the late 1990s (Landesa Rural Development Institute, 2011). In India, the most comprehensive study has estimated that 60 million people have been displaced from their land for development projects since independence, and that the rate of displacement has increased post-liberalization (Fernandes, 2008).

3 For the best analysis of the financial underpinnings of the recent farmland rush, see Fairbairn (2014).

4 From which derived the name for the seventeenth-century 'Levellers'.

5 For China and India alone, the estimates are 10 million and 16–28 million, respectively (WCD, 2000). These figures include only those displaced by reservoirs, not the millions more displaced by downstream effects, canals and related infrastructure.

6 Those dispossessed for the Nagarjuna Sagar Dam in the 1950s, for example, were offered Rs100–150 (about US$2–3 at the time) per acre (Singh and Samantray, 1992, p69). As late as the 1990s, oustees of the Tehri Dam in what is now Uttarakhand were offered Rs12,000 (US$274 at the time) per acre of *irrigated* land (Kedia, 2008, p121).

7 Men later admitted to Mehta that, had they consulted women, they probably would have identified the problems with the resettlement sites and rejected them.

8 Remarkably, however, his niece left home and joined the movement as a full-time activist.

9 In the case of dams in Africa, Braun's (2011) research shows the ways in dam construction sites are themselves characterized by discriminatory employment that marginalizes women in the informal economy.

10 For a particularly brutal (but not isolated) case of how World Bank-funded dams intersected with reactionary dictatorships supported by the US government during the Cold War, see the study of Guatemala's Chixoy Dam by Barbara Rose Johnston (2005).

11 Which means that they had received inside information about the SEZ's location, which would allow them to buy up cheap farmland that would dramatically appreciate the instant the SEZ was announced.

6

TRANSFORMATIVE INVESTMENTS FOR GENDER-EQUAL SUSTAINABLE DEVELOPMENT

Isha Ray

Introduction

This chapter develops an agenda for sustainable development, with particular emphasis on local priorities, poverty alleviation and gender equality. Sustainable development can take many different pathways, even within the dominant three-pillar paradigm (economy–environment–society) of sustainability (see Leach et al, Chapter 1 in this book). Following Sen, I adopt a capabilities-enhancement view of development, and argue that any sustainable development pathway must include an explicit commitment to gender equality in its conceptualization and implementation. To this end, I highlight four 'mundane' sectors in which socially transformative investments should be substantially increased: domestic water, safe sanitation, clean(er)-burning cookstoves, and domestic electricity services. These basic services are still thin for the lowest-income quintiles in low-income countries, and there is overwhelming evidence that their absence disproportionately affects women and girls. Inadequate access to these services prevents the realization of human rights for all, of gender equality and of environmental integrity.

I draw on the vast literature on access to basic services for the poor to argue that *universal and gender-equal access* cannot be guaranteed primarily by voluntary mechanisms (i.e. through market forces or through the non-governmental sector). Universal access needs low-cost innovations, certainly; it also needs a renewal of the civic contract between the state and its citizens; it requires strong public action for the protection of citizens and their environmental resources. As we move into the post-2015 era, promoting public action towards gender-equal development should become a priority for the 'sustainable development' agenda. I conclude with some thoughts on capabilities and the bodies they inhabit. Gender-equal sustainable development cannot be treated as a disembodied concept: an explicit recognition of the biological and the social body is necessary when setting targets and indicators towards water, sanitation and energy services goals.

Sustainable development with gender equality

'Sustainable development' was a disarmingly value- and gender-neutral concept from its very inception. The Brundtland Report *Our Common Future* (Brundtland, 1987), stating that sustainable development was development that met the needs of the current generation while not jeopardizing the needs of future generations, established the standard definition of the term. The report cemented the three-pillar approach to sustainability, in which sustainability has environmental, economic and social components. Because it had little to say on the tensions and trade-offs among these three dimensions, the Brundtland Report provided no guidance on social or regional priorities for sustainability, or on the difficulties of deciding which development initiatives were or were not sustainable, or what was to be sustained and for whom (Leach et al, Chapter 1 in this book).

The global overtones of the Brundtland Report are reflected in the current concepts of 'planetary boundaries' (Rockström et al, 2009b; UNEP, 2013b) and 'planetary stability' (Griggs et al, 2013) as frameworks for sustainable development. These frameworks rightly place the crisis of climate change front and centre, but they remain high-level. As a result, everyone is generally in favour of sustainable development, but the distribution of costs, benefits, risks and uncertainties inherent in different realizations of sustainability remains highly contentious.

In the spirit of this book, this chapter follows a more normative, more explicitly value-laden understanding of sustainable development. Economic development has followed not one grand trajectory, but multiple pathways, in diverse historical conditions (Hart, 1998). Sustainable development can also follow multiple pathways (Sneddon et al, 2006; Leach et al, 2010). Each sustainable development pathway can be assessed with respect to different criteria, such as poverty alleviation, environmental integrity, or distribution of risks. Some economically attractive pathways to development may be unsustainable altogether, from the perspective of resource use relative to availability, or of greenhouse gas emissions. Some ecologically sustainable pathways may be less equitable than others with respect to the alignment of risks, costs and benefits. In short, sustainable development means making choices from amongst a range of desirable objectives.

Defining and assessing sustainable development within a multiple-pathways framework makes development outcomes, and conflicts and complementarities amongst these outcomes, transparent. Specific societal investments, for example in energy or health or transportation, can be seen as economic and political choices along development pathways, as opposed to appearing as inevitable or natural solutions to sustainability challenges. This approach makes explicit the conceptual and political differences *within* the idea of sustainability.

As the Millennium Development Goals (MDG) era comes to an end, laudable progress has been made along many of its targets and indicators, especially those concerning human health (Sachs, 2013; UN, 2013b). But even when specific targets were achieved, many were not achieved in a gender-equal (or spatially even) manner (UN Women, 2013). This is to be expected within a multiple-pathways framework: target achievement by one metric might not lead to achievement by other desirable metrics. But gender equality is necessary for overall economic development (Seguino, 2000; Kabeer and Natali, 2013), and is fundamental to the fulfilment of universal human rights (CEDAW, 1979; Elson and Balakrishnan, 2012). The MDGs have been sharply critiqued for losing sight of the human rights framework that gave rise to them in the first place (Fukuda-Parr et al, 2013; Sen and Mukherjee, 2013). This chapter argues that the post-2015 sustainable development agenda, and the interventions and investments that are carried out in its name, should be firmly embedded within a gender equality-enhancing pathway.

We are interested here in substantive, as opposed to merely formal, gender equality. Whether gender equality should mean equality of opportunity or equality of outcome is an ongoing debate, but, in practice, the two are difficult to disentangle (UNDP, 2013b, p30; also World Bank, 2012c, p4). A sustainable development pathway with gender equality would improve women's (and girls') access to new opportunities and new possibilities. It would enhance women's capabilities, so they are more able 'to choose the lives they have reason to value' (Sen, 1999, p18). In Sen's framework, capability is not merely a skill set; it is akin to *freedom*, meaning the freedom and ability to lead a particular life as opposed to another. Capabilities prioritize choice and agency over wellbeing per se (Nussbaum, 2000; Vizard et al, 2011); they are thus only indirectly linked to specific bundles of goods and services.

A gender-equal development pathway can be assessed by the extent to which the relative capabilities of women, especially those of poor women and girls, can be (or have been) advanced as a result of societal investments. I use the term 'investment' to denote financial, social and institutional efforts aimed at a future stream of benefits – not exclusively monetary – for humans and their environments. Many investment domains could be socially transformative, as long as investments commensurate with the scale of the development challenge are made. But for the goal of gender equality we must ask: which domains affect women, especially poorer women, the most, relative to men? Here the gender, environment and development literature has repeatedly shown that the physical and emotional burdens of accessing daily necessities such as food, fuel and water (e.g. Cecelski, 1984; Agarwal, 1997; Ray, 2007), and the expectations of unpaid care work from girls and women (e.g. Elson and Çağatay, 2000; Razavi, 2007), reduce women's capabilities relative to their own potential and relative to those of men. This chapter therefore highlights four priorities for significantly higher investments in the service of sustainable development: domestic water services, sanitation, clean(er) cookstoves, and basic electricity services. The focus on these four sectors does not, of course, deny the importance of other services (such as education, health care and food security) that are necessary for gender equality.

These four domains offer strong transformative potential through which women's and girls' capabilities may be significantly expanded in low-income countries. All four have improved (meaning efficient, lower-carbon, lower-cost, or all of these) technological possibilities at their core, but cannot effectively go to scale based on technological interventions alone. As is the case with all technologies, interventions in these domains are at once technical, social and thoroughly gendered – so we cannot assume that improved technologies for use by women will automatically improve women's lives (see Bray, 2007). All four domains are directly connected to development and environment, and can be invested in along environmentally sustainable *or* unsustainable pathways. And all four are 'mundane' investments (cf. Kammen and Dove, 1997), in that they are concerned with everyday living and dying, they are the backbone of a decent quality of life, and yet they remain significantly under-invested in, relative to the global need.

The rest of this chapter is divided into five sections. First, I turn to the question of how we would assess (ex ante) or evaluate (ex post) a sustainable development intervention through the lens of gender equality. This section draws on the literature on the operationalization of capabilities and of wellbeing, and also argues that the gendered distribution of risks from societal investments is an important assessment criterion. I then discuss each of the four domains, focusing on technological and social approaches towards providing basic levels of service. The political and institutional barriers to services for low-income populations at scale, and in particular for ensuring gender equality or environmental integrity in their provision, are all too well known. The next section does not repeat the litany of barriers, but highlights the institutional contexts that may enable sustainable development pathways. It discusses the continued relevance of contractual theories of the state, and the public–private–civil alliances that are needed to support social investments at the necessary scales. The chapter concludes with some thoughts on female bodies, human capabilities and their implications for the goals and targets of sustainable development.

Assessing investments for gender equality

If we are going to promote some investments over others, we must have criteria for estimating their impacts before investing, or evaluating their impacts after the investment has been made. For gender equality, investments in the name of sustainable development should be assessed with *women's capability enhancement* as a necessary (though, of course, not sufficient) component of sustainability. No development pathway can be considered sustainable if it decreases female capabilities. Thus if an investment in a low-carbon and efficient energy technology intended for the poor inadvertently increases unpaid care work for women, or undermines their ability to earn or to innovate (Agarwal, 1983; Cecelski, 2000), then it is not on a sustainable development pathway. This is not to deny the clear and urgent need to decarbonize the global economy, but to argue that an emissions-centric or planetary boundaries view of sustainability is inadequate without a gender equality perspective.

There are clearly overlaps between human capabilities and real incomes (Evans, 2002). The simplest proxy for capability enhancement for the poor is the quintile axiom proposed by Basu (2006). Basu argues that to capture poverty and inequality, we should rank countries not by their overall GDP per capita, but by the per capita income of the lowest quintile. He argues that the quintile measure will track the broader indicators in the UN's Human Development Index,[1] such as life expectancy and gender-bias indicators, better than the traditional GDP per capita can do. The quintile axiom is easy to use and is explicitly oriented towards substantive equality. It emphasizes within-country inequality in addition to cross-country inequality. It could be used to assess the outcomes of specific investments in water, sanitation, energy or any other sector, at any scale from the regional to the local. But this one-dimensional proxy implicitly assumes that investments have the same impacts on poor women as they do on poor men, and we have already seen that this assumption is not justified. Capability enhancement is inherently a multi-indicator phenomenon (Nussbaum, 2000).

A better way to measure women's capability enhancement, while keeping the measure practical and parsimonious, is to choose a subset of indicators from those that already go into the UN's Human Development Index (HDI). The HDI is derived from Sen's influential capabilities and functionings approach (Sen, 1985; Ul-Haq, 1995), and can be seen as a way to operationalize capabilities. The HDI as a whole is very broad; socio-economic circumstances and local priorities will dictate which indicators of capability are most relevant, and for which domains, in specific cases. For instance, for investments in sanitation, we can imagine that an education indicator, such as secondary school enrolment for girls, might be a good metric of evaluation; field experience from Asia and Africa has shown that poor sanitary facilities keep girls out of school (UNDP, 2006). For investments in clean cooking energy for the poor, under-five infant mortality may be a better metric; indoor air pollution from burning solid fuels causes premature deaths throughout the global South (WHO, 2014b). The indicators of interest should be measured for the overall population, but also for the lowest quintiles, in the spirit of the quintile axiom. They can be measured at any scale, for the whole state or for a single community.

For water, sanitation, and energy services, two useful capability indicators for assessing whether investments are on a gender-equal pathway might be: the *female under-five mortality rate*; and the ratio of *female to male enrolment in secondary education*. These indicators are especially relevant for low-income communities or countries. Under-five mortality ratios, secondary school enrolment and anthropocentric measures of nutrition are themselves important capabilities, but are also the gateway to many other capabilities and functionings (Saith and Harris-White, 1999). Of these, anthropometric measures of nutrition are more difficult to measure, whereas child mortality and school enrolment data, imperfect though they may be (see Unterhalter, 2013), are routinely collected in a large number of countries.

The enrolment measure is the female-to-male ratio as this is a direct indicator of parity; however, the simple rate of female participation in secondary education is also a plausible capability metric. Secondary school enrolment is preferred to primary school enrolment: the literature has convincingly shown that more years in school are associated with girls being able to better articulate their rights and to better protect themselves and their families against illness (e.g. Unterhalter, 2013). The under-five female mortality indicator is not a female-to-male ratio, as child mortality by gender tends in the same direction in a given country (though not always). As with most HDI components, both measures can be operationalized at the regional, state and community levels, as well as stratified by income quintile, depending upon the scale of the investment.

Two is a small number of indicators for the purpose of measuring gender equality across four substantive domains. These criteria can be interpreted as the minimum constituents of a sustainable pathway; actual investments may be assessed through additional environmental and economic criteria. However, the larger the number of outcome indicators, the more complex it is to attribute a causal connection between investment and outcome. Fukuda-Parr (2003) contends that parsimony and simplicity are essential for indicators to gain policy traction. Indeed, just one of the HDI indicators may be an adequate gender-equality assessment criterion in some contexts, depending on the pre-investment baseline conditions. A more fundamental critique could be that choosing an indicator such as secondary school enrolment assumes that the quality of a woman's life and aspirations has the same components as the quality of a man's life and aspirations (see Nussbaum and Sen, 1993). I follow the position that universal accounts of human capabilities are indeed defensible (Annas, 1993), because the capabilities framework emphasizes choice and agency (Nussbaum, 2003; Vizard et al, 2011), and does not insist upon specific outcomes such as paid employment.

This chapter proposes one additional indicator for gender-equal development: the reduction of unpaid care work. Every economy is dependent on 'non-market based social reproduction' (Razavi, 2007, p5), or the unpaid care economy, comprising cooking, cleaning, caring for children, elders or the sick, and community-based volunteering. In low-income economies, care work also includes fetching water and fuel, often over long distances. This sort of unpaid work is heavily feminized, and it may go up or go down as a result of ostensibly sustainable interventions. Interventions may even be counted as sustainable *because* they rely on uncounted work; much-lauded programmes such as rainwater harvesting and community-based natural resource management have been critiqued on this ground (e.g. Jackson, 1993; Kabeer, 2005). Reduction of unpaid care work, particularly in low-resource households, is essential if women and girls are to develop the full range of their capabilities. This indicator is not a component of the HDI, but time-use data for several countries exist (Budlender, 2010; Esquivel, 2013). Though this criterion may lead to additional burdens of data collection on developing countries, time use and care work data need to be systematically collected to monitor improvements in gender equality. Country-level data collection should strive to include at least the minimum set of gender indicators proposed by the UN Statistical Commission.[2]

Innovative technologies and programmes have a range of attendant risks as well as a range of intended outcomes, and these risks are at least as important as future gains. For every investment in sustainable development, therefore, we must ask: What kinds of risks are we taking when we promote certain techno-social interventions, and who comprises the 'we'? Here I draw on the 'rights and risks' approach of the World Commission on Dams (WCD, 2000) – this work has been conceptually valuable in laying out a framework for responsible public investments, but it has been neglected in policy and practice. The Commission clearly distinguished risk-bearers from rights-bearers, arguing that risk-bearers often do not have rights with respect to investment decisions that are commensurate with their risks. The report presented examples of large dam projects, in which those without legal land title, such as poor women, the landless, or indigenous communities, were given no compensation for lost land and livelihoods in the submergence areas (WCD, 2000, pp104–105). In other words: when projecting the benefits of a specific intervention in any of our suggested domains, we must also make transparent who has the right to make investment choices, who is assessing the risks of these choices, and on whose behalf they are assessing them.

The WCD members concluded that the differential risk profiles and perceptions within and across communities call for public discussions with all the affected and the interested parties, recognizing that the two may not be the same, and acknowledging that unforeseen consequences are always possible. The broader risk literature on technology and social acceptance has indeed shown that risk cannot be understood simply as a probability distribution of known outcomes. People bring to their risk assessments not only the attributes of a technology, but also their cultural and political frames of reference (Rayner, 1984), their perspectives on 'how fair is safe enough' (Rayner and Cantor, 1987), and their own uncertainties and fears. These subjectively different perceptions are not a matter of better communication of technical risks (see Fischhoff, 1995); they require analysis of the multiple criteria by which the risks are perceived (Stirling, 2011). For many investments, risks, not just outcomes, will vary with the gender and class of the risk-bearer. Therefore assessing risks, with an emphasis on risk distribution, risk perception, and the voluntary or involuntary nature of the risks, is especially important for large-scale and irreversible investments.

Categories of investment for gender-equal sustainable development

I now turn to the four selected categories of investment for social transformation. These investments are reliable and affordable domestic water supplies, clean and dignified sanitation, cleaner cookstoves, and basic electricity services. All of these are 'basic' categories in two senses: they serve fundamental human needs regardless of socio-cultural characteristics, and their absence or inadequacy precludes the attainment of many other capabilities as well as human rights. They are the determinants of health and livelihood for the majority of women, whatever their class, and are the backbone of what has been called the 'environmentalism of the poor' (Guha, 2000; Martínez-Alier, 2002).

All four categories of investment have spillover effects that benefit users as well as non-users (e.g. safe sanitation for women increases overall community health, and efficient cookstoves improve household health as well as household budgets). Inadequate and unsafe water, unsafe sanitation, and indoor air pollution from solid fuels account for over 11 per cent of deaths in low-income countries (WHO, 2009). All four investments have a technological core, but investing in technology alone without a supporting social ecosystem cannot take them to a transformative scale. All four are merit goods, meaning that the social benefits from their provision are likely to exceed the private benefits. This means that all are candidates for investments in the public domain, though not exclusively so, and that markets alone will not deliver them at scale. All four categories are possible to invest in along *un*sustainable pathways that may not promote gender equality or environmental integrity, or along more sustainable and equitable pathways through which capabilities may be improved. For example, urban sanitation investments that provide a low toilet-to-user ratio preclude women from using them, because they cannot stand in long morning lines or walk to distant facilities at night. On the other hand, well designed cookstove interventions simultaneously improve household air pollution and women's health, especially if they replace coal-burning stoves.

The selected categories are 'mundane' investments, rather than technological innovations supposedly at the cutting edge of development practice (see Kammen and Dove, 1997). Absolutely everybody, whatever their age or gender or class, needs to drink water, go to the bathroom, breathe, eat cooked food, and see in the dark. It is mundane investments that touch everyone every day and expand everyday human capabilities. In addition, mundane quality-of-life innovations can occur anywhere, in low-income as well as high-income settings (e.g. Brokensha et al, 1980; Gadgil et al, 1993) they can be appropriated and modified by users, male as well as female, in line with local needs (e.g. Cecelski, 2000; de Laet and Mol, 2000); and they can occur at any scale, from national policy directives with centralized infrastructures, to decentralized community-based implementation. Furthermore, if an innovative technology or financing mechanism finds a local market, it can revitalize rural and urban economies. Mundane investments are, in this sense, potentially transformative with respect to local development processes as well as development outcomes.

Finally, in focusing on these categories, we cannot assume that more toilets or more stoves will inevitably lead to gender equality, or that these are the only worthwhile investments for sustainable development. This chapter emphasizes those investment categories that are directly linked to human and environmental health, and that can directly enhance the capabilities of poorer women, because they are disproportionately burdened with poor health and unpaid work in their absence (Cleaver, 1998; Antonopoulos and Hirway, 2010; Anenberg et al, 2013; Corbett and Mehta, 2013).

Water

A woman carrying water on her head or on her hips with the scorching sun in the background is the iconic image of development unmet. Well into the twenty-first century, close to a billion people live without access to improved water sources, defined by the WHO as water from a protected well, protected spring, collected rainwater or tap. Diarrhoea from inadequate water, sanitation and hygiene claims the lives of 1000 children a day (WHO, 2014a), and 140 million people are exposed to high levels of arsenic in their water (Ravenscroft et al, 2009). Many innovative approaches have been developed towards improving drinking water quality for the poor (Amrose et al, forthcoming), but I focus here on adequate, reliable and affordable quantities of water for domestic (i.e. productive and reproductive) use. For most poor women, a source of domestic water that is reliably and conveniently accessed is the first criterion of sustainable development.

Social expectations dictate that women and girls are the primary water carriers for their families; in over 70 per cent of households where water has to be fetched, women and girls do the fetching (WHO/UNICEF, 2013). Where rural water sources are distant, women may walk up to two hours to fetch water. Where urban water is from shared standpipes, they may wait in line for over an hour (see Ray, 2007 and references therein). The further the source of water, the less water the household uses (Howard and Bartram, 2003), and the more child health is likely to suffer (Pickering and Davis, 2012). Case studies from around the world show that water-related 'time poverty' translates to lost income for women and lost schooling for girls (UNDP, 2006). In addition, high levels of mental stress have been reported when water rights are insecure (Wutich and Ragsdale, 2008). All this fetching and carrying, usually from a young age, causes cumulative wear-and-tear to the neck, spine, back and knees; in effect, a woman's body becomes part of the water-delivery infrastructure, doing the work of pipes.

Global water access data conceal the many inequities in water access – all across the developing world, urban access to improved water is higher than rural access; core urban access is higher than peri-urban access; and access at the top quintile is much higher than at the bottom quintile (WHO/UNICEF, 2013). These trends are commensurate with the Human Development Report of 2006, which stated unequivocally that lack of access to water stemmed from inequality and lack of rights, and not from some generalized notion of 'scarcity' (UNDP, 2006). Even in urban areas, where the access percentages are usually higher, the reliability, quality and affordability of water for the lowest quintiles are all insecure (Ahlers et al, 2014). Continuous piped water has the greatest health benefits and lowest drudgery costs, but is technologically and financially viable only for densely populated communities. Piped water with a sewer connection for the developing world would have required US$136 billion a year (in 2007 US$) from 2000 to 2015 (just) to meet the MDGs; meeting the MDG targets using cheaper supply technologies, including low-cost pipes, roof-water capture, and wells, and without adding point-of-use treatments to improve water quality, was estimated at under US$2 billion annually (Hutton et al, 2007). According to the Joint Monitoring Program,[3] the UNICEF/WHO effort that is the source of global water and sanitation data, the water access target for the MDGs was met ahead of schedule. But this achievement falls short of universal access, falls short of water security, has been achieved largely through urban rather than rural access, and is quite compatible with continued time poverty for women, high costs of access, and other indicators of what has been called 'water poverty' (Sullivan et al, 2003).

In rural areas, modest quantities of water are needed not just for consumption, but for livelihoods. Zwarteveen (1997) argues that an exclusive focus on gender in the drinking water sector overlooks the increasing number of woman-headed farm households, and emphasizes the role of women as mothers rather than as producers as well. Rural systems that are 'multiple-use' – meaning that they provide water for domestic purposes, small plots and a few cattle or goats – are more likely to meet the range of basic needs that rural women must meet. They have a higher potential for cost recovery as they help to generate income (van Koppen et al, 2006), especially if credit is available. A drinking water-focused intervention, by contrast, such as a borehole with a pump, would have a *lifecycle* per person per year cost of US$20–60 (WASHCost, 2011), with little chance of cost recovery from its low-income user base. From a user-centred perspective, investing in water services that go beyond just drinking water will be more capability-enhancing; it may also enable partial cost recovery, which donors and governments increasingly demand.

In addition to large storage-based water projects, decentralized water-augmenting technologies exist, and have collectively reached many millions. Many would count as 'multiple use' in today's terminology. Some of these are modernized traditional approaches, often rural and community-based. The best known example is rainwater harvesting, which is now being taken to scale by communities in partnership with several governments (e.g. Bruins et al, 1986; Raju and Shah, 2000). Another is the treadle pump, a foot-powered pump that extracts shallow water for domestic purposes as well as for small farms and kitchen plots (Shah et al, 2000; Mangisoni, 2008). The revival (or development) of these techniques is owed partly to recurrent droughts, and partly to counter the narrative that large dams are the only channel to water security (Gleick, 2000). A wide range of barriers – such as financial and political marginalization, and unsustainable implementation practices – has prevented these approaches from reaching truly transformative scales (see Sovacool, 2012). This is an active area of action research around the world, and one that has (mostly) learned that even the most promising technology can only go to scale in a supportive social, ecological and financial ecosystem.

A final word on water and women is in order. Failed water projects in rural and urban areas are legion, and a frequently cited reason for failure is that women's voices and views were ignored before and during these efforts. Women are the water users, and therefore the ones with knowledge and stakes (van Wijk-Sijbesma, 1998; IBLF, 2004). However, it is naïve to suggest that women's 'participation' is either necessary or sufficient for gender-equality or sustainability of outcomes (Prokopy, 2004; Meinzen-Dick et al, 2014). Women's leadership, when real rather than tokenistic, has indeed been associated with more cost-effective water delivery, more households with access to water, and less corruption in water financing (e.g. Chattopadhyay and Duflo, 2004; Fisher, 2006). But, if mandated as part of a water investment, participation could as easily increase women's workload as their wellbeing (Agarwal, 1998; Cleaver, 1998; Ray, 2007). Everywhere water is another word for life; its reliable and affordable access for poor women is one of the highest priorities of development. But conflating women's participation in water investments with a sustainable water supply risks becoming another avenue to more (unpaid) work for women. Such a path cannot be considered 'sustainable'.

Sanitation

We now turn to sanitation. Everybody goes to the toilet. There is little choice about when to go, and often little choice about where to go. 'Improved' sanitation facilities, according to the WHO and UNICEF,[4] include pour flush or flush toilets into a sewer, ventilated improved pits, and composting toilets, through the use of which pathogenic waste is likely to be removed from human contact. Many different toilet designs, from the simple pit with slab, to more complex but locally producible dry ('ecological') toilets, exist for low-income households (Nelson and Murray, 2008), and sustainable toilet design is an active research area. But over 2.5 billion people still have no access to an improved latrine; of these, 700 million use shared facilities, which the Joint Monitoring Program does not consider 'improved'. Open defecation rates have gone down in all developing countries (WHO/ UNICEF, 2013), but it remains the norm for 1 billion people, 90 per cent of whom are rural residents.

Open defecation is a severe public health as well as environmental health hazard, causing widespread diarrhoeal disease and water pollution (Black and Fawcett, 2008). Relative to its previous neglect in comparison with drinking water programmes, sanitation programmes are on the rise, promoted vigorously by health researchers (e.g. Hutton and Bartram, 2008; Clasen et al, 2010), governments in concert with local communities, and international non-profits. It is still the case that for every US$4 spent on water and sanitation programmes, sanitation receives about US$1 (GLAAS, 2012). But a sea change has occurred in recent years with respect to recognizing sanitation as indispensable for 'health, dignity and development' (Lenton et al, 2005).

This chapter argues that basic sanitation that is clean, affordable to construct and to use, and safe to access is a particularly transformative investment for women's (and girls') capabilities. Women need more privacy than men when they use the facilities because of social norms, need more time in the toilet than men do (because they must sit or squat), need physical safety when they access outside toilets, and may need multiple daily visits during their menstrual period. For these reasons, sanitation access may be more germane to gender equality and dignity than even access to water. As with water access, sanitation access in low-income countries is highly unequal: urban coverage rates are significantly higher than rural coverage rates (WHO/UNICEF, 2013), and within rural regions access is lowest for communities far away from main roads (WHO/UNICEF, 2010). Overall, it is estimated that children in the poorest quintiles of low-income countries (in South Asia and sub-Saharan Africa) suffer 20 times the health burden of inadequate sanitation as children in the top quintiles within those same countries (Rheingans et al, 2012).

New directions in sanitation research and promotion emphasize extending access through innovative new technologies, encouraging toilet uptake, improving markets for sanitation products, and encouraging a larger role for non-state actors (Jenkins and Curtis, 2005; Black and Fawcett, 2008). Significant donor efforts (e.g. the Gates Foundation's 'Reinvent the Toilet' initiative) and government-community efforts (e.g. community-led total sanitation, CLTS, campaigns) are now focused on sustainable sanitation specifically for the poor. CLTS emphasizes rural sanitation, as this reflects both its origins (Kar and Chambers, 2008) as well as where open defecation mostly occurs. But there are also city-based examples of urban sanitation with community leadership at their centre, using sanitation as a community-building as well as toilet-building exercise, from South Asia, Central America and southern Africa (Satterthwaite et al, 2005). These methods, once pilot projects but now becoming mainstream, represent a major change from previous supply-driven and facilities-driven methods. It is still unclear if these demand-driven means can be sustained over time in multiple settings, or if they can adapt to the political economies of different countries well enough to go to scale (e.g. Harris et al, 2011 on Vietnam). CLTS in particular has been praised as a revolutionary, subsidy-free approach to community mobilization for sanitation, but mutual 'encouragement' (Chambers in *The Guardian*, 2011) has been critiqued for morphing into 'community-backed shaming' (Chatterjee in *The Guardian*, 2011).

The definition of improved (or reinvented) latrines in the leading efforts remains hardware- and uptake-oriented, saying little about wastewater treatment before disposal, or about sludge removal if the toilet is a dry toilet. Untreated sewage and faecal sludge from overflowing pits are highly polluting and unsustainable. Baum et al (2013) estimate that if improved sanitation required sewage to be treated before its discharge into the environment, 4.1 billion rather than 2.5 billion would be unserved. Sustainable toilet design and programmes have to include not only the reduction of open defecation, but also the removal of pathogenic waste and its disposal or re-use (Nelson and Murray, 2008). Financing sanitation at the required scale remains a global-scale challenge, with great uncertainty in existing cost estimates and almost no data on spending by private households. Hutton and Bartram (2008) estimated that about US$36 billion (2008 US$) annually would need to be invested for ten years to meet (and maintain) the MDG target of reducing by half the population without access to improved sanitation. If primary treatment of toilet waste and long-term maintenance costs are added, the cost of 'sustainable sanitation' can be 5 to 20 times the cost of building the latrine alone (WASHCost, 2011). Innovative social enterprises that safely convert human waste into reusable sludge or renewable energy, such as Sanergy,[5] are being piloted at the scale of urban slums, exploiting the cost recovery possibilities from productive re-use (see also Murray and Ray, 2010), but these efforts are still at the proof-of-concept or pilot stage.

The emphasis on eliminating open defecation is absolutely critical. But we have to ask: is this enough for sustainable or gender-equal sanitation? Clean and secure sanitation can enable girls' education, women's mobility and sexual security. But gender equality means that toilet programmes have to go well beyond defecation and disease management, and take equally seriously the requirements of dignity of access and menstrual hygiene management. Menstrual hygiene is so private that it has usually fallen through the cracks of national and international sanitation promotions (Bharadwaj and Patkar, 2004); it is only now being acknowledged as the critical programmatic gap as we move towards the post-2015 targets (WHO/UNICEF, 2013). Sanitation facilities and products that are safe and respect privacy enable girls to stay in school (e.g. Ali and Rizvi, 2010) and reduce their discomfort (and sometimes shame) during menstruation (McMahon et al, 2011). In short, men and women have very different sanitation needs, for biological and social reasons. Investments in this area have to be designed and implemented with these bodily needs and the social norms that surround them upfront and centre, and this means sanitation uptake programmes should not be focused on prevention of open defecation alone.

Cookstoves

The recently published *Resource Guide* from the Global Alliance for Clean Cookstoves (Hart and Smith, 2013) opens with a clear statement of the stoves and gender parity link: 'Often spending many hours per day searching for fuel and cooking over open flames emitting harmful smoke, women are disproportionately impacted by dirty and inefficient cooking practices and reliance on biomass for fuels.' Biomass-burning traditional cookstoves (i.e. using wood, charcoal, animal manure or crop residues), especially when used indoors, are the primary contributor to household air pollution (HAP). Globally HAP is responsible for over 4 million deaths (WHO, 2014b), and HAP and ambient air pollution jointly are now the leading global environmental health risk. In South Asia and China, solid-fuel cookstoves – biomass-based in India, but significantly coal-based in China – are the single largest contributor to HAP. The cumulative burdens from diseases, from black carbon and inhaled particulate matter, are manifest in respiratory infections, lung inflammation, low birth-weight and cardiac events (Fullerton et al, 2008).

It is still the norm for women to do the daily cooking for their families. It is a central part of the unpaid care economy. They and their children, especially younger ones who are with adult females all the time, therefore suffer disproportionately from 'the killer in the kitchen' (Bailis et al, 2009). The time spent in collecting fuelwood or charcoal, also a job mainly delegated to women, is onerous and sometimes dangerous, for the women and also for the children who must accompany them (Masud et al, 2007). In addition, rural households are often highly labour-constrained, especially during peak agricultural seasons, and the time that women spend collecting fuelwood has high opportunity costs (Dewees, 1989) – although empirical studies show wide variation on this front (see Cooke et al, 2008). Relative to water and sanitation, the data by country and by quintile on access to efficient cookstoves are rather sparse (Anenberg et al, 2013). In part, this is because cookstoves historically have not been a significant focus of public spending or routinely collected public data. The exception was China's massive and organized rural energy programme, the National Improved Stoves Program (NISP), which has since been discontinued, but which introduced 180 million improved stoves while it lasted (Sinton et al, 2004).

The health benefits from fewer diseases, and income benefits from saved fuel when households switch to cleaner-burning cookstoves, are important to communities overall. These investments, like those in water and sanitation, yield overall positive externalities well beyond gendered benefits. In South Asia and sub-Saharan Africa, for example, a large share of ambient (not just indoor) particulate matter is attributed to cooking with solid fuels (Zhou, 2011). Investing at scale in efficient solid-fuel stoves, especially in rural and peri-urban regions without liquefied petroleum gas (LPG) or natural gas for cooking, is simultaneously a gender-equal and a sustainable-pathway investment.

As with sanitation, there has been a welcome upsurge of attention to the need for clean(er) cookstoves in recent years. Despite this attention, these remain underinvested-in as public investments, as is generally the case with mundane technologies. First, the effects of cookstove interventions in the field have been widely varied – from no effect, to modest health improvements, to lower-than-anticipated improvements in indoor air pollution (Grieshop et al, 2011; Anenberg et al, 2013). The designs and combustion efficiencies of 'clean' cookstoves also vary widely, from those that include a chimney so that the smoke is pushed outdoors, to those that simply use less fuel but retain particulate pollution indoors. The income effects of efficient stoves are more likely to be consistently positive, as many improved stoves burn between 30 and 60 per cent less fuel than their unimproved counterparts; this is a significant saving for rural households that can spend nearly 10 per cent of their monthly income on energy (see e.g. Miah et al, 2009).

Second, producing cookstoves that women want to use, and marketing these to low-income families, has been hard. Most cookstove interventions, even when they report satisfaction with the stoves and use of the stoves, also report the continued use of the traditional stove for staple foods. In addition, there is anecdotal evidence that women are unwilling to give up the convenience of two stoves despite the benefits of consistently using the efficient one. This form of 'device stacking' makes it harder to see health impacts and also harder to sell new stoves (Ruiz-Mercado et al, 2011). In the cooking arena especially, men and women may value different aspects of clean stoves. It has been argued that women value stove aesthetics and smoke-free environments more than men, who are concerned about timely meals and the traditional taste of food (e.g. Cecelski, 2000). Such views are not necessarily in conflict, but they present marketing challenges. Though at-scale change remains elusive, encouraging stove uptake results have been reported by many NGOs, such as Practical Action and Potential Energy, working in Asia and Africa, and with women centrally involved in stove design, testing and social and conventional marketing (Hart and Smith, 2013).

The cookstove arena is now firmly enmeshed in the climate mitigation discourse. It is often asserted that with cleaner cookstoves we can empower poor women, improve human health *and* mitigate global warming, and therefore there is a win–win climate–energy–poverty nexus (e.g. Casillas and Kammen, 2010; Venkataraman et al, 2010). Reduced solid fuel use does reduce harmful emissions, even though all stoves in total produce a (very) small fraction of total emissions (1–3 tons of CO_2/year per stove: Lee et al, 2013). More troublesome than CO_2 is black carbon (BC, or plain old soot), which biomass and coal-burning stoves produce, and which is a forcing agent for near-term warming. In South Asia it is estimated that half the total emitted BC is from biomass-burning stoves (see Anenberg et al, 2013), and that BC disrupts the monsoons and therefore potentially threatens water availability. The most detailed research to date bounding BC from multiple sources shows that residential biofuel cooking has (maybe) a small positive net forcing from short-lived pollutants (about 0.025 W/m^2), and the uncertainty around this estimate is extremely wide around zero (Bond et al, 2013, p5504). Residential coal burning has a slightly higher forcing effect, but also 'with low certainty' (Bond et al, 2013, p5505).

The apparent forcing impacts have made it possible to finance and market stove programmes through public–private partnerships (PPPs), the Clean Development Mechanism, the Clean Cooking Loan Fund, and other new forms of creative carbon financing.[6] But the data (read carefully) give us little assurance that reducing biofuel-based cooking will meaningfully mitigate climate change. The so-called 'co-benefits' of climate mitigation from clean stoves, such as better health for (especially) women, and lower costs for fuel (in collection time or cash), in fact overwhelm the benefits of climate mitigation. This matters because discursive framings shape development practice (Cornwall and Brock, 2005). Development discourses around stoves promoting a climate-empowerment 'nexus', by placing a huge human health benefit alongside a relatively small and uncertain climate benefit, may reap a short-term financing advantage. But over time, they risk subtly and inadvertently linking the burden of climate mitigation with the daily actions of the poorest women.

Electricity

The final example of a transformative investment is electricity (see Goldemberg et al, 1985). Reliable, safe and affordable lighting, or a cell phone in an emergency, truly transforms lives. Electric lighting means that men and women can work longer or more flexible hours if needed, that children (or adults) can study in the evenings, and that cell phones, which have become an essential means of communication for the working poor, can stay charged (Alstone et al, 2015). Electric lighting is safer by far than kerosene lamps or candles (Mills, 2012). Open wick-based lighting, such as kerosene lamps without a surrounding cover, generates high levels of BC, an indoor pollutant and regional climate disruptor (see above; also Lam et al, 2012). Overall, not having basic electricity automatically puts a household in the category of 'poor', and over 1.3 billion people remain poor by this metric (IEA, 2012).

Basic electricity access is most commonly defined as having a connection in the home. Access to electricity services is a prerequisite for gender equality and not just for overall economic development (Cecelski, 2000; Cabraal et al, 2005). The primary target of MDG 3 (Promote gender equality) was the elimination of gender disparity in education, and access to electricity has allowed more women to read and watch television across all income classes (Pereira et al, 2011, and ESMAP, 2004 cited therein). While low-cost, stand-alone lighting is a necessary near-term intervention (see Alstone et al, 2015), it is access to electricity that improves night-time safety and health care infrastructure (because clinics can function after sunset, vaccines can be kept cold, etc.). The maternal mortality ratio (MMR) in particular is strongly correlated with access to electricity (Sovacool, 2012). A high MMR is not by itself a sign of gender inequality in health care, but we do know that women aged 15–34 years die in disproportionately high numbers on account of maternal mortality (Saith and Harris-White, 1999), and deliveries in the dark, or without functioning equipment, are known to be significant causes of infections and death. These data are evidence that basic electricity access is essential for the expansion of women's capabilities.

Cost estimates to bring modern electricity services to the 1.3 billion unserved vary widely, from US\$36 billion to US\$60 billion per year until 2030 (Guruswamy, 2011). The *World Energy Outlook* of the International Energy Association estimates US\$49 billion per year until 2030 (IEA, 2012). The range depends on how capital costs are estimated, but also on what is assumed about fuel prices and appliance efficiencies. Ongoing operations and maintenance are usually included for assessing grid electricity costs, but are most often left out of calculations for smaller home-based or community-based systems. Centralized grid extension remains most efficient for densely populated middle-income urban areas such as in China or South Africa. But capital cost considerations and low prospects for revenue recovery have prevented private sector utilities from entering low-income, sparsely populated, rural markets, even as many developing countries have been pushed, for reasons of efficiency but also of ideology, in the direction of privatizing their energy services (Williams and Ghanadan, 2006).

Many authors have noted the current tension between bringing electricity to the unconnected and increasing greenhouse gas emissions, because the conventional model of provision is a centralized grid based on fossil-fuel energy (e.g. Bazilian et al, 2011; Girod et al, 2013). Overall, the majority of those in the dark are rural residents, and their low capacity to pay, high level of need, and global climate change considerations have combined to make decentralized, renewables-based small systems a leading policy recommendation.[7] Microgrid systems can be extremely small, 10 W or so ('pico'), supporting simply a couple of lights and cell-phone charging; or solar home systems, supporting fans, four or five efficient lights, and a television, averaging about 30–40 W for commonly sold units; or mini-grid systems which offer several community-scale services, require higher upfront investments, but generate electricity at significantly lower cost than home systems (Alstone et al, 2015). Microgrid systems may be faster to scale up and replicate than a centralized grid in low-resource communities, but – as with water and sanitation – case studies show that costs and capacity for ongoing maintenance cannot be an afterthought in the cost–benefit analyses (Schnitzer et al, 2014). Hybrid renewable-conventional systems are also possible, at the community or multi-community scale, combining photovoltaics with wind, or even with (admittedly polluting) diesel, providing grid-like reliability and a range of productive applications beyond just residential use.

Basic electricity services for the 1.3 billion unserved, which could mean a fan (where it is hot), two fluorescent lights and a radio (or, moving up the ladder a bit, a television), all on for perhaps five hours a day, would add approximately 1 per cent a year to current global electricity consumption (Peter Alstone, personal communication). Therefore the climate is not in immediate danger from minimal service provision for the poor, even if their entire consumption were to be powered by fossil fuels. But integrating renewables into the grid, and expanding decentralized options using clean power sources that minimize local health impacts and particulate pollution (Markandya et al, 2009), are important for preventing the lock-down of new fossil fuel-based infrastructures. The provision of rock-bottom basic services is only a start, after all; poverty alleviation will require moving well beyond that (Sovacool, 2012; also Schnitzer et al, 2014). As with the cookstove arena, the discourses of sustainability for basic electricity services should more closely reflect the relative effects on climate versus on capabilities of on-grid and off-grid, conventional and renewable, options for the unserved.

As with all interventions, decentralized electrification programmes have succeeded in some areas, but have failed for financial, political and social reasons in others. And while basic electricity services remain essential for sustainable development, no technology, regardless of its cost, climate resilience or mode of dissemination, can ensure the electricity generated will, in fact, improve gender equality. Studies on women and electricity have reported that, once there are electric lights, women have more time to be with their children, perform their chores more quickly, and read more (Barnes and Foley, 2004; ESMAP, 2004). But with extremely small home systems, cooking, studying and television could compete for the limited electricity (Jacobson, 2004); intra-household allocation and power may determine who uses the watts and for which purposes (see Guyer and Peters, 1987; Agarwal, 1997). It is likely that systems with a higher capacity than simply 'pico' – somewhat higher per-user or lifecycle costs notwithstanding – will be needed for electricity services to actively promote gender equality in the home.

Transformative alliances for transformative investments

I turn now to a discussion of the institutional context of investing in sustainability and capabilities. Each of the four priority sectors identified depends on innovative and/or affordable technologies, and technologies can easily become the central actors in theories of access and in stories of social transformation. But technology is only a part of any investment story – technologies are disseminated (and even developed) in an institutional and financial context, to users with their own values and views, and within specific political economies. The institutional context significantly determines who has access, and on what terms. Projects on water, sanitation and energy are no longer parachuted into communities, but try to engage women users at every level – from design to marketing to finance. This is particularly true for market-based interventions such as clean cookstoves (Hart and Smith, 2013) or efficient off-grid lighting (Alstone et al, 2011); it is also increasingly the case for water and sanitation. But the institutional demands of going to scale for the approximately 1.3 billion without electricity or the approximately 2.5 billion without sanitation are truly daunting.

Water, sanitation and electricity historically have gone to scale through public sector investments, as networked utilities have traditionally been monopolies (see Hanemann, 2006). Since the 1980s, these services in developing countries have opened up to the private sector. In part this was because the public sector did not provide basic services to the low-income public, and the global political economy became more market-friendly and more state-sceptical (e.g. World Bank, 2004). Over the same period, civil society provision and decentralization became more and more mainstream in these service sectors. Cookstoves, our final priority area, were never developed and provided primarily in the public domain. Stoves have historically been seen as stand-alone consumer items, and, because of public health and climate considerations, are only now moving from the fully private to the partially public sphere. It is clear that public–private–civil alliances are needed for sustainable development, but what could these alliances look like along a gender-equitable pathway? And on whose terrain are these alliances taking place?

The post-1980s spate of PPPs in the centralized or semi-centralized utilities for developing countries has had mixed results for both water and electricity (Bakker, 2010; Bazilian et al, 2011). The literature in support of PPPs has argued that these partnerships are the only way forward as the state sector has neither cash nor capacity to expand provision beyond those already covered. However, a recent comprehensive study of water and sanitation financing in 17 countries, conducted by UN Water and WHO, shows that 80 per cent of the (non-household) funds for this sector continues to come from central, regional and local governments (GLAAS, 2012). The literature against PPPs argues that privatization is reducing the state to a mere upholder of private property and guarantor of private contracts (e.g. Miraftab, 2004), but this perspective sometimes glosses over the failure, and the implications of that failure, of many states to provide for their poor citizens (discussed in Linder, 1999; Osborne, 2006).

Though state-run programmes have been on the defensive in recent years, and though states are often very poorly governed, the evidence to date suggests that they remain pivotal to social investments at scale. A well known example is China's rural clean cookstove project (NISP, mentioned earlier); this programme transformed over 100 million households through improved stoves, with a coordinated effort by multiple national ministries, multiple county and village level officials, rural energy companies and local energy service enterprises (Smith et al, 1993; Sinton et al, 2004). An example of nationally led rural electricity access is the post-1994 National Electrification Program (NEP) of South Africa. This far-reaching programme was successful in that access to basic electricity, enough for three or four lights, a radio and a TV, increased for 2.7 million households between 1994 and 1999 (Pereira et al, 2011), with selected private sector concessionaires working, as it were, towards a largely public sector goal. The fee-for-service photovoltaic-based component, however, was apparently less successful than the on-grid aspects (Lemaire, 2011; Pereira et al, 2011). An older example of a drinking water PPP comes from India, implemented well before the term was coined; the government placed a guaranteed demand for handpumps to be installed all over rural India, national and international companies bid for the contracts for the pumps and pipes and drilling equipment, and NGOs educated communities about the importance of safe water and pump maintenance (Talbot, 1997).

Such at-scale examples are rare unless the state plays a central role, though not necessarily the role of direct service provider. Private enterprise, demand-driven services and finances, bottom-up NGO pressure, and the 'show-me' effects of pilot projects are all critical. But the literature on the importance and innovation of private actors in essential services seems to conclude that the state needs to set and enforce an enabling policy framework, provide direct assistance to the poorest, and direct the flow and targeting of collective goods – if water and energy services are to be universally provided. Several studies, even when promoting private sector participation, suggest that one reason for promising interventions failing to scale up is that the state did not provide subsidies, or killed the sustainability of the effort with too many subsidies, or did not enforce its own regulations, or did not otherwise promote sustainable interventions (e.g. Zhang and Smith, 2007; Bailis et al, 2009; Harris et al, 2011; Pereira et al, 2011; Sovacool, 2012). It is old news, after all, that private actors cannot capture spillover benefits, or provide services to an extremely poor user base, or guarantee environmental integrity. This is not their mandate.

At the same time, the nature of the private sector players in water, sanitation and energy has been rapidly changing, especially for providers working with the lowest quintiles. In addition to registered corporate entities, there are numerous small-scale and semi-formal entities, sometimes purely commercial, at other times social as well as commercial, who are agile and entrepreneurial. It is critical that the public sector engages with these private sector(s) in sustainable development efforts, and to regulate them while taking advantage of their service-creation and market-creation potential. Yet regulation and oversight is a capacity that smaller states may lack (Cairncross, 2003). Monitoring and oversight of the private and public sectors, therefore, are also the business of civil society and social movement representatives. These interest groups, heterogeneous though they may be, are often effective pressure groups and/or watchdogs on behalf of unserved communities. In a shifting institutional environment, transformative investments can only go to scale with transformative alliances amongst all the players in the development arena.

Contemporary efforts we can point to are not (yet) at the transformative scale, but they show that innovative alliances are indeed possible in the water, sanitation and energy space. Grameen Shakti is a private (but non-profit) sector actor in off-grid electricity in Bangladesh, and has installed over 1 million home solar systems. It uses financing provided by the International Finance Corporation and the Government of Bangladesh to extend micro-credit to its buyers (Martinot et al, 2001). The extensive networks of rainwater harvesting systems in India, pioneered by groups such as Tarun Bharat Sangh and Gravis, are now going to scale with government support – and in some cases government mandates – after thousands of successful demonstrations. Community-led total sanitation, a subsidy-free participatory approach to latrine building and use, seems to be expanding rapidly in sub-Saharan Africa with the support of international agencies and national governments (Musyoki, 2010; Rukuni, 2010). Cookstove projects with women's groups, social enterprises and for-profit stove makers are working with millions of customers in Africa, Central America, and South and Southeast Asia. These examples are proof that transformative alliances can and do exist, and that new forms of state–capital–society ties (see Evans, 2008) can enable gender-equal sustainable development.

Of course, financing pro-poor gender-equalizing investment in sustainable water, sanitation and energy services is a formidable proposition for countries with a low per capita GDP. Transformative investments through transformative institutional alliances are both critically needed and possible. But the difficulty of financing such investments to scale must be acknowledged, and budgetary competition with other sectors – health, defence, education, agriculture – must also be faced. Financing mundane but transformative investments for the lowest quintiles needs a refocusing of fiscal and political decision-making in developed and developing countries alike. Both traditional as well as non-traditional sources of financing water, sanitation and energy services could potentially be harnessed and re-directed towards sustainability and gender equality. These include direct (central or local) government financing, debt-forgiveness for highly indebted countries, raising development assistance to the long-standing goal of 0.7 per cent of the GNP of every country, and redirecting military budgets, possibly in concert with neighbouring countries, amongst other options (Schalatek, 2012). But financing or loan repayments that inadvertently increase the unpaid workload of low-income women would be capability-reducing, and thus not on a sustainable pathway.

In short, for all the failures of state-run efforts, and there are too many of these – and for all the states that govern badly or even brutally, and there are too many of these – the historical evidence points to the need for a state that is in a contract with its citizens, and a contract which it, at least in part, honours. This is an old model of the state, one with Aristotelian antecedents, and one that has been in and out of analytical fashion in recent decades. The modern version is akin to what Evans (1995) has called the 'developmental state', in which the state, in concert with other social actors, is ultimately accountable to the citizens. It is compatible with the call for all countries to progressively realize their commitments to human rights (UN, 1948) – which include gender equality, and the mundane means of life and dignity discussed here. This chapter certainly does not call for renewed dirigisme, but it does conclude that sustainable and capability-expanding development needs the contractual state.

Concluding thoughts

This chapter argues that sustainable development is a multi-dimensional, multi-pathway concept whose components may or may not all be simultaneously and equally achievable. Accepting that there are many sustainable pathways leads to greater transparency in the trade-offs that societies may have to make between one goal (e.g. lower carbon emissions) and another (e.g. poverty alleviation), both of which are desirable and defensible components of sustainable development. Sustainable development is, therefore, a negotiated concept in implementation.

Along with the other authors in this book, I have argued that, for sustainable development to be compatible with internationally accepted human rights norms, gender equality is a central component of any chosen pathway(s). Thus investments towards socially transformative development should consider women's capability enhancement, especially at the lowest quintile, as a non-negotiable goal. This means that sustainable development efforts, globally or regionally, must be directed towards key sectors from which poor women can disproportionately benefit.

The four sectors for socially transformative development proposed here are access to water, access to safe sanitation, access to clean cookstoves, and access to electricity. Each of these sectors could be transformative for women's health, dignity and work, and for poor women in particular. Effective investments at scale are certainly difficult and uncertain, and depend on gender-sensitive and context-sensitive design and financing. We have seen that transformative investments call for transformative alliances between policy-makers, donors and the state, as well as the private and civil sectors. However, investments at scale need the reach and organizing power of the state; and the state needs the mobilizing power and vigilance of social movements to push it to honour its social contracts.

I have argued that gender equality should be assessed through the outcome of Sen's enhanced 'capabilities', thus privileging freedoms and agency over traditional wellbeing measures such as income. Drawing on the 'rights and risks' framework (WCD, 2000), I suggest that any investment (local or national) should ensure that those who bear the risks of the intervention also hold the right to shape it. I draw on the vast literatures on operationalizing the concept of 'capability', and on feminist economics, that have shown unpaid care work to be a pillar of the paid economy everywhere, and a major constraint on women's capability enhancement. Investments in the four selected domains are, in effect, investments in the determinants of health and opportunity for all. Therefore they should be assessed, ex ante and ex post, through metrics of health and opportunity. I have suggested that under-five female mortality, gender parity in secondary education, and the reduction of unpaid care work for women and girls are illustrative metrics of assessment for these investments. In keeping with the spirit of the quintile axiom, investments should be prioritized for the lowest quintiles in communities where they are made.

This argument does not preclude the dominant focus on reducing carbon emissions or increasing pro-poor income as critical outcomes of sustainable development. But it does preclude a globalizing carbon-centric approach to sustainable water, sanitation and energy for the poor. Climate mitigation and women's wellbeing are fully compatible with one another. But the easy language of 'climate–gender nexus' places short-lived and hugely uncertain warming reductions in the same league as long-term and enormous wellbeing gains for women and for the poor. Its eventual discursive effect may be to require investments in reducing female mortality to be partially justified by evidence of reduced emissions – the development world has seen many times that discourse, once entrenched, has material effect. This chapter has made the case for *everyday sustainability for everyday equality* between men and women, and between boys and girls.

I end this chapter with some thoughts on the human body, human capabilities, and how these influence the way in which we should understand sustainable development going forward. Feminist political ecology has shown that the environment is first and foremost experienced in the body, and the body is therefore the first scale of environmental analysis (Rocheleau et al, 1996; Elmhirst, 2011). At least two of the priority sectors for transformative investment, water and stoves, are traditionally 'female' sectors. In no way do I intend to essentialize women's needs and values through these choices; we certainly cannot valorize socially constructed ideas of women as the natural drawers of water and preparers of meals. But I do want to argue that, to truly transform women's capabilities, we must recognize women's distinctive and embodied situations in their everyday lives. We must begin with the 'irreducible specificity of women's bodies' (Grosz, 1994).

For every target or 'beneficiary' of sustainable development, there is a body. That body is defined both by its biological characteristics and the social expectations of it. Without crossing into reductionist naturalizations, and without falling into the pernicious trap of one's-body-is-one's-destiny, we must explicitly recognize that the human body is the entity that houses human rights. What does this recognition mean for sustainable development? I argue that every development objective has, embedded within it, an assumption about the human body. We can call this assumption the 'prototype' body – it is always implicitly there. Sustainable development targets post-2015 cannot be finely tailored to the full range of different bodily needs and their associated social norms. They must therefore become explicit about the prototype body that they are (primarily) written for.

To illustrate this point, let us ask what explicitness means for two of our four priority sectors. What would the water and sanitation targets be for a body that must carry water where a pipe does not, must always sit or squat to use the toilet, will manage small children in the toilet, must wash her hands after defecation, must be safe from assault on her way to the facilities or the water source, and will bleed for four days a month for 40 years, except if she is pregnant or dies young? Gender equality in water and sanitation means designing sustainability targets for *that* body. Only then will sustainable development sustain human rights for all, along with the environmental resource base on which both development and rights depend.

Notes

1   http://hdr.undp.org/en/statistics/hdi
2   http://unstats.un.org/unsd/gender/default.html
3   www.wssinfo.org
4   www.wssinfo.org
5   e.g. http://saner.gy/about-us#
6   see http://carbonfinanceforcookstoves.org
7   www.se4all.org

7

GENDER EQUALITY AND SUSTAINABLE DEVELOPMENT

The limits and potential of global policy reports

Shahra Razavi and Seemin Qayum[1]

The original catalyst for this book was the process instigated by UN Women to inform the preparation of the 2014 *World Survey on the Role of Women in Development* (UN, 2014a; thereafter *World Survey*). As Chapter 1 in this book explains, several chapters originated as background papers for the *World Survey*, while the book project was inspired by the analysis and connections forged in the report's preparation workshops. It therefore seems fitting for this final chapter to address the *World Survey* more directly.

Here we provide our reflections on the research process behind the production of the report. We offer these reflections as feminist 'insiders' coordinating the research and writing the report, and as participants in similar processes of knowledge production at the interface of feminist research and policy. A number of the key arguments detailed in this book found their way into the *World Survey*, so this chapter provides an opportunity to summarize these messages, and to consider their potential for traction in global policy debates at the present moment. Yet the structure and process of a UN report also bring constraints of form, language and politics, which this book has not had to follow. Reflecting on these issues, we elaborate on the role of feminist ideas in charting development trajectories that are equitable and sustainable along multiple dimensions, as well as the reach and influence of policy reports and their potential to feed into broader processes of social change.

Calls for transformation and a new social contract: Feminist political economy and feminist political ecology

In the aftermath of the 'triple crisis' of finance, food and energy, and with rising concerns about global inequalities, climate change and environmental degradation, there has been greater receptivity to proposals for alternative development trajectories. This is evident not only in the mushrooming of social mobilizations and experiments around the world, in the form of 'social and solidarity economies', for example, but also in the number of publications appearing from within the UN system itself that call for structural change. The topics broached in recent UN reports are indicative of the changing *zeitgeist* or 'spirit of the time', with UNDP (2013b) writing about unprecedented inequality and 'humanity divided', while UNEP calls for a 'global green new deal' (2009), not to mention UNCTAD's (2014) proposals for an overhaul of the system of global economic governance. While the turn to Keynesian counter-cyclical policies was short-lived, in a moment when finance-led capitalism appeared to have lost legitimacy, if not power, the crisis seemed to have opened up space for 'sub- and counter-hegemonic discourses, projects and practices' (Jessop, 2012, p39).

A more conducive context has also emerged for the global deliberations on a new set of Sustainable Development Goals (SDGs). Despite serious political differences on a range of issues – from the role of the private sector and transnational corporations to questions of financing for the new goals, as well as on the obligations of northern countries for the negative impacts of their laws, policies and actions beyond their borders – there seems to be a rhetorical consensus at least on the limitations of a 'business-as-usual' approach and on the need for transformation. One of the lessons learnt from the MDG era – when the goal-setting was done behind closed doors, involving donors and a limited circle of UN technocrats – is the importance of wide-ranging consultations with national governments, civil society groups, academics and other actors, of which there have been many over the past few years. The other is the relevance of human rights to goal definition, policy elaboration, implementation and monitoring, even if critical aspects of human rights remain contested and absent from the current proposals for the SDGs (Balakrishnan and Saiz, 2014).

This more expansive intellectual space was conducive to bringing a feminist political economy and political ecology analysis to bear on issues of sustainability, and for this – and many of the key arguments elaborated in more depth in this book – to inform the 2014 *World Survey*. Indeed, the *World Survey* was able to delve into many multiple and rising inequalities at the intersection of gender, class and race; underline the ways in which market-driven strategies associated with under-regulated capitalism rely upon women's undervalued – and often unpaid – labour as well as their reproductive work; suggest that the same development trajectories also produce environmental crises through the overexploitation of natural resources and the pollution and degradation of land, water and climate; and propose a more regulated and rights-based development approach wherein the state plays a central role as an arbiter of people's rights, but is held firmly in check and accountable through a renewed social contract which includes women's and other rights advocates as key constituencies.

The *World Survey*, for example, provides a strong critique of dominant macroeconomic policy agendas and production patterns geared to export markets – a key area of policy-making that has changed very little over the past decades, despite the much-heralded softening of approach by the international financial institutions in acknowledging the importance of investments in social protection and social services, and of efforts at 'social inclusion'. The *World Survey* chapter on 'green economy, gender equality and care', echoing Braunstein and Houston (Chapter 2 in this book), underlines the systemic paradox of relying on export-oriented production processes coupled with wage stagnation as a strategy for delivering growth and development. It underlines the specific problems such a strategy poses for improving the earnings and employment conditions of women workers, who are often clustered into labour-intensive production processes, whether in manufacturing or agriculture and horticulture. While participation in global value chains can ease access to global markets for developing countries, it also intensifies competition, and through a 'fallacy of composition'[2] as UNCTAD (2002) pointed out many years ago, constrains wage growth and limits the expansion of domestic aggregate demand. These global relations of production are not only economically unsustainable, but also have failed to generate sufficient high-quality employment for both women and men, and have compromised the potential to advance gender equality through new opportunities in paid work.

Some of this analysis is not new. In fact, key elements of it were already elaborated in the 1999 *World Survey*, which focused on 'globalization, gender and work' – an analysis that was in many ways 'ahead of the curve' (Jolly et al, 2005). Interestingly, the 1999 report too was the product of another post-crisis juncture, released on the heels of the 1997 East Asian crisis. However, going beyond the 1999 report, the gender analysis of global production processes in the 2014 *World Survey* is much better integrated with an understanding of the unpaid reproductive economy (or unpaid care work, as it is now widely called). The chapter on 'green economy, gender equality and care', and indeed the report as a whole, make the important point that even if a gender-responsive green economy agenda is put in place that enhances women's employment prospects and the quality of their work, this is not going to be sufficient (see Braunstein and Houston, Chapter 2 in this book). To redress gender inequality and promote the three dimensions of sustainable development, policy-makers need to pay particular attention to investments in public goods and the care economy. This is one of the themes that is threaded throughout the report, as well as throughout this book – especially in the final section that charts key elements of 'investments for gender-responsive sustainable development' (see also Ray, Chapter 6 in this book). There can be no sustainability if the conditions of human existence are not constantly reproduced, on a day-to-day basis and from one generation to the next. 'Achieving sustainable development means not only reconciling economic and environmental sustainability, but also prioritizing social sustainability' (UN, 2014a, para 17).

The attention given in the *World Survey* to women's disproportionate share of unpaid care and domestic work is not surprising, with the increasing prominence that has been given to the care economy in global policy debates on economic and social development over the past decade or so. What started in the 1970s as a feminist concern in the context of a handful of mostly European welfare states, has become a theme with global relevance, including to low-income developing countries (Razavi, 2011). The interest in the topic has gone well beyond global research and policy initiatives by organizations such as the ILO, OECD and UNRISD, and is now discussed within the human rights community as well as in intergovernmental negotiations.[3] The 'Agreed Conclusions' of the 2014 Commission on the Status of Women (CSW58), for example, which reviewed the MDGs from a gender perspective, made specific references to the importance of care as a key societal function and the imperative of valuing this work, and reducing and redistributing its provision between women and men, and between households and society more broadly (UN, 2014b, para gg). Building on this recognition, the issue of care is also now one of the target areas in the proposed SDGs, under the gender equality goal. But it is not always clear how the redistribution of care between women and men, and between households and society, can be supported, and what policies are needed to make it happen.

The analysis of unpaid care and domestic work in the *World Survey*, especially in terms of priority investments for gender-responsive sustainable development, is biased towards the needs of poorer women in relatively poor communities. Hence the focus is on water, sanitation, cookstoves and electricity, which are the backbone of a decent quality of life, have a direct bearing on environmental sustainability, and when in short supply place a disproportionate burden on women, especially poorer women and girls. Women's time, labour and their very bodies are used up without these public goods and services: 'a woman's body becomes part of the water-delivery infrastructure, doing the work of pipes' (UN, 2014a, para 282; also Ray, Chapter 6 in this book).

The *World Survey* usefully reminds us that while the private sector, NGOs and public–private partnerships may be spearheading the innovative and/or affordable technologies needed to make investments in water, sanitation, cookstoves and electricity a success, the institutional demands of going to scale for over a billion people without electricity or 2.5 billion without sanitation are daunting. Scaling-up and -out requires state action: only the state can set and enforce an enabling policy framework, provide direct assistance to the poorest (through subsidized tariffs, for example), and direct the flow and targeting of collective goods, if water and energy services are to be universally provided. Noting the many deficiencies of 'actually existing states' – the fact that many states are poorly governed, do not respond to the needs of their poorer citizens, especially women citizens, and may have little capacity to regulate private actors – the report presents a nuanced political economy analysis that acknowledges the need for market regulation as a joint responsibility of states and civil society actors, which can be effective watchdogs on behalf of marginalized social groups.

This focus on basic public goods such as water and sanitation is not strictly speaking about care or person care – which has an interpersonal dimension – but about 'social reproduction' more broadly, that falls disproportionately on poorer women in under-served and marginalized communities. While the bias is justified given the key themes of the report – economic, environmental and social sustainability – very little is said about 'classic' care-giving (for young children, elderly parents and parents-in-law, husbands/partners, the ill and the disabled) undertaken by women, often on an unpaid basis in their capacities as mothers, wives, daughters, sisters and family members. The same is true of this book's analysis. Much more could also be said about how sexual divisions of labour, power inequalities, and violence and subordination are undergirded by the gendering and racialization of paid and unpaid care work – a set of issues that may be less directly amenable to policy treatment, but are nevertheless fundamental to how societies substantiate and reproduce intersecting hierarchies of gender, class and race (Ray and Qayum, 2009).

The filtering out of some feminist analyses

There are also areas where the *World Survey*'s analysis was constrained – and where this book has had the opportunity to go further. Questions of care naturally lead to questions of the body – the care, nourishment and protection of bodies, as well as the mistreatment, deprivations and violence inflicted on them. Bodily autonomy, integrity and control are, of course, at the heart of feminist scholarship and activism, as are gender identities, sexualities and politics embedded in multiple and intersecting inequalities. As such, the *World Survey* would maintain that gender-equal sustainable development cannot be treated as a disembodied concept (see Ray, Chapter 6 in this book). Since all policy recommendations are made based on a set of implicit assumptions about the 'prototype body' to which they apply, we must be explicit about that body, and its integrity and dignity in designing policies that meet her circumstances and needs in order to be sustainable. But, by and large, most policy reports have a binary and heteronormative notion of human beings closely related to fixed biological sex: male bodies (and male sexuality) and female bodies (and female sexuality). Gender is used as an umbrella term for two mutually exclusive and stable categories of men and women (and sometimes boys and girls), but most often refers euphemistically to women. Little attention, if any, is given to the construction of masculinities and femininities, and practically none to the assemblage of biologies and sexualities (cf. Butler, 1990).[4] Gender equality or inequality is most often presented as a comparative metric between the two sexes, with little reference to structural origins or relations of power and domination.

Feminist analysis has taken pains to refute the ostensibly Freudian 'biology is destiny' or rather 'anatomy is destiny' discourses (Moi, 2000) that essentialize the female body and sexuality and, divorced from history, geography, culture, and political economy, reduce women to their reproductive biology and fertility as bearers and carers of children. The policy implications of such reductionism are multifarious, for instance, that women are somehow closer to nature and therefore naturally suited to caring for and protecting the environment, reflected in the 'women, environment and development' discourse which continues to influence development funding and practice despite sustained feminist critique (Leach, 2007; see Leach et al, Chapter 1 in this book). Or the focus of the MDGs on improving maternal health (MDG 5) while pushing a range of other issues central to women's sexual and reproductive rights over the entire life course to the periphery of policy discourse and attention (Yamin and Boulanger, 2013b). In fact there has been a significant drop in maternal mortality ratios since 1990, even as the ratios remained many times higher in developing than in developed regions, and universal access to reproductive health is far from being achieved.[5] While recognizing life-saving advances, the *World Survey* chapter on 'population, sustainable development and gender equality' compellingly illuminates the discourses that instrumentally link women's fertility to overpopulation and thereby to poverty, resource scarcity, environmental degradation and climate change (see also Hartmann et al, Chapter 3 in this book). These discourses are dauntingly resilient and entrenched, as are the corresponding ones that propose reducing women's fertility as a policy option for sustainable development. Yet reproductive health policies and practices are frequently limited to basic family planning and contraception in the absence of a broader sexual and reproductive health and rights agenda, and support for women's agency, choice and autonomy. Moreover – as Hartmann et al (this book) highlight – the structural causes of poverty, resource scarcity, and environmental and climate crises are rooted in the unequal distribution of wealth and skewed consumption of resources, goods and services, rather than a matter of 'too many people'. These structural factors – which also help to produce gender inequality – are far more difficult to target through policy reforms than are women's bodies, which are constantly subject to state and market forces and 'reforming' discourses.

The imperative of numbers and 'agreed language'

The previous section elaborated some of the challenges in bringing an interpretive and discursive understanding of gender equality – which is intrinsic to the pathways approach applied and elaborated in this book, with its attention to diverse framings and narratives of gender and of sustainability – into a largely positivist report such as the *World Survey*. The reliance on statistics and validation and the sensitivities around 'agreed language' are some of the other peculiarities of producing such documents.

The *World Survey* is not a data-driven report – in fact, the report does not include any statistical annexes or even tables – but being a 'report of the Secretary-General' the text is closely scrutinized by both in-house and external reviewers to ensure that its analysis is empirically grounded, and the statistics that are peppered throughout the text meet quality standards. For example, commonly cited statistics – that 70 per cent of the world's poor are women – can turn out to be simply erroneous and misleading.

On the positive side, extensive rounds of revision in response to comments from academic peer reviewers, other UN agencies, in-house experts and senior management, and many rounds of 'fact-checking' help ensure the rigour of the arguments and claims put forth, as well as the statistics that are used and the adequacy of referencing. But what about the more constricting, and largely unintended, consequences of such a process? Does writing a report in this way limit the scope of the analysis by weighing it down to the 'lowest common denominator' on which there is consensus?

While reports of this nature can produce useful 'surveys' of the relevant literature, are they able to take a major analytical leap forward or to 'push the envelope' beyond what are already accepted positions within UN reports? Our inclination would be to say 'probably not' to the latter question. And yet, despite the many constraints that can limit the scope for innovation in report-writing, on many occasions the UN has led the way on alternative approaches to social and economic development – from the UNDP's *Human Development Reports* that have revitalized and operationalized the capability framework as an antidote to 'money metric' approaches centred on economic growth, to proposals for gradualist transitions put forward by the UN regional economic commissions as alternatives to the 'shock therapy' recipes of the international financial institutions, to UNESCO's reports advocating education for all within a largely universalist approach. Anchored within the UN's normative human rights framework, many of these reports have made the case for 'alternative' development strategies in an incremental manner.

With respect to the *World Survey*, it is worth underlining the consistent emphasis in the report on one of this book's key sets of arguments – the dangers of positioning women as 'sustainability saviours' and of overarching instrumentalist assumptions that gender equality and women's participation are good for the environment or for the economy – and that economic growth and environmental protection lead automatically to gains for women and for gender equality. In contradistinction, and articulated in keeping with its practical style, the *World Survey* proposes three criteria for assessing whether the policies, programmes and actions implemented in the name of sustainability actually support gender equality: whether they enhance the human rights and capabilities of women and girls, especially from disadvantaged groups; whether they reduce the burden of unpaid domestic and care work carried by women and girls; and whether they involve the full participation of women as actors, leaders and decision-makers.

What about the imperative of 'evidence-based policy-making'? Is this at odds with feminism as a transformative project? We agree with feminist critics who point to some of the limitations of evidence-based policy-making, especially the fact that what is often measurable and for which statistics already exist may not even capture what has most significance for transforming gendered structures of constraint. We know, for example, from the work of Mala Htun and Laurel Weldon (2012) that the best indicator of strong policy responses on a range of gender inequality issues is the strength of feminist organizing in civil society. Yet attempts at measuring women's political effectiveness invariably fall back on indicators such as the share of women in parliaments or in high levels of political office, because these are more readily available. Likewise, an indicator such as female labour force participation (compared with male labour force participation), which is routinely used to capture women's economic capabilities or economic empowerment, is grossly insufficient. We need much better evidence on the quality of the work that women do; whether a rise in labour force participation is merely adding paid work to a largely unchanged burden of unpaid domestic and care work (the 'double shift'); the relation between economic growth or green growth and gender equality measures, to name just a few issues. We also need to understand why gender pay gaps, for example, are reducing: is it because women are doing better and catching up with men, or is it because men's conditions of work and levels of pay have deteriorated? And we need to go beyond the binary 'women versus men' to get a better sense of the many inequalities that divide women, whether by class, race or location. As such we would agree with Liebowitz and Zwingler when they say 'Measurement attempts and their inherent logic of simplification and comparability may *serve* but cannot *replace* the logic of comprehensive and context-sensitive assessment and problem solving' (2014, p363).

However, the recognition of some of the limitations of quantitative indicators does not mean that we should 'throw out the baby with the bathwater'. Gender statistics can help capture a richer array of factors and forces that contribute to a 'context-sensitive assessment'. For example, data disaggregation by sex, age, income, location and the creation of nuanced gender statistics are necessary to be able to 'measure' a reduction in inequalities and progress towards 'universal and equitable' access to resources and services, which are clearly two aims of a transformative feminist project. In fact, as this text goes to press, one of the clearly contested issues in the negotiation of the SDGs is precisely whether the goals and targets with laudatory universal and equitable ambitions and scope will indeed require for their implementation indicators and data disaggregated by sex, age, income, location and other relevant factors. This would mean, of course, significant international and national investments in statistical capacities, collection and analysis. Or whether the SDGs – as the MDGs before them – will simply rely on the 'best available data' to construct indicators and monitoring measures, rather than heeding the calls for new and better data and data sources – a 'gender data revolution' for a truly transformative development agenda.

Another point worth making is that it is not just data limitations that constrain analytical reports. The pressure to cite concrete case studies to back up the analytical claims being made can also be paralysing. For a start, even though gender and sustainable development is often seen as a burgeoning research field, in compiling the *World Survey* we were struck by the difficulty of illustrating the analytical work with concrete case studies that are up-to-date, geographically diverse and clearly illustrative, without falling into the traps of what Cornwall et al (2007) have called 'gender myths and feminist fables'. The chapters in this book have succeeded in expanding the range, but not by much. It is not surprising, therefore, that in the gender and sustainable development field a small number of case studies get cited again and again, their findings selectively used and any contingencies or ambiguities they may have had filtered out. What is even more debilitating is the pressure to go beyond critique – where research is on much stronger ground – to propose 'best practices', without the many qualifications that would have to be made about why certain 'best practices' may be one-off outcomes dependent on very specific circumstances and therefore not *replicable* or *scalable* – both of which are generalized policy recommendations for development interventions.

We would like to include a few words about the significance of 'agreed language' – the language around which binding or non-binding inter-governmental policy negotiations are built, and which serves as the 'legal' antecedents for future policy formulation. The sensitivity around language is not altogether surprising, given that many UN documents are highly political and deal with issues on which there are very diverse and contested views. But agreed language, combined with the constraints of policy discourses, also elides difference and diversity in the interest of an identifiable, measurable and trackable policy subject, the undifferentiated mass of 'women and girls', always contrasted with its male comparator. Feminist scholars, for example, like other egalitarian thinkers, have tended to use 'equity' (rather than 'equality') in order to draw attention to existing gender differences, and to avoid a 'difference-blind' approach that demands 'same treatment'. Some feminists would insist that 'equity' is congruent with fairness and justice, that 'equalizing' the playing field is never enough given intersecting gender, race and class inequalities and multivalent gender difference. Within the broader literature, therefore, feminists continue to use both 'equality' and 'equity', sometimes with political or philosophical intent and at other times interchangeably for stylistic variation – as the various usages in this book's chapters illustrate.

However, in the context of UN debates, the terms have taken on a different significance and meaning. Feminists in this context have often advocated for the consistent use of the term gender 'equality', largely in response to the ways in which conservative religious forces (putting the accent on gender difference) appropriated the term 'equity' to deny women equal rights to resources, bodily integrity and decision-making. There are similar concerns about terms such as 'gender equitable' and 'gender sensitive', which are both seen as weak, while preference is given to terms such as 'gender responsive', which raise the bar and underline the need for stronger policy responses. While consistency in language may make for an anodyne and repetitive style of writing, it can avoid confusion and may even add to the clarity and accessibility of the text, especially for non-specialists.

A final point: recourse to or defence of agreed language is often made by 'feminists within the system' in order to sustain past gains for the realization of women's rights and gender equality, and to prevent erosion or reversals by the conservative forces of the moment. This is clearly an understandable tactical position, but it does pose the risk of turning previous achievements into stone and preventing progress on new and creative fronts and issues that are essential for dynamic and transformative feminist politics. The vital struggle to achieve sexual and reproductive health and rights (SRHR) for all, women and men, girls and boys, across gender identities and sexualities, is incompletely backed by agreed language enshrined in, for example, the International Conference on Population and Development (ICPD) Programme of Action (1994) or the Beijing Declaration and Platform for Action (1995) – both skirt the contentious issues of sexual rights – while the 20-year review of the ICPD (UNFPA, 2014) which did call for SRHR was heavily criticized in some quarters. This has led, in some global policy fora, to defence of the language on sexual and reproductive health and reproductive rights, and reluctance to advocate for policies on sexual rights for fear of opening up to scrutiny and potentially eroding past gains.

Contributing to social change: Through policies or social practices? Or both?

Needless to say, social actors, social movements and civil society networks are not constrained by such concerns. They can take, as they have, the advances of Cairo and Beijing as green lights for SRHR advocacy and for advancing an emancipatory agenda. Feminism is about change and transformation across all institutions and spaces for policy and practice, both personal/private/micro and political/public/macro, effectively melding the two realms. However, strategies for effecting change are highly varied, and feminists in different institutional locations (in states, global institutions, social movements, community organizations, research/academia) often engage in a multiplicity of strategies depending on their location (as 'insiders' or 'outsiders'), the contexts they are in and the nature of the moment (Miller and Razavi, 1998; Eyben and Turquet, 2013; Leach et al, Chapter 1 in this book). Change in real lives and social relations comes about as a result of change in policies (to which reports such as the *World Survey* can contribute), but also as a result of processes of social, cultural, political and economic change, which may be triggered by social actors and movements or, more often than not, by structural economic and political forces. Thus policy inevitably follows structural changes in real lives and places, whether due to social or economic forces, but it can influence identifying, managing, promoting, curtailing or redressing those changes, as the case may be.

These policy documents have both an explicit and implicit audience – the explicit audience of the *World Survey* is UN Member States; but it is implicit, and often hoped, that the report will reach a much more diverse set of change agents (including organized civil society, academic researchers, the private sector, and so on) through various ripple effects. Sometimes this happens when a report is picked up and championed by a social movement, a trade union, an NGO or a feminist organization, thereby amplifying its policy impact at different levels (global, regional, national, local). It is important, however, to remind ourselves that the policy route is but one channel for trying to effect social change. Other channels will involve different actors and different strategies.

What global policy reports can do at their best is condense the spirit of the time, and respond to the demands and aspirations of collectivities. It is rare that they can be the rallying point for social change. When they are at their best as potential instigators of change is when policy processes crystallize, even if incompletely, the assessments and expressions of a multiplicity of actors – grassroots, civil society, scientific and research, government, international – as did Cairo and Beijing for gender equality, and the Brundtland Report and Agenda 21 for sustainable development. In its modest way, the *World Survey* has tried to insert itself in a policy and social change process by reaching out to a wider audience with shared and urgent concerns, not least through this book, which builds on the report to engage academics, practitioners, activists and feminists.

Notes

1 The views and opinions expressed are the authors' and do not necessarily reflect the positions of UN Women.
2 'on its own a small developing country can substantially expand its exports without flooding the market and seriously reducing the prices of the products concerned, but this may not be true for developing countries as a whole, or even for large individual countries such as China and India. A rapid increase in exports of labour-intensive products involves a potential risk that the terms of trade will decline to such an extent that the benefits of any increased volume of exports may be more than offset by losses due to lower export prices' (UNCTAD, 2002, p114).
3 The link between human rights and the care economy has been clearly articulated in the report of the Special Rapporteur on extreme poverty and human rights, Magdalena Sepulveda (UN, 2013d).
4 'Gender ought not to be conceived merely as the cultural inscription of meaning on a pregiven sex... gender must also designate the very apparatus of production whereby the sexes themselves are established' (Butler, 1990, p7).
5 www.un.org/millenniumgoals/maternal.shtml. There are, however serious concerns about the accuracy of existing data sources. In the absence of comprehensive records of deaths and of causes of death, measuring maternal death accurately is difficult. Estimates are often used to fill the data gaps. However, these can vary widely depending on data sources and modelling methodologies.

REFERENCES

Acemoglu, D., Aghion, P., Bursztyn, L. and Hemous, D. (2009) *The Environment and Directed Technical Change*, NBER Working Paper 15451, National Bureau of Economic Research, Cambridge, MA.

Adams, V., Murphy, M. and Clarke, A. E. (2009) 'Anticipation: Technoscience, life, affect, temporality', *Subjectivity*, vol 28, pp246–265, doi 10.1057/sub.2009.18.

Adams, W. M. (2004) *Against Extinction: The Story of Conservation*, Earthscan, London.

ADB and FAO (2013) *Gender Equality and Food Security: Women's Empowerment as a Tool against Hunger*, Asian Development Bank and Food and Agriculture Organization, Manila and Rome.

Adhikari, R. and Yamamoto, Y. (2006) *Sewing Thoughts: How to Realise Human Development Goals in the Post-Quota World*, Tracing Report, Asia Pacific Trading Initiative, UNDP Regional Centre in Colombo.

Agarwal, B. (1983) 'Diffusion of rural innovations: Some analytical issues and the case of wood-burning cookstoves', *World Development*, vol 11, pp359–376.

Agarwal, B. (1988) 'Who sows? Who reaps? Women and land rights in India', *Journal of Peasant Studies*, vol 15, no 4, pp532–581.

Agarwal, B. (1992) 'The gender and environment debate: Lessons from India', *Feminist Studies*, vol 18, no 1, pp119–158.

Agarwal, B. (1994) *A Field of One's Own: Gender and Land Rights in South Asia*, Cambridge University Press, Cambridge.

Agarwal, B. (1997) 'Environmental action, gender equity and women's participation', *Development & Change*, vol 28, pp1–44.

Agarwal, B. (1998) 'Environmental management, equity and ecofeminism: Debating India's experience', *Journal of Peasant Studies*, vol 25, pp55–95.

Agarwal, B. (2001) 'Participatory exclusions, community forestry, and gender: An analysis for South Asia and a conceptual framework', *World Development*, vol 29, no 10, pp1623–1648.

Agarwal, B. (2002) 'Gender inequality, cooperation and environmental sustainability', paper presented at a workshop on 'Inequality, Collective Action and Environmental Sustainability', Working Paper 02-10-058, Santa Fe Institute, New Mexico.

Agarwal, B. (2010) *Gender and Green Governance: The Political Economy of Women's Presence Within and Beyond Community Forestry*, Oxford University Press, Oxford.

Agarwal, B. (2011) *Food Crises and Gender Inequality*, DESA Working Paper 107, UN Department of Economic and Social Affairs, New York.

Agarwal, B. (2014) 'Food sovereignty, food security and democratic choice: Critical contradictions, difficult conciliations', *Journal of Peasant Studies*, vol 41, no 6, pp1247–1268.

AGRA (2013) 'AGRA's policy program: Strengthening national policies to support Africa's Green Revolution', www.gatesfoundation.org/How-We-Work/Resources/Grantee-Profiles/Grantee-Profile-Alliance-for-a-Green-Revolution-in-Africa-AGRA, accessed 20 March 2013.

Ahlers, R., Cleaver, F., Rusca, M. and Schwartz, K. (2014) 'Informal space in the urban waterscape: Disaggregation and co-production of water services', *Water Alternatives*, vol 7, pp1–14.

Ali, T. S. and Rizvi, S. N. (2010) 'Menstrual knowledge and practices of female adolescents in urban Karachi, Pakistan', *Journal of Adolescence*, vol 33, pp531–541.

Allman, J., Geiger, S. and Musisi, N. (eds) (2002) *Women in African Colonial Histories*, Indiana University Press, Bloomington, IN.

Alstone, P., Niethammer, C., Mendonça, B. and Eftimie, A. (2011) 'Expanding women's role in Africa's modern off-grid lighting market', *Lighting Africa*, 4 October, http://lightingafrica.org, accessed 22 February 2015.

Alstone, P., Gershenson, D. and Kammen, D. K. (2015) 'Decentralized energy systems for clean electricity access', *Nature Climate Change*, vol 5, pp305–314, doi: 10.1038/nclimate2512.

Amrose, S., Burt, Z. and Ray, I. (forthcoming) 'Safe drinking water for low-income regions', *Annual Review of Environment and Resources*.

Anderson, D. and Grove, R. (1987) *Conservation in Africa: Peoples, Policies and Practice*, Cambridge University Press, Cambridge.

Anenberg, S. C., Balakrishnan, K., Jetter, J. J., Masera, O., Mehta, S., Moss, J. and Ramanathan, V. (2013) 'Cleaner cooking solutions to achieve health, climate and economic co-benefits', *Environmental Science and Technology*, vol 47, no 9, pp3944–3952.

Annas, J. (1993) 'Women and the quality of life: Two norms or one?', in M. Nussbaum and A. Sen (eds) *The Quality of Life*, WIDER Studies in Development Economics, Oxford University Press, New York.

Anseeuw, W., Boche, M., Breu, T., Giger, M., Lay, J., Messerli, P. and Nolte, K. (2012) *Transnational Land Deals for Agriculture in the Global South: Analytical Report based on the Land Matrix Database*, Centre for Development and Environment, Cirad and German Institute of Global and Area Studies, Bern, Montpelier and Hamburg.

Antonopoulos, R. and Hirway, I. (2010) *Unpaid Work and the Economy: Gender, Time and Poverty in Developing Countries*, Palgrave Macmillan, New York.

Appfell-Marglin, F. and Simon, S. (1994) 'Feminist orientalism and development', in W. Harcourt (ed) *Feminist Perspectives on Sustainable Development*, Zed Books, London, pp26–46.

Arora-Jonsson, S. (2011) 'Virtue and vulnerability: Discourses on women, gender and climate change', *Global Environmental Change*, vol 21, no 2, pp744–751.

Artecona, R. and Cunningham, W. (2002) *Effects of Trade Liberalization on the Gender Wage Gap in Mexico*, World Bank, Washington, DC.

Asher, K. (2004) 'Texts in context: Afro-Colombian women's activism in the Pacific Lowlands of Colombia', *Feminist Review*, vol 78, no 1, pp38–55.

Bacchetta, M., Ernst, E. and Bustamante, J. (2009) *Globalization and Informal Jobs in Developing Countries*, International Labour Organization and World Trade Organization, Geneva.

Badgett, M. V. L. and Folbre, N. (1999) 'Assigning care: Gender norms and economic outcomes', *International Labour Review*, vol 138, no 3, pp81–103.

Bahçe, S. A. K. and Memiş, E. (2013) 'Estimating the impact of the 2008–09 economic crisis on work time in Turkey', *Feminist Economics*, vol 19, no 3, pp181–207.

Bailis, R., Cowan, A., Berrueta, V. and Masera, O. (2009) 'Arresting the killer in the kitchen: The promises and pitfalls of commercializing improved cookstoves', *World Development*, vol 37, no 10, pp1694–1705.

Bakker, K. (2010) *Privatizing Water: Governance Failure and the World's Urban Water Crisis*, Cornell University Press, Ithaca, NY.

Balakrishnan, R. and Saiz, I. (2014) 'Transforming the development agenda requires more, not less, attention to human rights', Opendemocracy, 15 September, https://www.opendemocracy.net/openglobalrights-blog/radhika-balakrishnan-and-ignacio-saiz/transforming-development-agenda-requires, accessed 1 March 2015.

Bamber, P. and Fernandez-Stark, K. (2013) 'Global value chains, economic upgrading and gender in the horticulture industry', in C. Staritz and J. Guiherme Reis (eds) *Global Value Chains, Economic Upgrading, and Gender. Case Studies of the Horticulture, Tourism, and Call Center Industries*, World Bank, Washington, DC.

Banerji, P., Iyer, R., Rangachari, R., Sengupta, N. and Singh, S. (2000) *India Country Study Prepared for the World Commission on Dams*, World Commission on Dams, Cape Town.

Barnes, D. and Foley, G. (2004) *Rural Electrification in the Developing World: A Summary of Lessons from Successful Programmes*, Joint UNDP/World Bank Energy Sector Management Assistance Programme (ESMAP), World Bank, Washington, DC.

Barnosky, A., Hadly, A., Bascompte, J., Berlow, E., Brown, J., Fortelius, M., Getz, W. M., Harte, J., Hastings, A., Marquet, P. A., Martinez, N. D., Mooers, A., Roopnarine, P., Vermeij, G., Williams, J. W., Gillespie, R., Kitzes, J., Marshal, C., Matzke, N., Mindell, D. P., Revilla, E. and Smith, A. B. (2012) 'Approaching a state shift in Earth's biosphere', *Nature*, vol 486, pp52–58, doi 10.1038/nature11018.

Barrientos, S. (2007) 'Gender, codes of conduct and labour standards in global production systems', in I. van Staveren, D. Elson, C. Growth and N. Cagatay (eds) *The Feminist Economics of Trade*, Routledge, New York.

Barrientos, S. and Evers, B. (2013) 'Gender production networks: Push and pull on corporate responsibility?', in S. M. Rai and G. Waylen (eds) *New Frontiers in Feminist Political Economy*, Routledge, London, pp43–61.

Barrientos, S., Gereffi, G. and Rossi, A. (2011) 'Economic and social upgrading in global production networks: A new paradigm for a changing world', *International Labour Review*, vol 150, nos 3–4, pp319–340.

Basu, K. (2006) 'Globalization, poverty and inequality: What is the relationship? What can be done?', *World Development*, vol 34, no 8, pp1361–1373.

Baum, R., Luh, J. and Bartram, J. (2013) 'Sanitation: A global estimate of sewerage connections without treatment and the resulting impact on MDG progress', *Environmental Science & Technology*, vol 47, no 4, pp1994–2000.

Baviskar, A. (1995) *In the Belly of the River: Tribal Conflicts over Development in the Narmada Valley*, Oxford University Press, Oxford.

Bazilian, M., Hobbs, B. F., Blyth, W., MacGill, I. and Howells, M. (2011) 'Interactions between energy security and climate change: A focus on developing countries', *Energy Policy*, vol 39, pp3750–3756.

BBC News Africa (2012) 'Nigerian President Goodluck Jonathan urges birth control', BBC News, www.bbc.co.uk/news/world-africa-18610751, accessed 29 January 2015.

Behrman, J., Meinzen-Dick, R. and Quisumbing, A. (2012) 'The gender implications of large-scale land deals', *Journal of Peasant Studies*, vol 39, no 1, pp49–79.

Beinart, W. and McGregor, J. (2003) 'Social history and African environments', *Ecology and History Series*, Ohio University Press and James Currey, Athens, OH and Oxford.

Benería, L. and Roldan, M. (1987) *The Crossroads of Class and Gender: Industrial Homework, Subcontracting, and Household Dynamics in Mexico City*, University of Chicago Press, Chicago, IL.

Benería, L. and Sen, G. (1981) 'Accumulation, reproduction, and "women's role in economic development": Boserup revisited' *Signs*, vol 7, no 2 (Winter 1981), pp279–298.

Berik, G. and van der Meulen Rodgers, Y. (2009) 'Engendering development strategies and macroeconomic policies? What's sound and sensible?' in G. Berik, Y. van der Meulen Rodgers and A. Zammit (eds) *Social Justice and Gender Equality: Rethinking Development Strategies and Macroeconomic Policies*, Routledge for UN Research Institute for Social Development, New York.

Berik, G. and van der Meulen Rodgers, Y. (2010) 'Options for enforcing labour standards: Lessons from Bangladesh and Cambodia', *Journal of International Development*, vol 22, pp56–85.

Berik, G, van der Meulen Rodgers, Y. and Zveglich, J. E. (2004) 'International trade and gender wage discrimination. Evidence from East Asia' *Review of Development Economics*, vol 8, no 2, pp237–254.

Berkhout, F., Leach, M. and Scoones, I. (eds) (2003) *Negotiating Environmental Change: New Perspectives from Social Science*, Edgar Elgar, London.

Bernanke, B. S. (2011) 'Global imbalances: Links to economic and financial stability', Speech for the Banque de France Financial Stability Review Launch Event, Paris, France, 18 February.

Bernhardt, T. and Milberg, W. (2011) *Does Economic Upgrading Generate Social Upgrading? Insights from the Horticulture, Apparel, Mobile Phones and Tourism Sectors*, Capturing the Gains Working Paper 2011/07, Capturing the Gains, University of Manchester.

Bernstein, H. (2004) 'Changing before our very eyes: Agrarian questions and the politics of land today', *Journal of Agrarian Change*, vol 4, nos 1–2, pp190–225.

Bhanot, R. and Singh, M. (1992) 'The oustees of Pong Dam: Their search for a home', in E. G. Thukral (ed) *Big Dams, Displaced People*, Sage, New Delhi.

Bharadwaj, S. and Patkar, A. (2004) *Menstrual Hygiene and Management in Developing Countries: Taking Stock*, Junction Social Working Paper, IRC, The Hague, www.ircwash.org/resources/menstrual-hygiene-and-management-developing-countries-taking-stock, accessed 22 February 2015.

Bill & Melinda Gates Foundation (2012) 'Family planning: Strategy overview. Global Health Program', https://docs.gatesfoundation.org/Documents/family-planning-strategy.pdf, accessed 29 January 2015.

Bisht, T. C. (2009) 'Development-induced displacement and women: The case of the Tehri Dam, India', *Asia Pacific Journal of Anthropology*, vol 10, no 4, pp301–317.

Black, M. and Fawcett, B. (2008) *The Last Taboo: Opening the Door on the Global Sanitation Crisis*, Earthscan, London and Stirling, VA.

Black, S. E. and Brainerd, E. (2004) 'Importing equality? The impact of globalization on gender discrimination', *Industrial and Labour Relations Review*, vol 57, no 4, pp540–559.

Blecker, R. (2012) 'Global imbalances and U.S. trade in the great recession and its aftermath', in B. Cynamon, S. Fazzari and M. Setterfield (eds) *After the Great Recession: The Struggle for Economic Recovery and Growth*, Cambridge University Press, New York.

Blecker, R. A. and Seguino, S. (2002) 'Macroeconomic effects of reducing gender wage inequality in an export-oriented, semi-industrialized economy', *Review of Development Economics*, vol 6, no 1, pp103–119.

Bloom, D., Canning, D. and Sevilla, J. (2003) 'The demographic dividend: A new perspective on the economic consequences of population change', RAND, Santa Monica, CA, www.rand.org/content/dam/rand/pubs/monograph_reports/2007/MR1274.pdf, accessed 29 January 2015.

Blumberg, R. (1991) 'Income under female versus male control', in R. Blumberg (ed) *Gender, Family and Economy: The Triple Overlap*, Sage, Newbury Park, CA.

Bøås, M. and McNeill, D. (2003) *Global Institutions and Development. Framing the World?* Routledge, London.

Bond, T. C., Doherty, S. J., Fahey, D. W., Forster, P. M., Bemtsen, T., DeAngelo, B. J., Flanner, M. G., Ghan, S., Kärcher, B., Koch, D., Kinne, S., Kondo, Y., Quinn, P. K., Sarofim, M. C., Schultz, M. G., Schulz, M., Venkataraman, C., Zhang, H., Zhang, S., Bellouin, N., Guttikunda, S. K., Hopke, P. K., Jacobson, M. Z., Kaiser, J. W., Klimont, Z., Lohmann, U., Schwarz, J. P., Shindell, D., Storelvmo, T., Warren, S. G. and Zender, C. S. (2013) 'Bounding the role of black carbon in the climate system: A scientific assessment', *Journal of Geophysical Research: Atmospheres*, vol 118, pp5380–5552.

Borras, S. M. (2004) *La Via Campesina: An Evolving Transnational Social Movement*, Transnational Institute, Amsterdam.

Borras, S. M. and Franco, J. C. (2013) 'Global land grabbing and political reactions "from below"', *Third World Quarterly*, vol 34, no 9, pp1723–1747.

Borras, S. M., McMichael, P. and Scoones, I. (eds) (2010) 'The politics of biofuels, land and agrarian change', *Journal of Peasant Studies*, vol 37, no 4, pp575–962.

Borras Jr, S. M., Hall, R., Scoones, I., White, B. and Wolford, W. (2011) 'Towards a better understanding of global land grabbing: An editorial introduction', *Journal of Peasant Studies*, vol 38, no 2, pp209–216.

Boserup, E. (1970) *Woman's Role in Economic Development*, St Martin's Press, New York.

Boyce, J. (2011) 'The environment as our common heritage', acceptance speech for the Common Heritage Award from the Media Freedom Foundation and Project Censored, 8 February.

Boyce, J. K. and Ndikumana, L. (2011) *Africa's Odious Debts: How Foreign Loans and Capital Flight Bled a Continent*, Zed Books, London.

Braidotti, R. (1994) *Nomadic Subjects: Embodiment and Sexual Difference in Contemporary Feminist Theory*, Columbia University Press, New York.

Braidotti, R., Charkiewicz, E., Häusler, S. and Wieringa, S. (1994) *Women, the Environment and Sustainable Development: Towards a Theoretical Synthesis*, Zed Books, London.

von Braun, J. (2014) 'Aiming for food and nutrition security in a changed global context: Strategy to end hunger', in J. A. Alonso, G. Cornia and R. Vos (eds) *Alternative Development Strategies in the Post 2015 Era*, Bloomsbury Press and United Nations, New York and London, pp163–180.

Braun, Y. (2011) 'The reproduction of inequality: Race, class, gender, and the social organisation of work at sites of large-scale development projects', *Social Problems*, vol 58, no 2, pp281–303.

Braunstein, E. (2012) *Neoliberal Development Macroeconomics. A Consideration of its Gendered Employment Effects*, UNRISD Gender and Development Programme Paper 14, UN Research Institute for Social Development, Geneva.

Braunstein, E. and Brenner, M. (2007) 'Foreign direct investment and wages in urban China: The differences between women and men', *Feminist Economics*, vol 13, nos 3–4, pp213–237.

Braunstein, E., Van Staveren, I. and Tavani, D. (2011) 'Embedding care and unpaid work in macroeconomic modeling: A structuralist approach', *Feminist Economics*, vol 17, no 4, pp5–31.

Bray, F. (2007) 'Gender and technology', *Annual Review of Anthropology*, vol 36, pp37–53.

Brockington, D., Duffy, R. and Igoe, J. (2008) *Nature Unbound: Conservation, Capitalism and the Future of Protected Areas*, Earthscan, London.

Brokensha, D., Warren, D. M. and Werner, O. (eds) (1980) *Indigenous Knowledge Systems and Development*, University Press of America, Washington, DC.

Brooks, J. and Wiggins, S. (2010) 'The use of input subsidies in developing countries', *Global Forum on Agriculture*, Organisation for Economic Co-operation and Development, Paris.

Bruins, H. J., Evenaru, M. and Nessler, U. (1986) 'Rainwater-harvesting agriculture for food production in arid zones: The challenge of the African famine', *Applied Geography*, vol 6, pp13–32.

Brundtland, G. H. (1987) *Our Common Future: Report of the World Commission on Environment and Development*, Oxford University Press, Oxford.

Brundtland, G. H., Erhlich, P., Goldemberg, J., Hansen, J., Lovins, A., Likens, G., Manabe, S., May, B., Mooney, H., Robèrt, K., Salim, E., Sato, G., Solomon, S., Stern, N., M. S. Swaminathan Research Foundation, Watson, R., Barefoot College, Conservation International, International Institute for Environment and Development and International Union for the Conservation of Nature (2012) *Environment and Development Challenges: The Imperative to Act*, The Blue Planet Laureates, Asahi Glass Foundation, Tokyo, www.af-info.or.jp/en/bpplaureates/doc/2012jp_fp_en.pdf, accessed 29 January 2015.

Buckingham-Hatfield, S. (2002) 'Gender equality: A prerequisite for sustainable development', *Geography*, vol 87, no 3, pp227–233.

Budig, M. and Misra, J. (2010) 'How care-work employment shapes earnings in cross-national perspective', *International Labour Review*, vol 149, no 4, pp441–460.

Budlender, D. (2010) 'What do time use studies tell us about unpaid care work?', in D. Budlender (ed.) *Time Use Studies and Unpaid Care Work*, UNRISD, Geneva, www.unrisd.org/80256B3C005BCCF9/%28httpAuxPages%29/A1A49C425F95FE92C12578E100592F34?OpenDocument, accessed 22 February 2015.

Büscher, B., Sullivan, S., Neves, K., Igoe, J. and Brockington, D. (2012) 'Towards a synthesized critique of neoliberal biodiversity conservation', *Capitalism, Nature Socialism*, vol 23, no 2, pp4–30.

Busse, M. and Spielmann, C. (2006) 'Gender inequality and trade', *Review of International Economics*, vol 14, no 3, pp362–379.

Bussolo, M. and De Hoyos, R. E. (2009) 'Gender aspects of the trade and poverty nexus: Introduction and overview', in M. Bussolo and R. E. De Hoyos (eds) *Gender Aspects of the Trade and Poverty Nexus: A Macro-Micro Approach*, Palgrave Macmillan and World Bank, Washington, DC.

Butler, J. (1990) *Gender Trouble: Feminism and the Subversion of Identity*, Routledge, New York and London.

Butler, J. (1994) 'Gender as performance: An interview with Judith Butler', *Radical Philosophy*, no 67, pp32–39.

Cabraal, A., Barnes, D. F. and Agarwal, S. G. (2005) *Annual Review of Environment and Resources*, vol 30, no 1, pp117–144.

Cairncross, S. (2003) 'Water supply and sanitation: Some misconceptions', *Tropical Medicine and International Health*, vol 8, no 3, pp193–195.

Calas, M. and Smircich, L. (1999) 'From the "woman's" point of view: Feminist approaches to organization studies', in S. Clegg and C. Hardy (eds) *Studying Organization, Theory and Method*, Sage, London, pp212–251.

Campbell, C. (1996) 'Out on the front lines but still struggling for voice: Women in the rubber tappers' defense of the forest in Xapuri, Acre, Brazil', in D. Rocheleau, B. Thomas-Slayter and E. Wangari (eds) *Feminist Political Ecology: Global Issues and Local Experiences*, Routledge, London.

von Carlowitz, H. C. (1712 [1732]) *Sylvicultura Oeconomica*, Reprint of 2nd edn, Verlag Kessel, Eifelweg, Germany.

Carney, J. (2004) 'Gender conflict in Gambian wetlands', in R. Peet and M. Watts (eds) *Liberation Ecologies: Environment, Development, Social Movements*, Routledge, London.

Carney, J. and Watts, M. (1990) 'Manufacturing dissent: Work, gender and the politics of meaning in a peasant society', *Africa: Journal of the International African Institute*, vol 60, no 2, pp207–241.

Carson, R. (1962) *Silent Spring*, Houghton Mifflin, Boston, MA.

Casillas, C. and Kammen, D. (2010) 'The energy–poverty–climate nexus', *Science*, vol 330, no 6008, pp1181–1182.

Castañeda, I. and Gammage, S. (2011) 'Gender, global crises, and climate change', in D. Jain and D. Elson (eds) *Harvesting Feminist Knowledge for Public Policy*, Sage, New Delhi.

Cecelski, E. (1984) *The Rural Energy Crisis, Women's Work and Family Welfare: Perspectives and Approaches to Action*, WEP Research Working Paper, International Labour Organization, Geneva, www.ilo.org/public/libdoc/ilo/1984/84B09_233_engl.pdf, accessed 22 February 2015.

Cecelski, E. (2000) *The Role of Women in Sustainable Energy Development*, National Renewable Energy Laboratory, Golden, CO.

CEDAW (1979) *Convention on the Elimination of All Forms of Discrimination Against Women*, United Nations General Assembly, www.un.org/womenwatch/daw/cedaw/committee.htm, accessed 22 February 2015.

Census of India (2001) *Census of India*, Government of India, Ministry of Home Affairs, New Delhi.

Census of India (2011) *Census of India*, Government of India, Ministry of Home Affairs, New Delhi.

Cernea, M. (1999) *The Economics of Involuntary Resettlement: Questions and Challenges*, World Bank, Washington, DC.

Cernea, M. and Mathur, H. M. (eds) (2008) *Can Compensation Prevent Impoverishment?: Reforming Resettlement Through Investments and Benefit-Sharing*, Oxford University Press, New Delhi.

Cernea, M. and McDowell, C. (eds) (2000) *Risks and Reconstruction: Experiences of Resettlers and Refugees*, World Bank, Washington, DC.

CESCR (1999) *General Comment 12*, Committee on Economic, Social and Cultural Rights, UN Office of the High Commissioner on Human Rights, New York.

CESR (2008) *Derechos o Privilegios: El compromisso fiscal con la salud, la educación y la alimentación en Guatemala*, Center for Economic and Social Rights, Guatemala/España.

Chambers, J. D. (1953) 'Enclosure and labour supply in the Industrial Revolution', *Economic History Review*, vol 2, no 5, pp319–343.

Chambers, R. (2011) 'Sanitation MDG is badly off track, but a community-led approach could fix that', Global Development/Poverty Matters blog, *The Guardian*, www.guardian.co.uk/global-development/poverty-matters/2011/may/30/mdg-sanitation-offtrack-but-community-led-approach-is-working, accessed 22 February 2015.

Chan, C. K. and Ching Lam, M. (2012) 'The reality and challenges of green jobs in China: An exploration', *International Journal of Labour Research*, vol 4, no 2, pp189–207.

Chatterjee, L. (2011) 'Time to acknowledge the dirty truth behind community-led sanitation', Global Development/Poverty Matters blog, *The Guardian*, www.guardian.co.uk/global-development/poverty-matters/2011/jun/09/dirty-truth-behind-community-sanitation, accessed 22 February 2015.

Chattopadhyay, R. and Duflo, E. (2004) 'Women as policy makers: Evidence from a randomized policy experiment in India', *Econometrica*, vol 72, no 5, pp1409–1443.

Chen, Z., Ge, Y., Lai, H. and Wan, C. (2013) 'Globalization and gender wage inequality in China', *World Development*, vol 44, pp256–266.

Chu, J. (2011) 'Gender and "land grabbing" in sub-Saharan Africa: Women's land rights and customary tenure', *Development*, vol 54, no 1, pp35–39.

Clancy, J. (2009) 'Economy or environment? It's a false choice', National Union of Public and General Employees, Canada, http://nupge.ca/content/%5Bnid%5D/economy-or-environment-its-false-choice.

Clasen, T. F., Bostoen, K., Schmidt, W. P., Boisson, S., Fung, I. C., Jenkins, M. W., Scott, B., Sugden, S. and Cairncross, S. (2010) 'Interventions to improve disposal of human excreta for preventing diarrhoea', *Cochrane Database of Systematic Reviews*, Issue 6, doi: 10.1002/14651858.CD007180.pub2.

Cleaver, F. (1998) 'Choice, complexity and change: Gendered livelihoods and the management of water', *Agriculture and Human Values*, vol 15, pp293–299.

Colson, E. (1999) 'Gendering those uprooted by "development"', in D. Indra (ed) *Engendering Forced Migration: Theory and Practice*, Berghahn Books, New York.

Connelly, M. (2008) *Fatal Misconception: The Struggle to Control World Population*, Harvard University Press, Cambridge, MA.

Cooke, P., Köhlin, G. and Hyde, W. F. (2008) 'Fuelwood, forests and community management – Evidence from household studies', *Environment and Development Economics*, Cambridge University Press, Cambridge, pp103–135.

Corbera, E. and Brown, K. (2008) 'Building institutions to trade ecosystem services: Marketing forest carbon in Mexico', *World Development*, vol 36, no 10, pp1956–1979.

Corbera, E. and Schroeder, H. (2010) 'Governing and implementing REDD', *Environmental Science and Policy*, vol 14, no 2, pp89–99.

Corbett, H. and Mehta, L. (2013) *Ensuring Women's and Girls' Rights to Water and Sanitation Post-2015*, IDS Policy Briefing 38, Institute of Development Studies, Brighton, UK, http://mobile.opendocs.ids.ac.uk/opendocs/handle/123456789/3268?show=full, accessed 22 February 2015.

Cornwall, A. and Brock, K. (2005) 'What do buzzwords do for development policy? A critical look at "participation", "empowerment" and "poverty reduction"', *Third World Quarterly*, vol 26, no 7, pp1043–1060.

Cornwall, A., Harrison, E. and Whitehead, A. (2007) 'Gender myths and feminist fables: The struggle for interpretive power in gender and development', *Development and Change*, vol 38, no 1, pp1–20.

Cripps, F., Izurieta, A. and Singh, A. (2011) 'Global imbalances, under-consumption and over-borrowing: The state of the world economy and future policies', *Development and Change*, vol 42, no 1, pp228–261.

Croll, E. and Parkin, D. (1992) *Bush Base, Forest Farm: Culture, Environment and Development*, Routledge, London and New York.

CWGL (2013) *Towards the Realization of Women's Rights and Gender Equality: Post 2015 Sustainable Development*, Center for Women's Global Leadership, Rutgers School of Arts and Sciences, New Brunswick, NJ.

Dabelko, G. D. (2011) 'Population and environment connections: The role of US family planning assistance in US foreign policy', Council on Foreign Relations, New York.

Dankelman, I. E. and Davidson, J. (eds) (1988) *Women and Environment in the Third World: Alliance for the Future*, Earthscan, London.

De Hoyos, R. E. (2006) *Structural Modeling of Female Labour Participation and Occupation Decisions*: Cambridge Working Paper in Economics 0611, Faculty of Economics, University of Cambridge, Cambridge.

De Schutter, O. (2011) *The World Trade Organizaiton and the Post-Global Food Crisis Agenda: Putting Food Security First in the International Trade Agenda*, UN Special Rapporteur on the Right to Food, www.srfood.org, accessed 17 April 2014.

De Schutter, O. (2012) *United Nations Special Rapporteur on the Right to Food: The Right to Food as a Human Right*, Office of the United Nations High Commissioner for Human Rights – United Nations Office at Geneva.

De Schutter, O. (2014) *Final Report: The Transformative Potential of the Right to Food*, Report of the Special Rapporteur on the Right to Food, General Assembly, UN, New York.

Deere, C. D., Oduro, A. D., Swaminathan, H. and Doss, C. (2013) 'Property rights and the gender distribution of wealth in Ecuador, Ghana, and India', *Journal of Economic Inequality*, vol 11, no 2, pp249–265.

Deininger, K., Byerlee, D., Lindsay, J., Norton, A., Selod, H. and Stickler, M. (2011) *Rising Global Interest in Farmland: Can it Yield Sustainable and Equitable Benefits?*, World Bank, Washington, DC.

Demeke, M., Dawe, D., Tefft, J., Ferede, T. and Bell, W. (2012) *Stabilizing Price Incentives for Staple Grain Producers in the Context of Broader Agricultural Policies: Debates and Country Experiences*, ESA Working Paper 12-05, Agricultural Development Economics Division, FAO, Rome.

Demeny, P. (1988) 'Social science and population policy', *Population and Development Review*, vol 3, no 14, pp451–479, reprinted in *Demography in Development – Social Science or Policy Science?* PROP Publication Series, vol 3, Program on Population and Development in Poor Countries, Lund University, Sweden.

Denton, F. (2002) 'Climate change vulnerability, impacts, and adaptation: Why does gender matter?', *Gender & Development*, vol 10, no 2, pp10–20.

Derman, B., Odgaard, R. and Sjaastad, E. (eds) (2007) *Conflicts over Land and Water in Africa*, James Curry, Oxford.

Dewan, R. (2008) 'Development projects and displaced women', in H. Mohan Mathur (ed) *India Social Development Report 2008: Development and Displacement*, Oxford University Press, New Delhi.

Dewees, P. (1989) 'The woodfuel crises reconsidered: Observations on the dynamics of abundance and scarcity', *World Development*, vol 17, no 8, 1159–1172.

Dominguez-Villalobos, L. and Brown-Grossman, F. (2010) 'Trade liberalization and gender wage inequality in Mexico', *Feminist Economics*, vol 16, no 4, pp53–79.

Dorward, A. (2009) *Rethinking Agricultural Input Subsidy Programmes in a Changing World*, School of Oriental and African Studies, London.

Doss, C. (2011) 'If women hold up half the sky, how much of the world's food do they produce?', ESA Working Paper 11-04, Agricultural Development Economics Division, FAO, Rome.

Dow, K. and Downing, T. E. (2007) *The Atlas of Climate Change: Mapping the World's Greatest Challenge*, University of California Press, Berkeley, CA.

Dowie, M. (2001) *American Foundations: An Investigative History*, MIT Press, Cambridge, MA.

Doyle, T. (2005) *Environmental Movements in Minority and Majority Worlds: A Global Perspective*, Rutgers University Press, Brunswick, NJ.

Doyle, T. and Chaturvedi, S. (2011) 'Climate refugees and security: Conceptualizations, categories and contestations', in J. S. Dryzek, R. B. Norgaard and D. Schlosberg (eds) *Oxford Handbook of Climate Change and Security*, Oxford University Press, Oxford, pp278–291.

Dressler, W., Büscher, B., Schoon, M., Brockington, D., Hayes, T., Kull, C., McCarthy, J. and Streshta, K. (2010) 'From hope to crisis and back? A critical history of the global CBNRM narrative', *Environmental Conservation*, vol 37, no 1, pp1–11.

Drèze, J. and Sen, A. (1989) *Hunger and Public Action*, Clarendon Press, Oxford.

Duflo, E. and Pande, R. (2007) 'Dams', *Quarterly Journal of Economics*, vol 122, no 2, pp601–646.

Dwivedi, R. (2006) *Conflict and Collective Action: The Sardar Sarovar Project in India*, Routledge, London.

Dyson, T. (2010) *Population and Development: The Demographic Transition*, Zed Books, London.

ECOSOC (2007) *Strengthening Efforts to Eradicate Poverty and Hunger, Including Through the Global Partnership for Development*, Report of the Secretary-General, United Nations, New York.

Edelman, M. (2013) 'Messy hectares: Questions about the epistemology of land grabbing data', *Journal of Peasant Studies*, vol 40, no 3, pp485–502.

Edström, J., Das, A. and Dolan, C. (2014) 'Undressing patriarchy: Men and structural violence', *IDS Bulletin*, vol 45, no 1, pp1–10.

Ehrlich, P. R. (1968) *The Population Bomb*, Sierra Club/Ballantine Books, New York.

Elmhirst, R. (2011) 'Introducing new feminist political ecologies', *Geoforum*, vol 42, no 2, pp129–132.

Elson, D. (1996) 'Appraising recent developments in the world market for nimble fingers', in A. Chhachhi and R. Pittin (eds) *Confronting State, Capital and Patriarchy: Women's Organizing in the Process of Industrialization*, St Martin's Press, New York.

Elson, D. (1998) 'The economic, the political and the domestic: Businesses, states and households in the organization of production', *New Political Economy*, vol 3, no 2, pp189–208.

Elson, D. (2011) 'Economics for a post-crisis world. Putting social justice first', in D. Jain and D. Elson (eds) *Harvesting Feminist Knowledge for Public Policy*, Sage, New Delhi.

Elson, D. and Balakrishnan, R. (2012) 'The post 2015 development framework and the realization of women's rights and social justice', *Center for Women's Global Leadership*, Rutgers University, New Brunswick, NJ.

Elson, D. and Çağatay, N. (2000) 'The social content of macroeconomic policies', *World Development*, vol 28, no 7, pp1347–1364.

Elson, D. and Pearson, R. (1981) 'Nimble fingers make cheap workers: An analysis of women's employment in third world export manufacturing', *Feminist Review*, vol 7, pp87–107.

England, P., Budig, M. and Folbre, N. (2002) 'Wages of virtue: The relative pay of care work', *Social Problems*, vol 49, no 4, pp455–473.

ESMAP (2004) *The Impact of Energy on Women's Lives in Rural India*, World Bank, Energy Sector Management Assistance Program (ESMAP), Washington, DC.

Esquivel, V. (2013) *Care in Households and Communities*, Oxfam Research Reports, Oxfam International, Oxford.

Evans, P. (1995) *Embedded Autonomy: States and Industrial Transformation*, Princeton University Press, Princeton, NJ.

Evans, P. (2002) 'Collective capabilities, culture, and Amartya Sen's Development as Freedom', *Studies in Comparative International Development*, vol 37, no 2, pp54–60.

Evans, P. (2008) *In Search of the 21st Century Developmental State*, Working Paper 4, Centre for Global Political Economy, University of Sussex, Brighton, UK.

Eyben, R. and Turquet, L. (eds) (2013) *Feminists in Development Organizations: Change from the Margins*, Practical Action Publishers, Rugby.

Fairbairn, M. (2014) '"Like gold with yield": Evolving intersections between farmland and finance', *Journal of Peasant Studies*, doi 10.1080/03066150.2013.873977.

Fairhead, J. and Leach, M. (1996) *Misreading the African Landscape: Society and Ecology in a Forest–Savanna Mosaic*, Cambridge University Press, Cambridge.

Fairhead, J., Leach, M. and Scoones, I. (2012) 'Green grabbing: A new appropriation of nature?', *Journal of Peasant Studies*, vol 39, no 2, pp285–307.

FAO (1996) *Declaration and Agenda for Action of the World Food Summit*, Food and Agriculture Organization, Rome.

FAO (2010) *State of Food and Agriculture 2010/2011: Women in Agriculture – Closing the Gender Gap for Development*, Food and Agriculture Organization, Rome.

FAO (2013) *The State of Food Insecurity in the World: The Multiple Dimensions of Food Security*, Food and Agriculture Organization, Rome.

FAO (2014) *Food Security Indicators*, Food and Agriculture Organization, Rome.

FAO, IFAD, UNCTAD and the World Bank Group (2010) *Principles for Responsible Agricultural Investment that Respects Rights, Livelihoods and Resources*, http://siteresources.worldbank.org/INTARD/214574-1111138388661/22453321/Principles_Extended.pdf, accessed 20 February 2014.

FAO, IFAD, IFM, OECD, UNCTAD, WFP, World Bank, WTO, IFPRI and UN HLTF (2011) *Price Volatility in Food and Agricultural Markets: Policy Responses. Policy Report to the G-20*.

FAO, IFAD and WFP (2013) *The State of Food Insecurity in the World: The Multiple Dimensions of Food Security*, www.fao.org/docrep/018/i3434e/i3434e00.htm, accessed 22 February 2015.

Fares, J., Gauri, V., Jimenez, E. Y., Lundberg, M. K. A., McKenzie, D., Murthi, M., Ridao-Cano, C. and Sinha, N. (2006) *World Development Report 2007: Development and the Next Generation*, World Bank, Washington, DC, doi 10.1596/978-0-8213-6549-6.

Federici, S. (2004) *Caliban and the Witch: Women, The Body and Primitive Accumulation*, Autonomedia, Brooklyn.

Feenstra, R. C. and Hanson, G. H. (1997) 'Foreign direct investment and relative wages: Evidence from Mexico's maquiladoras', *Journal of International Economics*, vol 42, nos 3–4, pp371–393.

Feng, W., Cai, Y. and B. Gu. (2013) 'Population, policy and politics: How will history judge China's one-child policy?', *Population and Development Review*, no 38, pp115–129.

Fernandes, W. (2004) 'Rehabilitation for the displaced', *Economic and Political Weekly*, vol 39, no 12, pp1191–1193.

Fernandes, W. (2008) 'Sixty years of development-induced displacement in India', in H. Mohan Mathur (ed) *India Social Development Report 2008: Development and Displacement*, Oxford University Press, New Delhi.

Fernandes, W. (2009) 'Displacement and alienation from common property resources', in L. Mehta (ed) *Displaced by Development: Confronting Marginalisation and Gender Injustice*, Sage, New Delhi.

Fernandes, W. and Paranjpye, V. (eds) (1997) *Rehabilitation Policy and Law in India: A Right to Livelihood*, Indian Social Institute, New Delhi.

Fernandes, W. and Thukral, E. G. (eds) (1989) *Development, Displacement, and Rehabilitation: Issues for a National Debate*, Indian Social Institute, New Delhi.

Financial Times (2014) *The Business of Global Food Security*, special report, 11 April, www.ft.com/reports/global-food-security, accessed 18 February 2015.

Fischer, A. M. (2010) 'The demographic imperative', *The Broker*, www.thebrokeronline.eu/en/Articles/The-demographic-imperative, accessed 29 January 2015.

Fischer, A. M. (2014) *The Social Value of Employment and the Redistributive Imperative for Development*, UNDP Human Development Report Office, http://hdr.undp.org/sites/default/files/fischer_hdr_2014_final.pdf, accessed 29 January 2015.

Fischer-Kowalski, M., Swilling, M., von Weizsäcker, E. U., Ren, Y., Moriguchi, Y., Crane, W., Krausmann, F., Eisenmenger, N., Giljum, S., Hennicke, P., Romero Lankao, P. and Siriban Manalang, A. (2011) *Decoupling Natural Resource Use and Environmental Impacts from Economic Growth*, a Report of the Working Group on Decoupling to the International Resource Panel, UN Environment Programme, New York.

Fischhoff, B. (1995) 'Risk perception and communication unplugged: Twenty years of process', *Risk Analysis*, vol 15, no 2, pp137–145.

Fisher, J. (2006) *For her, it's the Big Issue: Putting Women at the Center of Water Supply, Sanitation and Hygiene*, Evidence Report, Water Supply and Sanitation Collaboration Council, Geneva.

Folbre, N. (1994) *Who Pays for the Kids? Gender and the Structures of Constraint*, Routledge, New York.

Folbre, N. (2001) *The Invisible Heart: Economics and Family Values*, New Press, New York.

Folbre, N. (2012) 'The political economy of human capital', *Review of Radical Political Economics*, vol 44, no 3, pp281–292.

Folke, C., Jansson, Å., Rockström, J., Olsson, P., Carpenter, S. R., Chapin, F. S., Crepín, A.-S., Daily, G., Danell, K., Ebbesson, J., Elmqvist, T., Galaz, V., Moberg, F., Nilsson, M., Österblom, H., Ostrom, E., Persson, Å., Peterson, G., Polasky, S., Steffen, W., Walker, B. and Westley, F. (2011) 'Reconnecting to the biosphere', *Ambio*, vol 40, pp719–738.

Fontana, M. (2007) 'Modeling the effects of trade on women, at work and at home: Comparative perspectives', in I. van Staveren, D. Elson, C. Grown and N. Cagatay (eds) *The Feminist Economics of Trade*, Routledge, London.

Fraser, N. (2013) *The Fortunes of Feminism: From State-Managed Capitalism to Neoliberal Crisis*, Verso, London.

Fukuda-Parr, S. (2003) 'The human development paradigm: Operationalizing Sen's ideas on capabilities', *Feminist Economics*, vol 9, pp301–317.

Fukuda-Parr, S. and Orr, A. (2014) 'The MDG hunger target and the contested visions of food security', *Journal of Human Development and Capabilities*, vol 15, nos 2–3, pp147–60.

Fukuda-Parr, S., Greenstein, J. and Stewart, D. (2013) 'How should MDG success and failure be judged: Faster progress or achieving the targets?', *World Development*, vol 41, pp19–30.

Fullerton, D. G., Bruce, N. and Gordon, S. B. (2008) 'Indoor air pollution from biomass fuel smoke is a major health concern in the developing world', *Transactions of the Royal Society of Tropical Medicine and Hygiene*, vol 102, no 9, pp843–851.

Gadgil, M., Berkes, F. and Folke, C. (1993) 'Indigenous knowledge for biodiversity conservation', *Ambio*, vol 22, pp151–156.

Genanet (ed) (2013) *Sustainable Economy and Green Growth: Who Cares?*, Genanet, Berlin.

Ghosh, J. (2007) 'Informalization, migration and women: Recent trends in Asia', in D. Banerjee and M. Goldfield (eds) *Labour, Globalization and the State: Workers, Women and Migrants Confront Neoliberalism*, Routledge, London.

Ghosh, J. (2010) 'The unnatural coupling: Food and global finance', *Journal of Agrarian Change*, vol 10, no 1, pp72–86.

Gilbert, C. (2011) 'International commodity agreements and their current relevance for grains price stabilization', in A. Prakash (ed) *Safeguarding Food Security in Volatile Markets*, FAO, Rome.

Gillespie, S., Haris, J. and Kadiyala, S. (2012) *The Agriculture–Nutrition Disconnect in India: What do we know?* IFPRI discussion paper 01187, International Food Policy Research Institute, Washington, DC.

Girod, B., van Vuuren, D. P. and Hertwich, E. G. (2013) 'Global climate targets and future consumption level: An evaluation of the required GHG intensity', *Environmental Research Letters*, vol 8, no 1, doi:10.1088/1748-9326/8/1/014016.

GLAAS (2012) *UN-Water Global Annual Assessment of Sanitation and Drinking-Water (GLAAS) 2012 Report: The Challenge of Extending and Sustaining Services*, World Health Organization, Geneva.

Gleick, P. H. (2000) 'The changing water paradigm. A look at twenty-first century water resources development', *Water International*, vol 25, no 1, pp127–138.

Global Health Watch (2011) *Maternal Mortality: Need for a Broad Framework of Intervention*, Global Health Watch 3: An Alternative World Health Report, Zed Books, London.

Goetz, A. M. (1997) *Getting Institutions Right for Women in Development*, Zed Books, London.

Goldberg, P. K. and Pavcnik, N. (2007) 'Distributional effects of globalization in developing countries', *Journal of Economic Literature*, vol 45, no 1, pp39–82.

Goldblatt, B. and McLean, K. (eds) (2011) *Women's Social and Economic Rights*, Juta, Cape Town.

Goldemberg, J., Johansson, T. B., Reddy, A. K. and Williams, R. H. (1985) 'Basic needs and much more with one kilowatt per capita', *Ambio*, vol 14, nos 4–5, pp190–200.

GRAIN (2013) 'G8 and land grabs in Africa', *Against the Grain*, GRAIN, Barcelona, Spain, www.grain.org/article/entries/4663-the-g8-and-land-grabs-in-africa, accessed 18 February 2015.

Greenhalgh, S. (1996) 'The social construction of population science: An intellectual, institutional, and political history of twentieth century demography', *Comparative Studies in Society and History*, vol 1, no 38, pp26–66.

Greenhalgh, S. (2005) 'Globalization and population governance in China', in A. Ong and S. J. Collier (eds) *Global Assemblages: Technology, Politics and Ethics as Anthropological Problems*, Blackwell, Malden, MA, pp254–271.

Greenhalgh, S. (2012) 'Patriarchal demographics? China's sex ratio reconsidered', *Population and Development Review*, vol 38S, pp130–149.

Grieshop, A., Marshall, J. and Kandlikar, M. (2011) 'Heath and climate benefits of cookstove replacement options', *Energy Policy*, vol 39, no 12, pp7530–7542.

Griggs, D., Stafford-Smith, M., Gaffney, O., Rockström, J., Öhman, M. C., Shyamsundar, P., Steffen, W., Glaser, G., Kanie, N. and Noble, I. (2013) 'Policy: Sustainable development goals for people and planet', *Nature*, vol 495, pp305–307.

Grosz, E. (1994) *Volatile Bodies: Toward a Corporeal Feminism*, Indiana University Press, Bloomington, IN.

Guha, R. (2000) *Environmentalism: A Global History*, Oxford University Press, Oxford.

Guruswamy, L. (2011) 'Energy poverty', *Annual Review of Environment and Resources*, vol 36, pp139–161.

Guyer, J. and Peters, P. (1987) 'Introduction to Special Issue on Households', *Development & Change*, vol 18, no 2, pp197–214.

Hall, D. (2012) 'Rethinking primitive accumulation: Theoretical tensions and rural Southeast Asian complexities', *Antipode*, vol 44, no 4, pp1188–2008.

Hall, D., Hirsch, P. and Li, T. (2011) *Powers of Exclusion: Land Dilemmas in Southeast Asia*, Nus Press, Singapore.

Hammond, J. L. and Hammond, B. (1913) *The Village Labourer, 1760–1832: A Study in the Government of England Before the Reform Bill*, Longmans, Green and Co., New York.

Hanemann, W. M. (2006) 'The economic conception of water', in P. P. Rogers, M. R. Llamas and L. Martinez-Cortina (eds) *Water Crisis: Myth or Reality?* London, Taylor & Francis.

Haraway, D. (1988) 'Situated knowledges: The science question in feminism and the privilege of partial perspective', *Feminist Studies*, vol 14, no 3, pp575–599.

Harcourt, W. (ed) (1994a) *Feminist Perspectives on Sustainable Development*, Zed Books, London.

Harcourt, W. (1994b) 'Negotiating positions in the sustainable development debate: Situating the feminist perspective', in *Feminist Perspectives on Sustainable Development*, Zed Books, London, pp11–26.

Hardin, G. (1968) 'The tragedy of the commons', *Science*, vol 162, no 3859, pp1243–1248.

Harris, B. (1995) 'The intrafamily distribution of hunger in South Asia', in J. Drèze, A. Sen and A. Hussain (eds) *The Political Economy of Hunger: Selected Essays*, Clarendon Press, Oxford, pp224–297.

Harris, D., Kooy, M. and Jones, L. (2011) *Analyzing the Governance and Political Economy of Water and Sanitation Service Delivery*, ODI Working Paper 334, Overseas Development Institute, London.

Harrison, A. and Hanson, G. (1999) 'Who gains from trade reform? Some remaining puzzles', *Journal of Development Economics*, vol 59, no 1, pp125–154.

Hart, C. and Smith, G. (2013) *Scaling Adoption of Clean Cooking Solutions through Women's Empowerment: A Resource Guide*, Global Alliance for Clean Cookstoves, Washington, DC.

Hart, G. (1991) 'Engendering everyday forms of resistance: Gender, patronage and production politics in rural Malaysia', *Journal of Peasant Studies*, vol 19, no 1, pp93–121.

Hart, G. (1998) 'Multiple trajectories: A critique of industrial restructuring and the new institutionalism', *Antipode*, vol 30, no 4, pp333–356.

Hartmann, B. (1995) *Reproductive Rights and Wrongs: The Global Politics of Population Control*, South End Press, Boston, MA.

Hartmann, B. (1997) 'Women, population and the environment: Whose consensus, whose empowerment?', in N. Visvanathan, L. Duggan, L. Nisonoff and N. Wiegersma (eds) *The Women, Gender and Development Reader*, Zed Books, London and New Jersey, pp293–302.

Hartmann, B. (2010) 'Rethinking climate refugees and climate conflict: Rhetoric, reality and the politics of policy discourse', *Journal of International Development*, vol 22, pp233–246.

Hartmann, B. (2014) 'Converging on disaster: Climate security and the Malthusian Anticipatory Regime for Africa', *Geopolitics*, vol 19, no 4, pp757–783.

Haub, C. (2011) 'China releases first 2010 census results', Population Reference Bureau, www.prb.org/Publications/Articles/2011/china-census-results.aspx, accessed 29 January 2015.

Hawkins, R. and Ojeda, D. (2011) 'Gender and environment: Critical tradition and new challenges', *Environment and Planning – Part D*, vol 29, no 2, pp237–253.

van Heemstra, C. (2013) 'Sustainable economy and care economy. Concepts, linkages, questions', in *Sustainable Economy and Green Growth: Who Cares?*, Genanet, Berlin.

Heffron, R., Donnell, D., Rees, H., Celum, C., Mugo, N., Were, E., de Bruyn, G., Nakku-Joloba, E., Ngure, K., Kiarie, J., Coombs, R. W. and Maeten, J. M. (2012) 'Use of hormonal contraceptives and risk of HIV-1 transmission: A prospective cohort study', *The Lancet*, vol 12, pp19–26, doi http://dx.doi.org/10.1016/S1473-3099(11)70247-X.

Heintz, J. (2006) 'Low-wage manufacturing and global commodity chains: A model in the unequal exchange tradition', *Cambridge Journal of Economics*, vol 30, no 4, pp507–520.

Hendrixson, A. (2004) *Angry Young Men, Veiled Young Women: Constructing a New Population Threat*, Briefing 34, The Corner House, Sturminster Newton, UK, www.thecornerhouse.org.uk/sites/thecornerhouse.org.uk/files/34veiled.pdf, accessed 29 January 2015.

Hendrixson, A. (2014) 'Beyond bonus or bomb: Upholding the sexual and reproductive health of young people', *Reproductive Health Matters*, vol 22, no 23, pp125–134.

Herren, H., Bassi, A., Tan, Z. and Binns, W. P. (2011) *Green Jobs for a Revitalized Food and Agriculture Sector*, Food and Agriculture Organization, Rome.

Hildyard, N. (2010) '"Scarcity" as political strategy: Reflections on three hanging children', in L. Mehta (ed) *The Limits to Scarcity: Contesting the Politics of Allocation*, Earthscan, London, pp149–164.

HLPE (2011) *Price Volatility and Food Security, a Report by the High Level Panel of Experts on Food Security and Nutrition*, High Level Panel of Experts, Committee on World Food Security, Rome.

Hoang, D. and Jones, B. (2012) 'Why do corporate codes of conduct fail? Women workers and clothing supply chains in Vietnam', *Global Social Policy*, vol 12, no 1, pp67–85.

Hoddinott, J. (1999) *Operationalizing Household Security and Development Strategies. An Introduction*, Technical guideline no 1, International Food Policy Research Institute, Washington, DC.

Hoddinott, J., Alderman, H. and Haddad, L. (eds) (1998) *Intrahousehold Resource Allocation in Developing Countries: Methods, Models and Policy*, Johns Hopkins University Press, Baltimore, MD.

Hodgson, D. (1983) 'Demography as social science and policy science', *Population and Development Review*, vol 9, no 1, pp1–34.

Hodgson, D. and Watkins, S. C. (1997) 'Feminists and neo-Malthusians: Past and present alliances', *Population and Development Review*, vol 23, no 3, pp469–523.

Höhler, S. (2005) 'A "law of growth": The logistic curve and population control since World War II', presented at the *Technological and Aesthetic (Trans)Formations of Society* conference, 12–14 October, Darmstadt Technical University, Germany.

Hossain, N., King, R. and Kelbert, A. (2013) *Squeezed: Life in a Time of Food Price Volatility, Year 1 Results*, Institute of Development Studies and Oxfam International, Brighton and Oxford, UK.

Howard, G. and Bartram, J. (2003) *Domestic Water Quantity, Service Level and Health*, World Health Organization, Geneva.

Hsing, Y. (2010) *The Great Urban Transformation: The Politics of Land and Property in China*, Oxford University Press, Oxford.

Htun, M. and Weldon, J. L. (2012) 'The civic origins of progressive policy change: Combating violence against women in global perspective, 1975–2005', *American Political Science Review*, vol 106, no 3, pp548–569.

Humphries, J. (1990) 'Enclosures, common rights, and women: The proletarianization of families in the late eighteenth and early nineteenth centuries', *Journal of Economic History*, vol 50, no 1, pp17–42.

Hutton, G. and Bartram, J. (2008) 'Global costs of attaining the Millennium Development Goal for water supply and sanitation', *Bulletin of the World Health Organization*, vol 86, pp13–19.

Hutton, G., Haller, L. and Bartram, J. (2007) 'Global cost benefit analysis of water supply and sanitation interventions', *Journal of Water and Health*, vol 5, no 4, pp481–502.

Hvistendahl, M. (2011) 'Where have all the girls gone?' *Foreign Policy*, 27 June, http://foreignpolicy.com/2011/06/27/where-have-all-the-girls-gone/, accessed 29 January 2015.

IBGE (2010) *Pesquisa Nacional de Amostra de Domicilios (PNAD): seguranca alimentar 2004 e 2009*, Instituto Brasileiro de Geografia e Estatistica, Rio de Janeiro.

IBLF (2004) 'Community-based solutions to water, and sanitation challenges: Rainwater harvesting', International Business Leaders Forum, London, http://199.189.253.101/$sitepreview/globalrainwaterharvesting.org/article1.pdf, accessed 22 February 2015.

ICTSD (2009) 'Research: the latest studies and briefs from ICTSD', International Centre for Trade and Sustainable Development, Geneva, www.ictsd.org/research, accessed 18 April 2014.

IEA (2012) *World Energy Outlook 2012*, Organisation for Economic Co-operation and Development/International Energy Agency, www.worldenergyoutlook.org/publications/weo-2012, accessed 22 February 2015.

IFPRI (2009) *Climate Change: Impact on Agriculture and Costs of Adaptation*, International Food Policy Research Institute, Washington, DC.

IFPRI (2013a) *Global Food Policy Report 2013*, International Food Policy Research Institute, Washington, DC.

IFPRI (2013b) *Global Hunger Index 2013*, International Food Policy Research Institute, Washington, DC.

ILFSD (2009) 'Green jobs and women workers. Employment, equity, equality', Draft Report for the International Labour Foundation for Sustainable Development and UNEP.

Ilkkaracan, I. (2013) 'The purple economy: A call for a new economic order beyond the green economy', in *Sustainable Economy and Green Growth: Who Cares?* Genanet, Berlin.

ILO (2008) *ILO Declaration on Social Justice for a Fair Globalization*, International Labour Organization, Geneva.

ILO (2012) *Working Towards Sustainable Development: Opportunities for Decent Work and Social Inclusion in a Green Economy*, International Labour Organization, Geneva.

ILO (2013) 'Promoting green jobs through the inclusion of informal waste pickers in Chile', ILO Fact Sheet, International Labour Organization, Geneva, www.ilo.org/global/topics/green-jobs/publications/WCMS_216961/lang--en/index.htm, accessed 20 January 2014.

IPCC (2013) *Climate Change 2013: The Physical Science Basis, Summary for Policymakers*, Working Group 1 Contribution to the IPCC Fifth Assessment Report: Changes to the underlying Scientific/Technical Assessment, IPCC, Geneva, www.ipcc.ch/report/ar5/wg1/, accessed 18 February 2014.

IUCN (2013) *The Environment and Gender Index (EGI) 2013 Pilot*, International Union for Conservation of Nature, Washington, DC.

Jackson, C. (1993) 'Doing what comes naturally? Women and environment in development', *World Development*, vol 21, no 12, pp1947–1963.

Jackson, C. (1998) 'Gender, irrigation and environment: arguing for agency', *Agricultural and Human Values*, vol 15, pp313–324.

Jackson, C. (2003) 'Gender analysis of land: Beyond land rights for women?', *Journal of Agrarian Change*, vol 4, no 3, pp453–480.

Jackson, T. (2009) *Prosperity without Growth: Economics for a Finite Planet*, Earthscan, London.

Jacobs, M. (2012) 'Green growth: Economic theory and political discourse', in R. Falkner (ed) *Handbook of Global Climate and Environmental Policy*, Wiley Blackwell, Oxford.

Jacobson, A. (2004) *Connective Power: Solar Electrification and Social Change in Kenya*, PhD thesis, Energy and Resources Group, University of California, Berkeley.

Jain, D. and Elson, D. (eds) (2011) *Harvesting Feminist Knowledge for Public Policy*, Sage, New Delhi.

Jaquette, J. S. and Staudt, K. A. (1985). 'Politics, population, and gender: A feminist analysis of US population policy in the third world', in K. B. Jones and A. G. Jonasdottir (eds) *The Political Interests of Gender*, Sage, London, pp214–243.

Jasanoff, S. (2004) *States of Knowledge: The Co-Production of Science and Social Order*, Routledge, London and New York.

Jenkins, M. and Curtis, V. (2005) 'Achieving the "good life": Why some people want latrines in rural Benin', *Social Science & Medicine*, vol 61, pp2446–2459.

Jenkins, R., Kennedy, L. and Mukhopadhyay, P. (2014) *Power, Policy and Protest: The Politics of India's Special Economic Zones*, Oxford University Press, Oxford.

Jenson, J. (2010) 'Diffusing ideas for after neoliberalism: The social investment perspective in Europe and Latin America', *Global Social Policy*, vol 10, no 1, pp59–84.

Jessop, B. (2012) 'Narratives of crisis and crisis response: Perspectives from North and South', in P. Utting and S. Razavi (eds) *The Global Crisis and Transformative Social Change*, Palgrave/UN Research Institute for Social Development, Basingstoke, UK.

Joekes, S., Green, C. and Leach, M. (1996) *Integrating Gender into Environmental Research and Policy*, Working Paper 27, Institute of Development Studies, Brighton, UK.

Johnson, K. (2014) 'China's one child policy: Not yet in the dustbin of history', *DifferenTakes*, no 83, http://popdev.hampshire.edu/projects/dt/83, accessed 29 January 2015.

Johnsson-Latham, G. (2007) *A Study on Gender Equality as a Prerequisite for Sustainable Development*, Report to the Environment Advisory Council, Sweden.

Johnston, B. R. (2005) 'Chixoy dam legacy issues study', Center for Political Ecology, Santa Cruz, www.centerforpoliticalecology.org/chixoy-legacy-issues-study/, accessed 15 January 2014.

Jolly, R., Emmerij, L. and Weiss, T. G. (2005) *The Power of UN Ideas. Lessons from the First 60 Years*, United Nations Intellectual History Project, New York.

Juhn, C., Ujhelyi, G. and Villegas-Sanchez, C. (2014) 'Men, women, and machines: How trade impacts gender inequality', *Journal of Development Economics*, vol 106, no 1, pp179–193.

Julia and White, B. (2012) 'Gendered experiences of dispossession: Oil palm expansion in a Dayak Hibun community in West Kalimantan', *Journal of Peasant Studies*, vol 39, nos 3–4, pp995–1016.

Kabeer, N. (1994) *Reversed Realities: Gender Hierarchies in Development Thought*, Verso, London.

Kabeer, N. (2005) 'Gender inequality and women's empowerment: A critical analysis of the third Millennium Development Goal', *Gender and Development*, vol 13, no 1, pp13–24.

Kabeer, N. (2011) *Contextualising the Economic Pathways of Women's Empowerment: Findings from a Multi-Country Research Programme*, Pathways Policy Paper, Pathways of Women's Empowerment Research and Communications Programme, Institute of Development Studies, Brighton, UK.

Kabeer, N. and Murthy, R. K. (1999) 'Gender, poverty and institutional exclusion: Insights from integrated rural development programme (IRDP) and development of women and children in rural areas (DWCRA)', in N. Kabeer and R. Subrahmanian (eds) *Institutions,*

Relations and Outcomes: A Framework and Case Studies for Gender-aware Planning, Kali for Women, New Delhi.

Kabeer, N. and Natali, L. (2013) *Gender Equality and Economic Growth: Is there a Win–Win?*, IDS Working Paper 417, Institute of Development Studies, Brighton, UK.

Kammen, D. and Dove, M. (1997) 'The virtues of mundane science', *Environment*, vol 39, no 6.

Kandiyoti, D. (1988) 'Bargaining with patriarchy', *Gender and Society*, vol 2, no 3, pp274–290.

Kar, K. and Chambers, R. (2008) *Handbook on Community Led Total Sanitation*, Plan International, London.

Kar, K. and Pasteur, K. (2005) *Subsidy or Self-Respect? Community Led Total Sanitation. An Update on Recent Developments*, IDS Working Paper 257, Institute of Development Studies, Brighton, UK.

Kedia, S. (2008) 'Nutrition and health impacts of involuntary resettlement: The Tehri Dam experience', in H.M. Mathur (ed) *India Social Development Report 2008: Development and Displacement*, Oxford University Press, New Delhi.

Khagram, S. (2004) *Dams and Development: Transnational Struggles for Water and Power*, Cornell University Press, Ithaca, NY.

Khan, A. (2014) 'Paid work as a pathway of empowerment: Pakistan's Lady Health Worker programme', in A. Cornwall and J. Edwards (eds) *Feminisms, Empowerment and Development: Changing Women's Lives*, Zed Books, London.

Kongar, E. (2007) 'Importing equality or exporting jobs? Competition and gender wage and employment differentials in U.S. manufacturing', in I. van Staveran, D. Elson, C. Grown and N. Cagatay (eds) *The Feminist Economics of Trade*, Routledge, London and New York.

van Koppen, B., Moriarty, P. and Boelee, E. (2006) *Multiple-use Water Services to Advance the Millennium Development Goals*, Research Report 98, International Irrigation Management Institute, Colombo, Sri Lanka.

Krause, E. (2006) *Dangerous Demographies and the Scientific Manufacture of Fear*, Briefing 36, The Corner House, Sturminster Newton, UK, www.thecornerhouse.org.uk/resource/dangerous-demographies, accessed 29 January 2015.

de Laet, M. and Mol, A. (2000) 'The Zimbabwe bush pump: Mechanics of a fluid technology', *Social Studies of Science*, vol 30, no 2, pp225–263.

Lafferty, W. M. and Eckerberg, K. (1998) *From the Earth Summit to Local Agenda 21: Working Towards Sustainable Development*, Earthscan, London.

Lam, N. L., Chen, Y., Weyant, C., Venkataraman, C., Sadavarte, P., Johnson, M. A., Smith, K. R., Brem, B. T., Arineitwe, J., Ellis, J. E. and Bond, T. C. (2012) 'Household light makes global heat: High black carbon emissions from kerosene wick lamps', *Environmental Science & Technology*, vol 46, no 24, pp13531–13538.

Lambrou, Y. and Paina, G. (2006) *Gender: The Missing Component of the Response to Climate Change*, Food and Agriculture Organization, Rome.

Landesa Rural Development Institute (2011) 'Summary of 2011 seventeen-province survey's findings', www.landesa.org/news/6th-china-survey/, accessed 25 February 2012.

Leach, M. (1992) 'Gender and the environment: Traps and opportunities', *Development in Practice*, vol 2, no 1, pp12–22.

Leach, M. (1994) *Rainforest Relations: Gender and Resource Use Among the Mende of Gola, Sierra Leone*, Edinburgh University Press, Edinburgh.

Leach, M. (2007) 'Earth mother myths and other ecofeminist fables: How a strategic notion rose and fell', *Development and Change*, vol 38, no 1, pp67–85.

Leach, M. and Mearns, R. (1996) *The Lie of the Land: Challenging Received Wisdom on the African Environment*, James Currey, Oxford.

Leach, M. and Scoones, I. (2013) 'Carbon forestry in West Africa: The politics of models, measures and verification processes', *Global Environmental Change*, vol 23, no 5, pp957–967.

Leach, M., Mearns, R. and Scoones, I. (1999) 'Environmental entitlements: Dynamics and institutions in community-based natural resource management', *World Development*, vol 27, no 2, pp225–247.

Leach, M., Scoones, I. and Stirling, A. (2010) *Dynamic Sustainabilities: Technology, Environment, Social Justice*, Earthscan, London.

Leach, M., Raworth, K. and Rockström, J. (2013) *Between Social and Planetary Boundaries: Navigating Pathways in the Safe and Just Space for Humanity*, World Social Science Report 2013: Changing Global Environments, UNESCO and International Social Science Council, Paris.

Lee, C., Chandler, C., Lazarus, M. and Johnson, F. X. (2013) *Assessing the Climate Impacts of Cookstoves Projects: Issues in Emissions Accounting*, Stockholm Environment Institute, Working Paper 2013-01, Stockholm Environment Institute, Stockholm, www.goldstandard.org/wp-content/uploads/2013/02/SEI-WP-2013-01-Cookstoves-Carbon-Markets.pdf, accessed 22 February 2015.

Lemaire, X. (2011) 'Off-grid electrification with solar home systems: The experience of a fee-for-service concession in South Africa', *Energy for Sustainable Development*, vol 15, no 3, pp277–283.

Lenton, R., Wright, A. M., Lewis, K. (2005) *Health, Dignity and Development: What Will It Take? UN Millennium Project Task Force on Water and Sanitation*, Earthscan, London and Stirling, VA.

Levien, M. (2011) 'Special Economic Zones and accumulation by dispossession in India', *Journal of Agrarian Change*, vol 11, no 4, pp454–483.

Levien, M. (2012) 'The land question: Special Economic Zones and the political economy of dispossession in India', *Journal of Peasant Studies*, vol 39, nos 3–4, pp933–969.

Levien, M. (2013a) 'The politics of dispossession: Theorizing India's "land wars"', *Politics & Society*, vol 41, no 3, pp351–394.

Levien, M. (2013b) 'Regimes of dispossession: From steel towns to Special Economic Zones', *Development and Change*, vol 44, no 2, pp381–407.

Li, T. (2011) 'Centering labor in the land grab debate', *Journal of Peasant Studies*, vol 38, no 2, pp281–298.

Li, T. (2014) *Land's End: Capitalist Relations on an Indigenous Frontier*, Duke University Press, Durham, NC.

Liebowitz, D. and Zwingler, S. (2014) 'Gender equality oversimplified: Using CEDAW to counter the measurement obsession', *International Studies Review*, vol 16, pp362–389.

Linder, S. (1999) 'Coming to terms with the public–private partnership: A grammar of multiple meanings', *American Behavioral Scientist*, vol 43, no 1, pp35–51.

Link Up (2013) 'Family planning 2013: Vision, voices and priorities of young people living with and affected by HIV', International HIV/AIDS Alliance, www.aidsalliance.org/assets/000/000/568/90666-Visions_-voices_-and-priorities_original.pdf?1406035833, accessed 29 January 2015.

Lohmann, L. (2005) 'Malthusianism and the terror of scarcity', in B. Hartmann, B. Subramaniam and C. Zerner (eds) *Making Threats: Biofears and Environmental Anxieties*, Rowman & Littlefield, Lanham, MD, pp81–98.

Longhurst, R. (2010) *Global Leadership for Nutrition: The UN's Standing Committee on Nutrition (SCN) and its Contributions*, Discussion Paper 390, Institute of Development Studies, Brighton, UK.

Maas, P. (2010) *Crude World: The Violent Twilight of Oil*, Vintage Books, New York.

MacGregor, S. (2010) '"Gender and climate change": From impacts to discourses', *Journal of the Indian Ocean Region*, vol 6, no 2, pp223–238.

Mackenzie, F. (1998) *Land, Ecology and Resistance in Kenya*, Edinburgh University Press for International African Institute, Edinburgh.

Mangisoni, J. (2008) 'Impact of treadle pump irrigation technology on smallholder poverty and food security in Malawi: A case study of Blantyre and Mchinji districts', *International Journal of Agricultural Sustainability*, vol 6, no 4, pp248–266.

Manning, R. (1988) *Village Revolts: Social Protest and Popular Disturbances in England, 1509–1640*, Clarendon Press, Oxford.

Markandya, A., Armstrong, B. G., Hales, S., Chiabai, A., Criqui, P., Mima, S., Tonne, C. and Wilkinson, P. (2009) 'Public health benefits of strategies to reduce greenhouse-gas emissions: Low-carbon electricity generation', *The Lancet*, vol 374, no 9706, pp2006–2015.

Markham, V. (2012) 'Live from Rio+20, day four: "Plenary floor, demographic dividend and the youth bulge"', *RH Reality Check*, www.rhrealitycheck.org/article/2012/06/22/live-from-rio20-day-four-plenary-floor-demographic-dividend-and-youth-bulge, accessed 29 January 2015.

Martínez-Alier, J. (2002) *The Environmentalism of the Poor: A Study of Ecological Conflicts and Valuation*, Edward Elgar, Cheltenham.

Martinot, E., Cabraal, A. and Mathur, S. (2001) 'World Bank/GEF solar home system projects: Experiences and lessons learned 1993–2000', *Renewable and Sustainable Energy Reviews*, vol 5, pp39–57.

Marx, K. (1977) *Capital, Volume I*, Vintage, New York.

Masud, J., Sharan, D. and Lohani, B. N. (2007) *Energy For All: Addressing the Energy, Environment, and Poverty Nexus in Asia*, Asian Development Bank, Manila.

Maxwell, S. (2001) 'The evolution of thinking about food security', in S. Devereux and S. Maxwell (eds) *Food Security in sub-Saharan Africa*, Intermediate Technology Development Group, London.

Maxwell, S. and Frankenberger, T. (eds) (1992) *Household Food Security: Concepts, and Measurements: A Technical Review*, UNICEF and International Fund for Agricultural Development, New York, NY and Rome.

May, J. (forthcoming) 'Changes in food security in South Africa since the end of Apartheid: Evidence using child malnourishment', in S. Fukuda-Parr and V. Taylor (eds) *Food Security in South Africa: Human Rights and Entitlement Perspectives*, UCT Press/Juta, Cape Town.

McMahon, S., Winch, P. J., Caruso, B. A., Obure, A. F., Ogutu, E. A., Ochari, I. A. and Rheingans, R. D. (2011) '"The girl with her period is the one to hang her head": Reflections on menstrual management among schoolgirls in rural Kenya', *BMC International Health and Human Rights*, vol 11, no 7, www.biomedcentral.com/1472-698X/11/7, accessed 22 February 2015.

McMichael, P. (2009) 'Food sovereignty, social reproduction and the agrarian question', in A. H. Akram-Lodhi and C. Kay (eds) *Peasants and Globalization, Political Economy, Rural Transformation and the Agrarian Question*, Routledge, London, pp288–311.

Meadows, D. H., Meadows, D., Randers, J. and Behrens III, W. W. (1972) *The Limits to Growth: A Report for the Club of Rome's Project on the Predicament of Mankind*, Universe Books, New York.

Mehra, R. and Gammage, S. (1999) 'Trends, countertrends, and gaps in women's employment', *World Development*, vol 27, no 3, pp533–550.

Mehta, L. (ed) (2009a) *Displaced by Development: Confronting Marginalisation and Gender Injustice*, Sage, New Delhi.

Mehta, L. (2009b) 'The double bind: A gender analysis of forced displacement and resettlement', in L. Mehta (ed) *Displaced by Development: Confronting Marginalisation and Gender Injustice*, Sage, New Delhi.

Mehta, L. (ed) (2010) *The Limits to Scarcity: Contesting the Politics of Allocation*, Earthscan, London.

Mehta, L. and Movik, S. (eds) (2011) *Shit Matters: The Potential of Community-Led Total Sanitation*, Practical Action Publishing, Rugby.

Mehta, L. and Srinivasan, B. (2000) 'Balancing pains and gains: A perspective chapter on gender and large dams', *World Commission on Dams Thematic Review*, World Commission on Dams Secretariat, Cape Town.

Mehta, L., Veldwisch, G. J. and Franco, J. (2012) 'Introduction to the Special Issue: Water grabbing? Focus on the (re)appropriation of finite water resources', *Water Alternatives*, vol 5, no 2, pp193–207.

Meinzen-Dick, R., Kovarik, C. and Quisumbing, A. (2014) 'Gender and sustainability', *Annual Review of Environment and Resources*, vol 39, pp29–55.

Mellor, M. (2009) 'Ecofeminist political economy and the politics of money', in A. Salleh (ed) *Eco-Sufficiency and Global Justice: Women Write Political Ecology*, Pluto Press, London.

Menon, N. and Rodgers, Y. (2009) 'International trade and the gender wage gap: New evidence from India's manufacturing sector', *World Development*, vol 37, no 5, pp965–981.

Merchant, C. (1980) *The Death of Nature: Women, Ecology, and the Scientific Revolution*, Harper and Row, San Francisco, CA.

Miah, Md. D., Sirajul Kabir, Md. R. R., Koike, M., Akhter, S., Shin, M. Y. (2009) 'Rural household energy consumption pattern in the disregarded villages of Bangladesh', *Energy Policy*, vol 38, no 2, pp997–1003.

Mies, M. (1986) *Patriarchy and Accumulation on a World Scale: Women in the International Division of Labour*, Zed Books, London.

Mies, M. and Shiva, V. (1993) *Ecofeminism*, Zed Books, London.

Mies, M., Bennholdt-Thomsen, V. and Von Werlhof, C. (1988) *Women: The Last Colony* (vol 8), Zed Books, London.

Milberg, W. and Winkler, D. (2013) *Outsourcing Economics: Global Value Chains in Capitalist Development*, Cambridge University Press, New York.

Miller, C. and Razavi, S. (1998) *Missionaries and Mandarins: Feminist Engagement with Development Institutions*, Intermediate Technology Publishers/UN Research Institute for Social Development, Geneva.

Mills, E. (2012) *Health Impacts of Fuel Based Lighting*, Lawrence Berkeley National Laboratory Lumina Project, University of California, CA.

Milner, C. and Wright, P. (1998) 'Modeling labour market adjustment to trade liberalization in an industrialization economy', *Economic Journal*, vol 108, no 447, pp509–528.

Miraftab, F. (2004) 'Public–private partnerships: The Trojan horse of neoliberal development?', *Journal of Planning Education and Research*, vol 24, no 1, pp89–101.

Moi, T. (2000) 'Is anatomy destiny? Freud and biological determinism', in P. Brooks and A. Woloch (eds) *Whose Freud? The Place of Psychoanalysis in Contemporary Culture*, Yale University Press, New Haven, pp71–92.

Movik, S. (2011) 'The dynamics and sustainability of Community-Led Total Sanitation (CLTS): Mapping challenges and pathways', in L., Mehta and S. Movik (eds) (2011) *Shit*

Matters: The Potential of Community-Led Total Sanitation, Practical Action Publishing, Rugby.

MSPAS, INE and CDC (2010) *Informe Final. V Encuesta Nacional de Salud Materno Infantil (ENSMI 2008–2009)*, Government of Guatemala, Ministerio de Salud Pública y Asistencia Social, Instituto Nacional de Estadística and Centros de Control y Prevención de Enfermedades.

Muro, M., Rothwell, J. and Saha, D. with Battelle Technology Partnership Practice (2011) *Sizing the Clean Economy. A National and Regional Green Jobs Assessment*, Brookings Institution, Washington, DC.

Murphy, M. (2009) 'Avertable life, investable futures: A Cold War story of sex and economy', presented at Society for Social Studies of Science annual meeting, Washington, DC.

Murray, A. and Ray, I. (2010) 'Back-end users: The unrecognized stakeholders in demand-driven sanitation', *Journal of Planning Education and Research*, vol 30, no 1, pp94–102.

Murtaugh, P. and Schlax, M. G. (2009) 'Reproduction and the carbon legacies of individuals', *Global Environmental Change*, no 19, pp14–20.

Musyoki, S. M. (2010) 'Scaling up CLTS in Kenya: Opportunities, challenges and lessons', in Bongartz, P., Musyoki, S. M., Milligan, A. and Ashley, H. (eds) *Tales of Shit: Community-Led Total Sanitation in Africa*, Participatory Learning and Action 61, International Institute for Environment and Development, London.

Mutunga, C., Zulu, E. and De-Souza, R. (2012) *Population Dynamics, Climate Change, and Sustainable Development in Africa*, Population Action International and African Institute for Development Policy, Washington, DC, http://populationaction.org/wp-content/uploads/2012/09/Sustainable-Development-in-Africa.pdf, accessed 29 January 2015.

Myers, N. (1995) *Environmental Exodus: An Emergent Crisis in the Global Arena*, Climate Institute, Washington, DC.

Naret Guerrero, M. and Stock, A. (2012) 'Green economy from a gender perspective', www.academia.edu/1604568/Green_economy_from_a_Gender_perspective, accessed 19 February 2015.

Natural Capital Committee (2013) *The State of Natural Capital: Towards a Framework for Measurement and Valuation*, Defra, London www.defra.gov.uk/naturalcapitalcommittee, accessed 19 February 2015.

Neeson, J. M. (1993) *Commoners: Common Right, Enclosure and Social Change in England, 1700–1820*, Cambridge University Press, Cambridge.

Nelson, J. A. and England, P. (2002) 'Feminist philosophies of love and work', *Hypatia*, vol 17, no 2, pp1–18.

Nelson, K. and Murray, A. (2008) 'Sanitation for underserved populations: Technologies, implementation challenges, and opportunities', *Annual Review of Environment and Resources*, vol 33, pp119–151.

Nelson, N., Geltzer, A. and Hilgartner, S. (2008) 'Introduction: The anticipatory state: Making policy-relevant knowledge about the future', *Science and Public Policy*, vol 35, no 8, pp546–550.

Ness, G. (2001) *Governance and Changing Aid Structures*, ESCP 7 Report, Woodrow Wilson Center, Washington, DC.

Neumayer, T. and Plumper, E. (2007) 'The gendered nature of natural disasters: The impact of catastrophic events on the gender gap in life expectancy, 1981–2002', *Annals of the Association of American Geographers*, vol 97, no 3, pp551–566.

Nicita, A. and Razzaz, S. (2003) *Who Benefits and How Much? How Gender Affects Welfare Impacts of a Booming Textile Industry*, Policy Research Working Paper 3029, World Bank, Washington, DC.

Nightingale, A. J. (2006) 'The nature of gender: Work, gender, and environment', *Environment and Planning D: Society and Space*, vol 24, pp165–185.

Nightingale, A. J. (2011) 'Bounding difference: Intersectionality and the material production of gender, caste, class and environment in Nepal', *Geoforum*, vol 42, no 2, pp153–162.

Nilsen, A. G. (2010) *Dispossession and Resistance in India: The River and the Rage*, Routledge, London.

Nordas, H. K. (2003) 'The impact of trade liberalization on women's job opportunities and earnings in developing countries', *World Trade Review*, vol 2, no 2, pp221–231.

Nussbaum, M. (2000) *Women and Human Development: The Capabilities Approach*, Cambridge, Cambridge University Press.

Nussbaum, M. (2003) 'Capabilities as fundamental entitlements: Sen and social justice', *Feminist Economics*, vol 9, nos 2–3, pp33–59.

Nussbaum, M. and Sen, A. (1993) *The Quality of Life*, WIDER Studies in Development, Oxford University Press, New York.

O'Neill, B., Dalton, M., Fuchs, R., Jiang, L., Pachauri, S. and Zigova, K. (2010) 'Global demographic trends and future carbon emissions', *Proceedings of the National Academy of Sciences, USA*, doi 10.1073/pnas.1004581107.

Obi, C. (2010) 'The petroleum industry: A paradox or (sp)oiler of development?', *Journal of Contemporary African Studies*, vol 28, no 4, pp443–457.

OECD (2009) *Eco-Innovation in Industry: Enabling Green Growth*, Organisation for Economic Co-operation and Development, Paris and Washington, DC.

OECD (2013a) *Interconnected Economies: Benefiting from Global Value Chains – Synthesis Report*, Organisation for Economic Co-operation and Development, Geneva.

OECD (2013b) *Putting Green Growth at the Heart of Development*, OECD Green Growth Studies, Organisation for Economic Co-operation and Development, Paris.

OECD, WTO and UNCTAD (2013) *Implications of Global Value Chains for Trade, Investment, Development and Jobs*, prepared for the G-20 Leaders Summit, Saint Petersburg (Russian Federation), September, Organisation for Economic Co-operation and Development, Paris.

Okonofua, F. (2010) 'Reducing maternal mortality in Nigeria: An approach through policy research and capacity building', *African Journal of Reproductive Health*, vol 14, no 3, pp9–10.

Oostendorp, R. H. (2009) 'Globalization and the gender wage gap', *World Bank Economic Review*, vol 23, no 1, pp141–161.

Ortiz, I. and Cummins, M. (2013) 'Austerity measures in developing countries: Public expenditure trends and the risks to children and women', *Feminist Economics*, vol 19, no 3, pp55–81.

Osborne, S. P. (2006) 'The new public governance?', *Public Management Review*, vol 8, no 3, pp377–387.

Ostrom, E. (2000) 'Collective action and the evolution of social norms', *Journal of Economic Perspectives*, vol 14, no 3, pp137–158.

Ostrom, E. (2010) 'Beyond markets and states: Polycentric governance of complex economic systems', *American Economic Review*, vol 100, no 3, pp641–672.

Otzelberger, A. (2011) 'Gender-responsive strategies on climate change: Recent progress and ways forward for donors', Institute of Development Studies, Brighton, UK, http://reliefweb.int/sites/reliefweb.int/files/resources/Full_Report_1973.pdf, accessed 19 February 2015.

Oxfam (2011) *Preparing for Think Cows: Why the G20 Should Keep Buffer Stocks on the Agenda*, Briefing Note 21, Oxfam, Oxford.

Oya, C. (2013) 'Methodological reflections on "land grab" databases and the "land grab" literature "rush"', *Journal of Peasant Studies*, vol 40, no 3, pp503–520.

Page, B. and Valone, D. A. (eds) (2007) *Philanthropic Foundations and the Globalization of Scientific Medicine and Public Health*, University Press of America, Lanham, MD.

Palit, C. (2009) 'Displacement, gender justice and people's struggles', in L. Mehta (ed) *Displaced by Development: Confronting Marginalisation and Gender Injustice*, Sage, New Delhi.

Pandey, B. and Rout, B. K. (2004) *Development Induced Displacement in India: Impact on Women*, National Commission for Women, New Delhi.

Patel, R. (2013) 'The Long Green Revolution', *Journal of Peasant Studies*, vol 40, no 1, pp1–63.

PATH (2012) 'Innovative partnership to deliver convenient contraceptives to up to three million women', www.path.org/news/press-room/170, accessed 29 January 2015.

Paul-Mazumdar, P. and Begum, A. (2002) *The Gender Imbalances in the Export-Oriented Garment Industry in Bangladesh*, Policy Research Report on Gender and Development, Working Paper 12, World Bank, Washington, DC.

Pearce, F. (2011) 'Dubious assumptions prime population bomb', *Nature*, p. 473, doi 10.1038/473125a.

Pearce, T. (2000) 'Death and maternity in Nigeria', in M. Tursen (ed) *African Women's Health*, Africa World Press, Trenton, NJ, pp1–26.

Peng, I. (2012) 'The boss, the worker, his wife and no babies: South Korean political and social economy of care in a context of institutional rigidities', in S. Razavi and S. Staab (eds) *Global Variations in the Political and Social Economy of Care: Worlds Apart*, Routledge, New York.

Pereira, M. G., Sena, J. A., Freitas, M. A. V. and da Silva, N. F. (2011) 'Evaluation of the impact of access to electricity: A comparative analysis of South Africa, China, India and Brazil', *Renewable and Sustainable Energy Reviews*, vol 15, pp1427–1441.

Petchesky, R. P. (1995) 'From population control to reproductive rights: Feminist fault lines', *Reproductive Health Matters*, vol 3, no 6, pp152–161.

Pew Global Stewardship Initiative (1993) *Pew Global Stewardship Initiative White Paper*, Pew Charitable Trusts.

Pickering, A. and Davis, J. (2012) 'Freshwater availability and water fetching distance affect child health in sub-Saharan Africa', *Environmental Science and Technology*, vol 46, no 4, pp2391–2397.

Piketty, T. (2014) *Capital in the Twenty-First Century*, Harvard University Press, Cambridge, MA.

Plumwood, V. (1986) 'Ecofeminism: An overview and discussion of positions and arguments', *Australian Journal of Philosophy*, vol 64, pp120–138.

Pollin, R., Epstein, G. and Heintz, J. (2009) 'Pro-growth alternatives for monetary and financial policies in sub-Saharan Africa', in T. McKinley (ed) *Economic Alternatives for Growth, Employment and Poverty Reduction*, Palgrave Macmillan for United Nations Development Programme, New York.

Prokopy, L. (2004) 'Women's participation in rural water supply projects in India: Is it moving beyond tokenism and does it matter?', *Water Policy*, vol 6, pp103–116.

Quisumbing, A., Meinzen-Dick, R. and Bassett, L. (2008) *Helping Women Respond to the Global Food Price Crisis*, IFPRI Policy Brief 7, International Food Policy Research Institute, Washington, DC.

Rai, S. and Waylen, G. (eds) (2013) *New Frontiers in Feminist Political Economy*, Routledge, London.

Raju, K. V. and Shah, T. (2000) 'Revitalization of irrigation tanks in Rajasthan', *Economic & Political Weekly*, vol 35, pp1930–1936.

Ralph, L. J., McCory, S. I., Shiu, K. and Padian, N. S. (2015) 'Hormonal contraceptive use and women's risk of HIV acquisition: A meta-analysis of observational studies', *The Lancet*, vol 15, no 2, pp181–189, http://dx.doi.org/10.1016/S1473-3099(14)71052-7.

Ramkuwar (2009) '"We will never forgive the Government": A personal testimony', in L. Mehta (ed) *Displaced by Development: Confronting Marginalisation and Gender Injustice*, Sage, New Delhi.

Rao, A. (2006) 'Making institutions work for women', *Development*, vol 49, no 1, pp63–67.

Rao, M. and Sexton, S. (eds) (2010) *Markets and Malthus: Population, Gender and Health in Neo-liberal Times*, Sage, New Delhi.

Ravenscroft, P., Brammer, H. and Richards, K. (2009) *Arsenic Pollution: A Global Synthesis*, John Wiley & Sons, Chichester.

Raworth, K. (2012) *A Safe and Just Space for Humanity: Can We Live Within the Doughnut?*, Oxfam Discussion Paper, Oxfam, Oxford.

Ray, I. (2007) 'Women, water and development', *Annual Review of Environment and Resources*, vol 32, pp421–449.

Ray, R. and Qayum, S. (2009) *Cultures of Servitude: Modernity, Domesticity, and Class in India*, Stanford University Press, Stanford, CA.

Rayner, S. (1984) 'Disagreeing about risk: The institutional cultures of risk management', in S. G. Hadden (ed) *Risk Analysis Institutions and Public Policy*, Associated Faculty Press, Port Washington, NY.

Rayner, S. and Cantor, R. (1987) 'How fair is safe enough? The cultural approach to societal technology choice', *Risk Analysis*, vol 7, pp3–9.

Razavi, S. (2003) 'Introduction: Agrarian change, gender and land rights', *Journal of Agrarian Change*, vol 3, nos 1–2, pp2–32.

Razavi, S. (2007) *The Political and Social Economy of Care in a Social Context*, UNRISD Gender and Development Programme Paper 3, UN Research Institute for Social Development, Geneva.

Razavi, S. (2009) 'Engendering the political economy of agrarian change', *Journal of Peasant Studies*, vol 36, no 1, pp197–226.

Razavi, S. (2011) 'Rethinking care in a development context', *Development and Change*, vol 42, no 4, pp873–903.

Razavi, S. and Staab, S. (2010) 'Underpaid and overworked: A cross-national perspective on care workers', *International Labour Review*, vol 149, no 4, pp407–422.

Resurreccion, B. P. (2006) 'Rules, roles and rights: Gender, participation and community fisheries management in Cambodia's Tonle Sap Region', *International Journal of Water Resources Development*, vol 22, no 3, pp39–53.

Resurreccion, B. P. and Elmhirst, R. (2008) *Gender and Natural Resource Management*, Earthscan, London.

Rheingans, R., Cumming, O., Anderson, J. and Showalter, J. (2012) *Estimating Inequities in Sanitation-related Disease Burden and Estimating the Potential Impacts of Pro-poor Targeting*, London School of Hygiene & Tropical Medicine, London.

Richey, L. (2008) *Population Politics and Development: From the Policies to the Clinics*, Palgrave Macmillan, New York.

Ridgeway, C. (2011) *Framed by Gender: How Gender Inequality Persists in the Modern World*, Oxford University Press, Oxford and New York.

Robles, M., Torero, M. and von Braun, J. (2009) *When Speculation Matters*, International Food Policy Research Institute, Washington, DC.

Rocheleau, D. (1988) 'Gender, resource management and the rural landscape: Implications for agroforestry and farming systems research', in S. Poats, M. Schmink and A. Spring (eds) *Gender Issues in Farming Systems Research and Extension*, Westview Press, Boulder, CO.

Rocheleau, D., Thomas-Slayter, B. and Wangari, E. (eds) (1996) *Feminist Political Ecology. Global Issues and Local Experiences*, Routledge, London.

Rockström, J., Steffen, W., Noone, K., Persson, Å., Chapin, III, F. S., Lambin, E. F., Lenton, T. M., Scheffer, M., Folke, C., Schellnhuber, H. J., Nykvist, B., de Wit, C. A., Hughes, T., van der Leeuw, S., Rodhe, H., Sörlin, S., Snyder, P. K., Costanza, R., Svedin, U., Falkenmark, M., Karlberg, L., Corell, R. W., Fabry, V. J., Hansen, J., Walker, B., Liverman, D., Richardson, K., Crutzen, P. and Foley, J. A. (2009a) 'A safe operating space for humanity', *Nature*, vol 461, pp472–475.

Rockström, J., Steffen, W., Noone, K., Persson, Å., Chapin, III, F. S., Lambin, E. F., Lenton, T. M., Scheffer, M., Folke, C., Schellnhuber, H. J., Nykvist, B., de Wit, C. A., Hughes, T., van der Leeuw, S., Rodhe, H., Sörlin, S., Snyder, P. K., Costanza, R., Svedin, U., Falkenmark, M., Karlberg, L., Corell, R. W., Fabry, V. J., Hansen, J., Walker, B., Liverman, D., Richardson, K., Crutzen, P. and Foley, J. A (2009b) 'Planetary boundaries: Exploring the safe operating space for humanity', *Ecology and Society*, vol 14, no 2, www.ecologyandsociety.org/vol14/iss2/art32/, accessed 22 February 2015.

Rodda, A. (1991) *Women and the Environment*, Zed Books, London.

Rodrik, D. (1997) *Has Globalization Gone Too Far?*, Institute for International Economics, Washington, DC.

Rodrik, D. (2006) 'Goodbye Washington consensus, hello Washington confusion? A review of the World Bank's economic growth in the 1990s: Learning from a decade of reform', *Journal of Economic Literature*, vol 44, no 4, pp969–983.

Roe, E. M. (1995) 'Except Africa: Postscript to a special section on development narratives', *World Development*, vol 23, no 6, pp1065–1069.

Ruiz-Mercado, I., Masera, O., Zamora, H. and Smith, K. R. (2011) 'Adoption and sustained use of improved cookstoves', *Energy Policy*, vol 39, pp7557–7566.

Rukuni, S. (2010) 'Challenging mindsets: CLTS and government policy in Zimbabwe', in Bongartz, P., Musyoki, S. M., Milligan, A. and Ashley, H. (eds) *Tales of Shit: Community-Led Total Sanitation in Africa*, Participatory Learning and Action 61, International Institute for Environment and Development, London.

Rulli, M. C., Saviori, A. and D'Odorico, P. (2013) 'Global land and water grabbing', *Proceedings of the National Academy of Sciences, USA*, vol 110, no 3, pp892–897.

Rustico, L. and Sperotti, F. (2012) 'Working conditions in "green jobs": Women in the renewable energy sector', *International Journal of Labour Research*, vol 4, no 2, pp209–229.

Sachs, J. (2013) 'The next frontier', *The Economist*, 21 September, www.economist.com/news/finance-and-economics/21586512-guest-article-jeffrey-sachs-director-earth-institute-columbia, accessed 22 February 2015.

Saith, R. and Harris-White, B. (1999) 'The gender sensitivity of well-being indicators', *Development & Change*, vol 30, no 3, pp465–497.

Salleh, A. (ed) (2009) *Eco-sufficiency and Global Justice: Women Write Political Ecology*, Pluto Press, London.

Sampat, P. (2010) 'Special Economic Zones in India: Reconfiguring displacement in a neoliberal order?', *City & Society*, vol 22, no 2, pp166–182.

Samson, M. (ed) (2009) *Refusing to be Cast Aside: Waste Pickers Organising Around the World*, Women in Informal Employment: Globalizing and Organizing (WIEGO), Cambridge, MA.

Sandler, J. and Rao, A. (2012) *Strategies of Feminist Bureaucrats: United Nations Experiences*, IDS Working Paper 397, Institute of Development Studies, Brighton, UK.

Sangari, K. (1995) 'Politics of diversity: Religious communities and multiple patriarchies', *Economic and Political Weekly*, vol 30, no 51, pp3287–3310.

Sangvai, S. (2002) *The River and Life: People's Struggle in the Narmada Valley*, Earthcare Books, Mumbai.

Sasser, J. (2012) 'Empower women, save the planet? Science, strategy, and population–environment advocacy', PhD thesis, University of California, Berkeley, CA.

Sasser, J. (2014a) 'From darkness into light: Race, population, and environment', *Antipode*, vol 46, no 5, pp1240–1257.

Sasser, J. (2014b) 'The wave of the future? Youth advocacy at the nexus of population and climate change', *Geographical Journal*, vol 180, no 2, pp102–110.

Satterthwaite, D. (2009) 'The implications of population growth and urbanization for climate change', *Environment & Urbanization*, vol 21, no 2, pp545–567.

Satterthwaite, D. with McGranahan, G. and Mitlin, D. (2005) *Community-Driven Development for Water and Sanitation in Urban Areas*, WSSCC–IIED Report, Water Supply and Sanitation Collaborative Council and International Institute for Environment and Development, www.sdinet.org/media/upload/documents/water,_sanitation,_hygene_mitlin.pdf, accessed 22 February 2015.

Satterthwaite, D., Mitlin, D. and Patel, S. (2011) *Engaging with the Urban Poor and their Organizations for Poverty Reduction and Urban Governance*, issues paper for the United Nations Development Programme, New York.

Sayre, N. F. (2008) 'The genesis, history and limits of carrying capacity', *Annals of the Association of American Geographers*, vol 98, no 1, pp120–134.

Schalatek, L. (2012) *Climate Financing for Gender Equality and Women's Empowerment: Challenges and Opportunities*, Expert Panel Presentation, UN Women, 56th Commission on the Status of Women, www.un.org/womenwatch/daw/csw/csw56/panels/panel4-Liane-Schalatek.pdf, accessed 22 February 2015.

Schalatek, L. (2013) *The Post-2015 Framework: Merging Care and Green Economy Approaches to Finance Gender-Equitable Sustainable Development*, Heinrich Boell Foundation, Berlin.

Schnitzer, D., Lounsbury, D. S., Carvallo, J. P., Deshmukh, R., Apt, J. and Kammen, D. (2014) *Microgrids for Rural Electrification: A Critical Review of Best Practices Based on Seven Case Studies*, United Nations Foundation, Washington, DC, http://energyaccess.org/images/content/files/MicrogridsReportFINAL_low.pdf, accessed 22 February 2015.

Scoones, I., Hall, R., Borras, S. M., White, B. and Wolford, W. (2013) 'The politics of evidence: Methodologies for understanding the global land rush', *Journal of Peasant Studies*, vol 40, no 3, pp469–484.

Scoones, I., Leach, M. and Newell, P. (eds) (2015) *The Politics of Green Transformations*, Routledge, Abingdon, UK.

Scott, J. C. (1985) *Weapons of the Weak: Everyday Forms of Peasant Resistance*, Yale University Press, New Haven, CT.

Seguino, S. (2000) 'Gender inequality and economic growth: A cross-country analysis', *World Development*, vol 28, pp1211–1230.

Seguino, S. (2010) 'Gender, distribution, and balance of payments constrained growth in developing countries', *Review of Political Economy*, vol 22, no 3, pp373–404.

Seguino, S. (2011) '"Rebooting" is not an option. Towards equitable social and economic development', in D. Jain and D. Elson (eds) *Harvesting Feminist Knowledge for Public Policy*, Sage, New Delhi.

Seguino, S. and Grown, C. (2006) 'Gender equity and globalization: Macroeconomic policy for developing countries', *Journal of International Development*, vol 18, pp1081–1114.

Selman, P. (1998) 'Local Agenda 21: Substance or spin?' *Journal of Environmental Planning and Management*, vol 41, no 5, pp533–553.

Sen, A. (1982) *Poverty and Famines: An Essay on Entitlement and Deprivation*, Oxford University Press, Oxford and New York.

Sen, A. (1985) 'Well-being, agency and freedom: The Dewey Lectures 1984', *Journal of Philosophy*, vol 82, no 4, pp169–221.

Sen, A. (1999) *Development as Freedom*, Oxford, Oxford University Press.

Sen, G. and Mukherjee, A. (2013) *No Empowerment without Rights, No Rights without Politics*, Working Paper Series: The Power of Numbers, http://fxb.harvard.edu/wp-content/uploads/sites/5/2013/09/Goal-3_Sen-and-Mukherjee_final_linked0625.pdf, accessed 22 February 2015.

Sen, G. and Nayar, A. (2013) 'Population, environment and human rights: A paradigm in the making', in B. Cela, I. Dankelman, and J. Stern (eds) *Powerful Synergies: Gender Equality, Economic Development and Environmental Sustainability*, United Nations Development Program, New York, www.undp.org/content/dam/undp/library/gender/f_PowerfulSynergies2013_Web.pdf, accessed 29 January 2015.

Shah, T., Alam, M., Kumar, D., Nagar, R. K. and Singh, M. (2000) *Pedaling out of Poverty: Social Impact of a Manual Irrigation Technology in South Asia*, Research Report 45, International Irrigation Management Institute, Colombo, Sri Lanka.

Sharpless, J. (1997) 'Population science, private foundations, and development aid: The transformation of demographic knowledge in the United States, 1945–1965', in F. Cooper and R. Packard (eds) *International Development and the Social Sciences: Essays on the History and Politics of Knowledge*, University of California Press, Berkeley, CA, pp176–202.

Shiva, V. (1988) *Staying Alive: Women, Ecology, and Development*, Zed Books, London.

Sidner, S. (2011) 'Solar panels power profit in Bangladesh', CNN, 12 April, http://edition.cnn.com/2011/BUSINESS/04/11/bangladesh.solar.power.kalihati/, accessed 25 January 2014.

Silliman, J. (2009) 'In search of climate justice: Refuting dubious linkages, affirming rights', *ARROWs for Change: Women's, Gender, and Rights Perspectives in Health Policies and Programmes*, vol 15, no 1, pp1–12.

Singh, M. and Samantray, R. K. (1992) 'Whatever happened to Muddavat Chenna? The tale of Nagarjunasagar', in E. G Thukral (ed) *Big Dams, Displaced People*, Sage, New Delhi.

Singh, S. (2008) 'Towards a just resettlement and rehabilitation policy for India', in H. M. Mathur (ed) *India Social Development Report 2008: Development and Displacement*, Oxford University Press, New Delhi.

Sinton, J., Smith, K. R., Peabody, J. W., Yapling, L., Xiliang, Z., Edwards, R. and Quan, G. (2004) 'An assessment of programs to promote improved household stoves in China', *Energy for Sustainable Development*, vol 8, pp33–52.

Sivaramakrishnan, K. (1999) *Modern Forests: Statemaking and Environmental Change in Colonial Eastern India*, Stanford University Press, Stanford, CA.

Skinner, E. (2011) *Gender and Climate Change – Overview Report*, Institute of Development Studies, Brighton, UK.

Skutsch, M. M. (2002) 'Protocols, treaties, and action: The climate change process viewed through gender spectacles', *Gender & Development*, vol 10, no 2, pp30–39.

Smith, K., Gu, S., Huang, K. and Qiu, D. (1993) 'One hundred million improved cookstoves in China: How was it done?', *World Development*, vol 21, no 6, pp941–961.

Smyth, I. (1996) 'Gender analysis of family planning: Beyond the feminist vs. population control debate', *Feminist Economics*, vol 2, no 2, pp63–86.

Smyth, I. and Turquet, L. (2012) *Strategies of Feminist Bureaucrats: Perspectives from International NGOs*, IDS Working Paper 396, Institute of Development Studies, Brighton, UK.

Sneddon, C., Howarth, R. and Norgaard, R. (2006) 'Sustainable development in a post-Brundtland world', *Ecological Economics*, vol 57, no 2, pp253–268.

Snell, K. D. M. (1985) *Annals of the Labouring Poor: Social Change and Agrarian England, 1660–1900*, Cambridge University Press, Cambridge.

Sovacool, B. K. (2012) 'The political economy of energy poverty: A review of key challenges', *Energy for Sustainable Development*, vol 16, no 3, pp272–282.

Srinivasan, B. (2007) *Negotiating Complexities: Collection of Feminist Essays*, Promilla and Co., New York.

Standing, G. (1989) 'Global feminization through flexible labour', *World Development*, vol 17, no 7, pp1077–1095.

Standing, G. (1999) 'Global feminization through flexible labour: A theme revisited', *World Development*, vol 27, no 3, pp583–602.

Staritz, C. (2013) 'Global value chains, economic upgrading and gender', in C. Staritz and J. Guiherme Reis (eds) *Global Value Chains, Economic Upgrading, and Gender. Case Studies of the Horticulture, Tourism, and Call Center Industries*, World Bank, Washington, DC.

Staritz, C. and Guiherme Reis, J. (eds) (2013) *Global Value Chains, Economic Upgrading, and Gender. Case Studies of the Horticulture, Tourism, and Call Center Industries*, World Bank, Washington, DC.

Statistics South Africa (2013) *General Household Survey Data 2013*, Statistics South Africa, Pretoria.

Steffen, W., Sanderson, A., Tyson, P. D., Jäger, J., Matson, P. A., Moore III, B., Oldfield, F., Richardson, K., Schellnhuber, H. J., Turner II, B. L. and Wasson, R. J. (2004) *Global Change and the Earth System: A Planet Under Pressure*, Springer, Berlin.

Steffen, W., Richardson, K., Rockström, J., Cornell, S. E., Fetzer, I., Bennett, E. M., Biggs, R., Carpenter, S. R., de Vries, W., de Wit, C. A., Folke, C., Gerten, D., Heinke, J., Mace, G. A., Persson, L. M., Ramanathan, V., Reyers, B. and Sörlin, S. (2015) 'Planetary boundaries: Guiding human development on a changing planet', www.sciencemag.org 16 January.

Stiglitz, J. (2008) 'Is there a post-Washington consensus consensus?', in N. Serra and J. Stiglitz (eds) *The Washington Consensus Reconsidered*, Oxford University Press, Oxford.

Stiglitz, J. E. (2012) *The Price of Inequality*, Penguin, London.

Stirling, A. (2011) 'Risk at a turning point?', *Journal of Risk Research*, vol 1, no 2, pp97–109.

Stockhammer, E. (2013) *Why Have Wage Shares Fallen? A Panel Analysis of the Determinants of Functional Income Distribution*, ILO Conditions of Work and Employment Series 35, International Labour Organization, Geneva.

Strietska-Ilina, O., Hofmann, C., Haro, M. D. and Jeon, S. (2011) *Skills for Green Jobs: A Global View*, International Labour Organization, Geneva.

Sullivan, C. A., Meigh, J. R., Giacomello, A. M., Fediw, T., Lawrence, P., Samad, M., Mlote, S., Hutton, C., Allan, J. A., Schulze, R. E., Dlamini, D. J. M., Cosgrove, W., Delli Priscoli, J., Gleick, P., Smout, I., Cobbing, J., Calow, R., Hunt, C., Hussain, A., Acreman, M. C., King, J., Malomo, S., Tate, E. L., O'Regan, D. O., Milner, S. and Steyl, I. (2003) 'The water poverty index: Development and application at the community scale', *Natural Resources Forum*, vol 27, no 3, pp189–199.

Sultana, F. (2011) 'Suffering for water, suffering from water: Emotional geographies of resource access, control and conflict', *Geoforum*, vol 42, no 2, pp163–172.

SUN (2012) 'SUN Movement Strategy 2012–2015', SUN (Scaling Up Nutrition), http://scalingupnutrition.org/wp-content/uploads/2012/10/SUN-MOVEMENT-STRATEGY-ENG.pdf, accessed 10 February 2013.

Szreter, S. (1993) 'The idea of demographic transition and the study of fertility change: A critical intellectual history', *Population and Development Review*, vol 19, no 4, pp659–701.

Tacoli, C. (2011) *Not only Climate Change: Mobility, Vulnerability and Socio-Economic Transformations in Environmentally Fragile Areas of Bolivia, Senegal and Tanzania*, IIED Human Settlements Working Paper Series, Rural–Urban Interactions and Livelihood Strategies, vol 28, International Institute for Environment and Development, London, http://pubs.iied.org/10590IIED.html, accessed 29 January 2015.

Talbot, R. (1997) 'Goals, roles and innovations in India', 23rd WEDC Conference, Durban, South Africa.

Tejani, S. and Milberg, W. (2010) *Global Defeminization? Industrial Upgrading, Occupational Segmentation and Manufacturing Employment in Middle-Income Countries*, SCEP Working Paper 2010-1, Schwartz Center for Economic Policy Analysis and Department of Economics, New School for Social Research, New York.

Terry, G. (2009) 'No climate justice without gender justice: An overview of the issues', *Gender & Development*, vol 17, no 1, pp5–18.

Thompson, E. P. (1966) *The Making of the English Working Class*, Vintage, New York.

Thukral, E. G. (ed) (1992) *Big Dams, Displaced People*, Sage, New Delhi.

Thukral, E. G. (1995) 'Development, displacement and rehabilitation: Is there a need for a gender perspective?', *Mainstream*, vol 33, no 51, pp24–26.

Thukral, E. G. (1996) 'Development, displacement and rehabilitation: Locating gender', *Economic and Political Weekly*, vol 31, no 24, pp1500–1503.

Thukral, E. G. (2009) 'Displacement and protecting the lives of children', in L. Mehta (ed) *Displaced by Development: Confronting Marginalisation and Gender Injustice*, Sage, New Delhi.

Tiba, Z. (2011) 'Targeting the most vulnerable: Implementing input subsidies', in Prakash, A. (ed) *Safeguarding Food Security in Volatile Markets*, Food and Agriculture Organization, Rome.

Tomlinson, I. (2013) 'Doubling food production to feed the 9 billion: A critical perspective on a key discourse of food security in the UK', *Journal of Rural Studies*, vol 29, pp81–90.

True, J. (2003) 'Mainstreaming gender in global public policy', *International Feminist Journal of Politics*, vol 5, no 3, pp368–396.

Truelove, Y. (2011) '(Re-)conceptualizing water inequality in Delhi, India through a feminist political ecology framework', *Geoforum*, vol 42, no 2, pp143–152.

Truman, H. S. (1949) Inaugural Address, Harry S. Truman Library & Museum, www.trumanlibrary.org/whistlestop/50yr_archive/inagural20jan1949.htm, accessed 29 January 2015.

Turse, N. (2013) 'The pivot to Africa: The startling size, scope, and growth of U.S. military operations on the African continent', *TomDispatch*, 5 September, www.tomdispatch.com/blog/175743, accessed 29 January 2015.

Tzannatos, Z. (1999) 'Women and labour market changes in the global economy: Growth helps, inequalities hurt and public policy matters', *World Development*, vol 27, no 3, pp551–569.

Ul-Haq, M. (1995) *Reflections on Human Development*, Oxford University Press, New York.

UN (1948) *Universal Declaration of Human Rights*, United Nations, Geneva.

UN (1975) *Report of the World Food Conference, Rome, 5–16 November 1974*, United Nations, New York.

UN (1992) *Report of the United Nations Conference on Environment and Development*, A/CONF.151/26, Vol. I–III, United Nations, New York.

UN (1999) *World Survey on the Role of Women in Development. Globalization, Gender and Work*, A/54/227, United Nations, New York.

UN (2013a) *World Population Prospects: The 2012 Revision*, Department of Economic and Social Affairs of the United Nations, New York.

UN (2013b) *The Millennium Development Goals Report 2013*, United Nations, New York.

UN (2013c) *A New Global Partnership: Eradicate Poverty and Transform Economies Through Sustainable Development – The Report of the High-Level Panel of Eminent Persons on the Post-2015 Development Agenda*, United Nations, New York.

UN (2013d) *Report of the Special Rapporteur on Extreme Poverty and Human Rights*, A/68/293, United Nations, New York.

UN (2014a) *World Survey on the Role of Women in Development*, A/69/156, United Nations, New York.

UN (2014b) *Commission on the Status of Women. Report on the Fifty-Eighth Session*, E/2014/27, United Nations, New York.

UN-NGLS (2013) *UN-NGLS Policy Briefs for the OWG on SDGs*, UN Non-Governmental Liaison Service, New York and Geneva, www.un-ngls.org/spip.php?article4371, accessed 22 February 2015.

UN TST (2014) *Population Dynamics*, Issue Brief 11, UN General Assembly, UN Technical Support Team, https://sustainabledevelopment.un.org/index.php?page=view&type=400&nr=1554&menu=35, accessed 29 January 2015.

UN Women (2013) *Challenges and Achievements in the Implementation of the Millennium Development Goals for Women and Girls*, Expert Group Meeting on Structural and Policy Constraints in Achieving the MDGs for Women and Girls, Mexico City, www.unwomen.org/~/media/Headquarters/Attachments/Sections/CSW/58/CSW58-2013-EGM-Report-en.pdf, accessed 22 February 2015.

UN Women (2014) *Gender Equality and Sustainable Development. World Survey on the Role of Women in Economic Development*, United Nations, New York.

UNCTAD (2002) *Trade and Development Report 2002*, UN Conference on Trade and Development, Geneva.

UNCTAD (2009) *Trade and Development Report 2009*, UN Conference on Trade and Development, Geneva.

UNCTAD (2010) *Trade and Development Report, 2010: Employment, Globalization and Development*, UN Conference on Trade and Development, New York and Geneva.

UNCTAD (2013a) *Trade and Development Report 2013: Adjusting to the Changing Dynamics of the World Economy*, UN Conference on Trade and Development, New York and Geneva.

UNCTAD (2013b) *World Investment Report 2013: Global Value Chains: Investment and Trade for Development*, UN Conference on Trade and Development, Geneva and New York.

UNCTAD (2014) *Trade and Development Report 2014: Global Governance and Policy Space for Development*, UN Conference on Trade and Development, Geneva.

UNDECA (2015) *Sustainable Development Goals*, United Nations Department of Economic and Social Affairs, https://sustainabledevelopment.un.org/topics/sustainabledevelopment goals, accessed 12 February 2015.

UNDP (2000) *Economic Reforms, Globalization, Poverty and the Environment*, D. Reed and H. Rosa (eds), UN Development Programme, New York.

UNDP (2006) *Human Development Report*, Oxford University Press, UN Development Programme, New York.

UNDP (2012) *Powerful Synergies: Gender Equality, Economic Development and Environmental Sustainability*, UN Development Programme, New York, www.undp.org/content/dam/undp/library/gender/Gender%20and%20Environment/Powerful-Synergies.pdf, accessed 19 February 2015.

UNDP (2013a) *Human Development Report 2013. The Rise of the South: Human Progress in a Diverse World*, UN Development Programme, New York.

UNDP (2013b) *Humanity Divided: Confronting Inequality in Developing Countries*, UN Development Programme, New York.

UNEP (2000) *Global Environmental Outlook 2000*. Clarke, R. (ed), UN Environment Programme, Nairobi.

UNEP (2009) *Global Green New Deal*, Policy Brief, UN Environment Programme, Nairobi.

UNEP (2011) *Towards a Green Economy: Pathways to Sustainable Development and Poverty Eradication*, UN Environment Programme, Nairobi.

UNEP (2013a) *What is the Green Economy Initiative?*, UN Environment Programme, www.unep.org/greeneconomy/AboutGEI/WhatisGEI/tabid/29784/Default.aspx, accessed 19 February 2015.

UNEP (2013b) *Embedding the Environment in Sustainable Development Goals*, UNEP Post 2015 Discussion Paper I, 19 July, UN Environment Programme, Nairobi.

UNEP, ILO, IOE and ITUC (2008) *Green Jobs: Towards Decent Work in a Sustainable, Low Carbon World*, UN Environment Programme, International Labour Organization, International Organisation of Employers and International Trade Union Confederation, Nairobi.

UNFPA (1992) *Women, Population and the Environment*, UNFPA (UN Population Fund), New York.

UNFPA (1995) *Report of the International Conference on Population and Development*, A/CONF.171/13/Rev.1, UNFPA (UN Population Fund), New York.

UNFPA (2014) *Framework of Actions for the Follow-up to the Programme of Action of the International Conference on Population and Development Beyond 2014*, UNFPA (UN Population Fund), New York, http://icpdbeyond2014.org/uploads/browser/files/icpd_global_review_report.pdf, accessed 29 January 2015.

Unmüßig, B., Sachs, W. and Fatheuer, T. (2012) *Critique of the Green Ecology – Toward Social and Environmental Equity*, Ecology Series 22, Heinrich Böll Stiftung, Berlin.

UNRISD (2005) *Gender Equality: Striving for Justice in an Unequal World*, UN Research Institute for Social Development, Geneva.

UNRISD (2010) *Combating Poverty and Inequality: Structural Change, Social Policy and Politics*, UN Research Institute for Social Development, Geneva.

Unterhalter, E. (2013) *The MDGs, Girls' Education, and Gender Equality*, Expert Paper for UN Women on Structural and Policy Constraints in Achieving the MDGs for Women and Girls, Mexico City, www.unwomen.org/~/media/Headquarters/Attachments/Sections/CSW/58/EP4-Elaine-Unterhalter%20pdf.pdf, accessed 22 February 2015.

Urdal, H. (2012) *A Clash of Generations?: Youth Bulges and Political Violence*, Expert Paper 2012, UN Department of Economic and Social Affairs, Population Division, New York, www.un.org/esa/population/publications/expertpapers/Urdal_Expert%20Paper.pdf, accessed 29 January 2015.

US Department of Defense (2014) *Quadrennial Defense Review 2014*, Washington, DC, www.defense.gov/pubs/2014_Quadrennial_Defense_Review.pdf, accessed 29 January 2015.

US Department of Defense Science Board (2011) *Report of the Defense Science Board Task Force on Trends and Implications of Climate Change and National and International Security*, Washington, DC, www.fas.org/irp/agency/dod/dsb/climate.pdf, accessed 29 January 2015.

USDA (2014) 'Food Security in the US: Key Statistics and Graphics', www.ers.usda.gov/topics/food-nutrition-assistance/food-security-in-the-us/key-statistics-graphics.aspx#foodsecure, accessed 13 June 2014.

Vaughan, G. (ed) (2007) *Women and the Gift Economy: A Radically Different Worldview is Possible*, Inanna Publications and Education Incorporated, Toronto.

Venkataraman, C., Sagar, A. D., Habib, G., Lam, N. and Smith, K. R. (2010) 'The Indian national initiative for advanced biomass cookstoves: The benefits of clean combustion', *Energy for Sustainable Development*, vol 14, pp63–72.

Verhoeven, H. (2011) 'Climate change, conflict and development in Sudan: Global neo-Malthusian narratives and local power struggles', *Development and Change*, vol 42, no 3, pp679–707.

Via Campesina (2014a) 'Chile: Women farmers to teach the region agroecology', 30 January, http://viacampesina.org/en/index.php/main-issues-mainmenu-27/women-mainmenu-39/1549-chile-women-farmers-to-teach-the-region-agroecology, accessed 3 February 2015.

Via Campesina (2014b) www.viacampesina.org, accessed 12 April 2014.

Viegas, P. (1992) 'The Hirakud oustees: Thirty years after', in E. G. Thukral (ed) *Big Dams, Displaced People*, Sage, New Delhi.

Vizard, P., Fukuda-Parr, S. and Elson, D. (2011) 'The capability approach and human rights', *Journal of Human Development and Capabilities*, vol 12, no 1, pp1–22.

Vogt, W. (1948) *Road to Survival*, William Sloane Associates, New York.

Wakabi, W. (2013) 'Nigeria aims to boost fight against maternal mortality', *The Lancet*, vol 381, no 9879, p. 1708.

WASHCost (2011) *Life-cycle Costs in Ghana: Briefing Note 4: Access to Water Services in Rural Areas and Small Towns*, International Water and Sanitation Centre (IRC), The Hague.

WCD (2000) *Dams and Development. A New Framework for Decision-Making*, World Commission on Dams and Earthscan, London and Sterling, VA.

West, P., Igoe, J. and Brockington, D. (2006) 'Parks and peoples: The social impact of protected areas', *Annual Review of Anthropology*, vol 35, pp251–277.

WFP (n.d.). 'Hunger', World Food Programme, Rome, www.wfp.org/hunger, accessed 21 April 2014.

White, B., Borras, S. M., Hall, R., Scoones, I. and Wolford, W. (eds) (2012) 'Special issue on the new enclosures: Critical perspectives on corporate land deals', *Journal of Peasant Studies*, vol 39, nos 3–4, pp619–1101.

White, G. (2011) *Climate Change and Migration: Security and Borders in a Warming World*, Oxford University Press, Oxford.

WHO (2009) *Global Health Risks: Mortality and Burden of Disease Attributable to Selected Major Risks*, World Health Organization, Geneva.

WHO (2014a) *Preventing Diarrhoea through Better Water Sanitation and Hygiene: Exposures and Impacts in Low- and Middle-Income Countries*, World Health Organization, Geneva.

WHO (2014b) '7 million deaths annually linked to air pollution', World Health Organization, Geneva, www.who.int/phe/health_topics/outdoorair/databases/en/, accessed 22 February 2015.

WHO/UNICEF (2010) *Progress on Sanitation and Drinking Water. 2010 Update*, World Health Organization and UNICEF, Geneva and New York.

WHO/UNICEF (2013) *Progress on Sanitation and Drinking Water. 2013 Update.* World Health Organization and UNICEF, Geneva and New York.

Wichterich, C. (2012) *The Future We Want. A Feminist Perspective*, Ecology Series 21, Heinrich Böll Stiftung, Berlin.

Wichterich, C. (2015) 'Contesting green growth, connecting care, commons and enough', in W. Harcourt and I. Nelson *Practicing Feminist Political Ecology: Going beyond the Green Economy*, Zed Books, London.

WIEGO (2014) 'Waste Pickers', Women in Informal Employment: Globalizing and Organizing, http://wiego.org/informal-economy/occupational-groups/waste-pickers, accessed 24 January 2014.

van Wijk-Sijbesma, C. (1998) *Gender in Water Resources Management, Water Supply and Sanitation: Roles and Realities Revisited*, International Water and Sanitation Center (IRC), The Hague.

Williams, G. (1995) 'Modernizing Malthus: World Bank, population control and the African environment', in J. Crush (ed) *Power of Development*, Routledge, London, pp158–175.

Williams, J. and Ghanadan, R. (2006) 'Electricity reform in developing and transition countries: A reappraisal', *Energy*, vol 31, pp815–844.

Wilmoth, J. R. and Ball, P. (1992) 'The population debate in American popular magazines', *Population and Development Review*, vol 18, no 4, pp631–668.

Wilson, K. (2012) *Race, Racism and Development*, Zed Books, London.

Wiltshire, R. (1992) *Environment and Development*, Grassroots' Women's Perspectives, Development alternatives with Women for a New era (DAWN), Barbados.

Wise, T.A. and Murphy, S. (2012) *Resolving the Food Crisis: Assessing Global Policy Reforms Since 2007*, Institute for Agriculture and Trade Policy/Global Development and Environment Institute at Tufts University, Medford, MA.

Witsenburg, K. and Roba, A. W. (2007) 'The use and management of water sources in Kenya's drylands: Is there a link between scarcity and violent conflicts?', in B. Derman, R. Odgaard and E. Sjaastad (eds) *Conflicts over Land and Water in Africa*, James Currey, Oxford, pp215–283.

Wong, E. (2013) 'Population control is called big revenue source in China', *New York Times*, 26 September, www.nytimes.com/2013/09/27/world/asia/chinese-provinces-collected-billions-in-family-planning-fines-lawyer-says.html?smid=pl-share, accessed 29 January 2015.

Wong, S. (2009) 'Climate change and sustainable technology: Re-linking poverty, gender, and governance', *Gender & Development*, vol 17, no 1, pp95–108.

Wood, A. (1991) 'North–south trade and female labour in manufacturing: An asymmetry', *Journal of Development Studies*, vol 27, no 2, pp168–189.

World Bank (2001) *Engendering Development Through Equality in Rights, Resources, and Voice*, Oxford University Press, New York.

World Bank (2004) *World Development Report: Making Services Work for Poor People*, World Bank and Oxford University Press, Washington, DC and Oxford.

World Bank (2006) *Rajasthan: Closing the Development Gap*, World Bank, Washington, DC.

World Bank (2007) *World Development Report 2008: Agriculture for Development*, World Bank, Washington, DC.

World Bank (2011) *Gender and Climate Change: Three Things You Should Know*, World Bank, Washington, DC.

World Bank (2012a) *Inclusive Green Growth: The Pathway to Sustainable Development*, World Bank, Washington, DC.

World Bank (2012b) 'Rural Population', World Bank Data, http://data.worldbank.org/indicator/SP.RUR.TOTL, accessed 15 March 2013.

World Bank (2012c) *World Development Report: Gender Equality and Development*, Washington, DC, World Bank.

World Bank (2013) *World Development Indicators*, World Bank, Washington, DC, http://data.worldbank.org/data-catalog/world-development-indicators, accessed 19 February 2015.

World Bank (2014) *World Development Indicators*, http://data.worldbank.org/data-catalog/world-development-indicators, accessed 19 February 2015.

WOW (2012) *WANTO: Women in Apprenticeship and Nontraditional Occupations Act*, Wider Opportunities for Women, Washington, DC, www.wowonline.org/documents/WANTOFactSheet.pdf, accessed 27 January 2014.

Wright, B. (2012) 'International grain reserves and other instruments to address volatility in grain markets', *World Bank Research Observer*, vol 27, no 12, pp222–260.

Wright, M. W. (2010) 'Geography and gender: Feminism and a feeling of justice', *Progress in Human Geography*, vol 34, no 6, pp818–827.

Wutich, A. and Ragsdale, K. (2008) 'Water insecurity and emotional distress: Coping with supply, access and seasonal variability of water in a Bolivian squatter settlement', *Social Science and Medicine*, vol 67, pp2116–2125.

Yamin, A. E. and Boulanger, V. M. (2013a) 'Embedding sexual and reproductive health and rights in a transformational development framework: Lessons learned from the MDG targets and indicators', *Reproductive Health Matters*, vol 21, no 42, pp74–85.

Yamin, A. E. and Boulanger, V. M. (2013b) *From Transforming Power to Counting Numbers: The Evolution of Sexual and Reproductive Health and Rights in Development, and where we want to go from here*, Working Paper Series, The Power of Numbers, Harvard School of Public Health and New School, http://fxb.harvard.edu/wp-content/uploads/sites/5/2013/09/Yamin-and-Boulanger_final-WP-with-cover-sheet_92413.pdf, accessed 1 March 2015.

Young, K., Wolkowitz, C. and McCullagh, R. (1984) *Of Marriage and the Market: Women's Subordination Internationally and Its Lessons*, Routledge & Kegan Paul, London.

Zhang, J. and Smith, K. (2007) 'Household air pollution from coal and biomass fuels in China: Measurements, health impacts, and interventions', *Environmental Health Perspectives*, vol 115, no 6, pp848–855.

Zhou, Z., Dionisio, K. L., Arku, R. E., Quaye, A., Hughes, A. F., Vallarino, J., Spengler, J. D., Hill, A., Agyei-Mensah, S. and Ezzati, M. (2011) 'Household and community poverty, biomass use, and air pollution in Accra, Ghana', *Proceedings of the National Academy of Sciences, USA*, vol 108, no 27, pp11028–11033.

Zwarteveen, M. (1997) 'Water: from basic need to commodity: A discussion on gender and water rights in the context of irrigation', *World Development*, vol 25, no 8, pp1335–1349.

INDEX